Artistic Needle Felting

Illustrator Mary Engelbreit has created some of today's most recognized and beloved designs. Mary's famous drawings have found their way onto thousands of products, including greeting cards, dishes, and accessories. And now you can add her signature look to textiles with needle felting or appliqué! Transform ordinary fabrics with soft accents or bold graphics made of colorful wool roving, felt, or yarn. The needle felting tool lets you incorporate fibers of wool into other fabrics, creating a permanent bond. Give your favorite pair of blue jeans a "breit" punch of color and pattern. Create dimension with layers of felt, easy embroidery, and bead embellishments. Whether you enjoy appliquéing felt shapes or choose to use this newest needle felting technique, you'll find lots of inspiring ways to decorate pillows, wall art, table runners, purses, and more.

Visit www.leisurearts.com to see a Webcast demonstration of the exciting technique of needle felting!

Mary Engelbreit

Growing up in St. Louis, Missouri, Mary Engelbreit adored drawing. She began sketching as soon as she could hold a crayon, and by the age of 11 she knew without a doubt that she wanted to be an artist.

After short-lived careers at an art store, an ad agency, and the *St. Louis Post-Dispatch*, Mary began illustrating fantasy greeting cards. But she really found her niche after her first son was born, when her artistic focus turned to more "everyday" moments.

Now an internationally known artist, Mary has created more than 4,000 images featuring whimsical quotes, precocious children, and, of course, her trademark cherries and Scottie dogs. In Mary's lovely, nostalgic world, life is richly detailed and "to imagine is everything!"

LEISURE ARTS, INC.
Little Rock, Arkansas

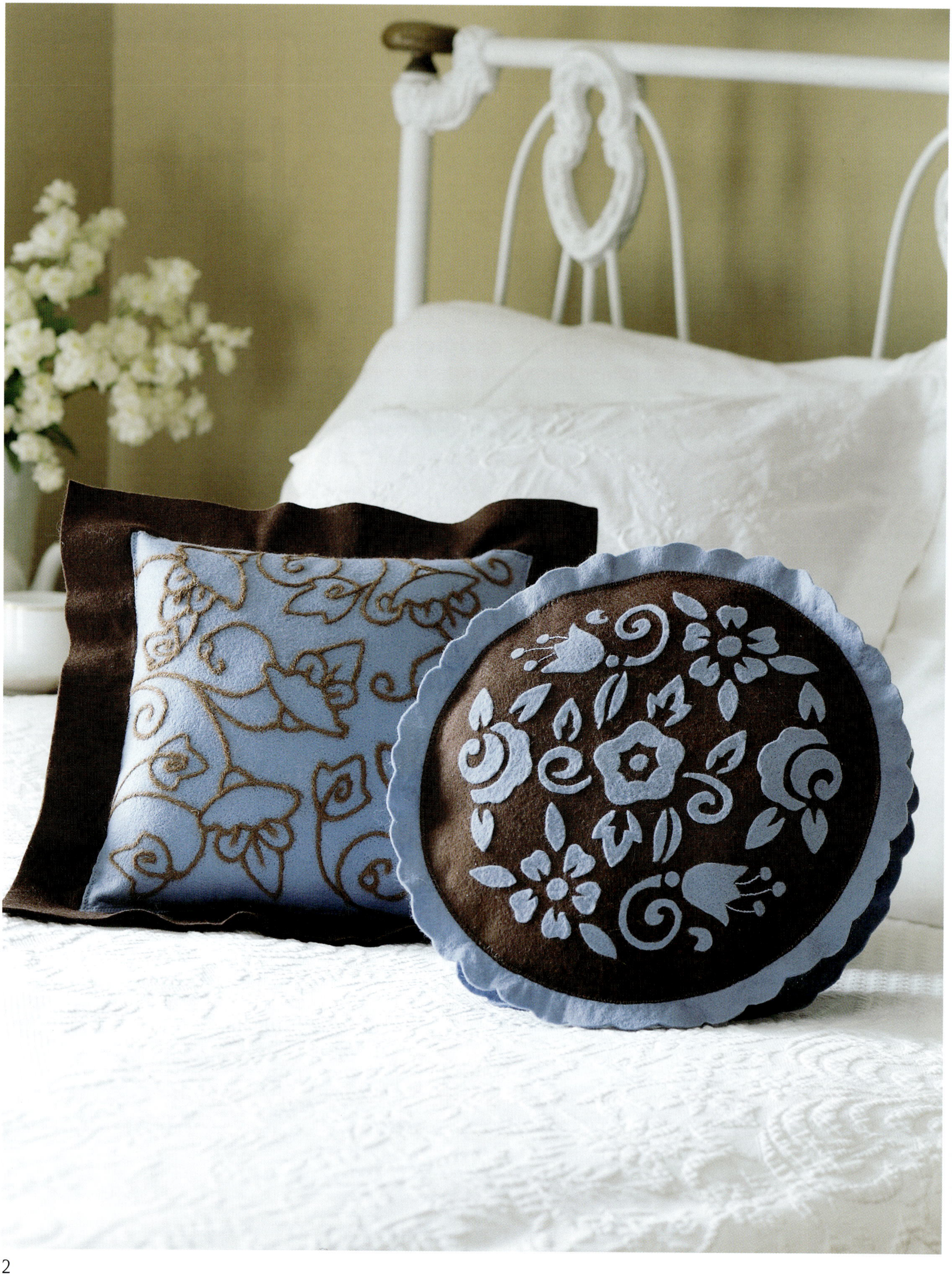

Square Pillow

Pattern, page 23, enlarged to 140%
Basic Instructions, pages 21-22

Supplies
- one 11" square of blue felt
- two 14" squares of brown felt for the pillow front and back
- tissue paper
- mesh transfer canvas
- white colored pencil
- felting needle tool and mat
- brown wool yarn
- liquid fray preventative
- clear nylon thread
- polyester fiberfill

Transfer the pattern to the center of the blue felt square. Needle felt with yarn along the pattern lines, cutting and dabbing the yarn ends with fray preventative. To complete the pillow front, center and zigzag the blue square on one brown felt square and press, using a pressing cloth. Leaving an opening for stuffing, match wrong sides and sew the pillow front to the pillow back along the same seam. Stuff the pillow and sew the opening closed.

Round Pillow

Pattern, page 24, enlarged to 110%
Basic Instructions, pages 21-22

Supplies
- one $11^{1}/_{2}$" square of brown wool felt
- two 13" squares, one 10" square, and one 2" x $33^{1}/_{2}$" strip of blue wool felt
- string
- thumbtack
- white colored pencil
- tissue paper
- freezer paper
- mesh transfer canvas
- felting needle tool and mat
- blue embroidery floss
- clear nylon thread
- polyester fiberfill

1. Using a $5^{1}/_{4}$" string measurement, follow Cutting a Fabric Circle (page 22) to cut one $10^{1}/_{2}$" dia. circle from brown felt. Use a 6" string measurement and cut two 12" circles from blue felt for the pillow front and back; scallop the edges.
2. Cut the appliqué pieces from the 10" blue felt square.
3. Transfer the pattern to the center of the brown felt circle for the placement of the appliqué pieces. Needle felt the appliqués in place and press, using a pressing cloth.
4. Use 2 strands of floss and stem stitch the tulip pistils.
5. Center and draw around the brown circle on one blue circle for the pillow back; set aside. Center and zigzag the brown circle on the remaining blue circle for the pillow front.
6. Use a $1/2$" seam allowance and sew the ends of the felt strip together to form the side band. Using the zigzag stitching as a guide, pin the band to the wrong side of the pillow front; zigzag in place. Leaving an opening for stuffing, pin, then zigzag the band to the pillow back along the drawn line.
7. Stuff the pillow and sew the opening closed.

Rectangular Pillow

Pattern, page 25
Basic Instructions, pages 21-22

Supplies
- two 11½" x 15" pieces of cream wool felt
- coral, green, yellow, and rose wool felt
- tissue paper
- freezer paper
- mesh transfer canvas
- water-soluble pen
- felting needle tool and mat
- green embroidery floss
- oval and bugle beads
- polyester fiberfill

Match right sides and use a ½" seam allowance unless otherwise indicated.

1. Cut two ½" x 15" coral felt strips. Cut the appliqué pieces from felt.
2. Transfer the pattern to the center of one cream felt piece for the placement of the appliqué pieces on the pillow front. Needle felt the appliqués in place. Needle felt one strip 2" from each long edge of the pillow front and press, using a pressing cloth.
3. Use 3 strands of floss and stem stitch the vines. Sew beads along the vines.
4. Leaving an opening for stuffing, sew the pillow front and back together; trim the corners. Turn the pillow right side out, stuff, and sew the opening closed.

Framed Pieces

Patterns, pages 26-27, enlarged to 115%
Basic Instructions, pages 21-22

Supplies
- three 14" squares of black felt
- tissue paper
- mesh transfer canvas
- white colored pencil
- felting needle tool and mat
- 3 shades of green, 2 reds, 2 yellows, orange, aqua, blue, purple, and lavender wool roving
- white E beads
- white thread
- three black frames with $5^{5}/_{8}$" square front openings and background mats

For each framed piece, transfer the pattern (including the shading lines) to the center of one felt square. Needle felt with wool roving in the pattern areas and press, using a pressing cloth. Sew beads where desired. Trim the felt and insert the design in a frame.

Wall Hanging

Patterns, pages 27-28, enlarged to 140%
Basic Instructions, pages 21-22

Supplies
- 10½" x 30" piece of tan wool fabric
- 13½" x 38" piece of brown wool fabric
- tissue paper
- mesh transfer canvas
- colored pencil
- felting needle tool and mat
- brown, green, yellow, and dark pink wool roving

Match right sides and use a ½" seam allowance unless otherwise indicated.

1. With the bottom of the pattern 1" from the bottom of the tan wool piece, center and transfer the floral pattern. Center and transfer the geometric pattern 2½" above the floral pattern. Needle felt with wool roving in the pattern areas and press, using a pressing cloth.
2. With the bottom of the tan piece 2½" from the bottom of the brown wool piece, sew the long sides together. Turn right side out and press, forming a ¾" wide brown border on the front along each side edge.
3. Turn the bottom end ½", then 1¼" to the front and topstitch. To form the hanging pocket, turn the top end ½", then 2¾" to the front and topstitch.

Dresser Scarf

Pattern, page 29, enlarged to 171%
Basic Instructions, pages 21-22

Supplies
- 19" x 40" piece of natural linen
- two 4½" x 19" border strips of brown linen
- yellow, blue, coral, watermelon, rose, lavender, and 3 shades of green felt
- corresponding embroidery floss colors
- tissue paper
- freezer paper
- mesh transfer canvas
- colored pencil
- fabric glue
- 3 yds of ⅛"w beige ribbon with white topstitching

Match right sides and use a ½" seam allowance unless otherwise indicated.

1. Sew a brown border strip on each end of the natural linen; press.
2. Cut two ¼" x 19" yellow felt strips. Cut the appliqué pieces from felt, extending each stem 4".
3. Center and transfer the pattern on each end of the linen for the placement of the appliqué pieces. Glue 5 ribbon lengths along the center of the linen, joining the large flower patterns.
4. Embroider the appliqués with 3 strands of floss for the stem stitch vines and 2 strands for all other stitching. Work blanket stitches around the larger pieces and on the left side of the felt stem and use whipstitches for the smaller pieces. Stem stitch along the right side of the felt stem and add veins to the large leaves. Add straight stitch veins to the small leaves.
5. Glue one felt strip over each border seam.
6. Match long edges and leave an opening for turning; sew the long edges together. Press the seam allowances open. With the seam at the center back, sew the short ends together. Trim the corners, turn the scarf right side out, and press, using a pressing cloth. Sew the opening closed. Topstitch around the edges of the scarf.

7

Journals

Supplies for each journal
- two 19½" x 13" pieces of felt
- two 9" x 11½" pieces of white mat board
- fabric glue
- 60" length of ½"w twill tape
- ¼" dia. hole punch
- 8½" x 11" paper sheets
- binder clips
- 1¾ yds of ¼"w ribbon for binding
- needle with large eye

1. For each cover, match short ends and fold one felt piece in half. Insert one mat board in the folded felt and glue the side, then top and bottom felt edges to the back. Covering the raw edges and mitering at the corners, glue twill tape along 3 sides of the cover.
2. Use a pencil to mark the hole placement ⅜" from the untaped edge of the front cover, beginning ¾" from the top and marking every 2". Punch the holes. Using the punched cover as a template for the back cover and the inside pages, punch the remaining holes.
3. Place the pages inside the covers and hold the layers together with the binder clips. Thread the needle with ribbon. Leaving an 18" tail, begin at the top front and lace the ribbon through the holes to the bottom and then up to the top. Knot at the top and use the tails as bookmarks.

Pink & Cream Cover

Pattern, page 30, enlarged to 110%
Basic Instructions, pages 21-22

Supplies
- 6" x 8" piece of pink wool felt
- 7" x 9¼" piece of cream felt (cut with pinking shears)
- pink and cream embroidery floss
- tissue paper
- freezer paper
- mesh transfer canvas
- water-soluble pen
- felting needle tool and mat
- pink glass seed beads
- fabric glue

1. Cut the appliqué pieces from pink felt.
2. Transfer the pattern to the center of the cream felt piece for the placement of the appliqué pieces. Needle felt the appliqués in place and press, using a pressing cloth.
3. Embroider the appliqués with 2 strands of cream floss, working blanket and stem stitches as desired. Sew beads on the flower centers, and along the stems and tips of the leaves.
4. Using 3 strands of pink floss, sew a running stitch around the outer edge of the cream piece. Glue the cover design to the front of the journal.

Bohemian Cover

Pattern, page 31
Basic Instructions, pages 21-22

Supplies
- 7" x 9½" piece of light yellow felt
- 7½" x 10" piece of blue felt
- blue, gold, pink, dark pink, green, and black wool felt scraps
- corresponding embroidery floss colors
- tissue paper
- freezer paper
- mesh transfer canvas
- water soluble pen
- felting needle tool and mat
- blue, pink, and green seed beads
- blue, pink, and green E beads
- fabric glue

1. Cut the appliqué pieces from felt scraps.
2. Transfer the pattern to the center of the light yellow felt piece for the placement of the appliqué pieces. Use a single needle to needle felt the appliqués (this will hold them in place for embroidering). Press, using a pressing cloth.
3. Embroider the appliqués with 3 strands of floss, working blanket, straight, stem, and running stitches on the design as desired. Sew beads on the design.
4. Blanket stitch the embroidered piece to the blue felt piece. Glue the cover design to the front of the journal.

Scalloped Runner

Patterns, page 30
Basic Instructions, pages 21-22

Supplies
- 11½" x 35" piece of yellow felt
- two 3½" x 11½" strips of green felt
- two 1¼" x 11½" strips of black felt
- two 2" x 11½" strips of orange felt
- eleven ¾" dia. black wool felt circles
- black and orange thread
- tissue paper
- mesh transfer canvas
- water soluble pen
- felting needle tool and mat
- red, orange, green, and yellow wool roving
- black embroidery floss

1. Place one green strip on each end of the yellow felt piece, overlapping the piece by ½"; zigzag in place. Center one black strip over each seam and topstitch along the long edges.
2. Using the scallop pattern, cut two scalloped strips from orange felt. Place one orange strip on the end of each green piece, overlapping the piece by ½"; topstitch in place.
3. Transfer the floral pattern on the runner where desired. Needle felt with wool roving in the pattern areas, starting with the leaves and working toward the center. Press, using a pressing cloth.
4. Needle felt the wool felt circles onto the runner.
5. Using 6 strands of floss, add French knots around the flower centers.

Cherry Purse Charm

Pattern, page 32
Basic Instructions, pages 21-22

Supplies
- red, green, and light green wool roving
- felting needle tool and mat
- two 1" diameter foam balls
- tissue paper
- brown pearl cotton
- key ring

1. To make each cherry from wool roving, place strips of roving across the felting needle mat and cross them with more strips. Needle felt the pieces together, adding roving as needed to make the felted piece large enough to wrap around a foam ball. Needle felt one corner of the felted piece to the foam ball. Wrap the piece around the ball, needle felting until the ball is covered. Trim away any extra roving and needle felt to blend in the cut edges.

2. To make the leaf from wool roving, place strips of roving across the felting needle mat and cross them with more strips. Needle felt the pieces together, folding the roving until it is a little larger than the leaf pattern.

3. Pin the leaf pattern cut from tissue paper to the felted roving; cut out the shape. Needle felt small thin strips of light green roving to the leaf for highlights.

4. Leave a 3" tail and thread a 15" length of pearl cotton through one cherry from top to bottom. Catch a bit of the roving and thread the needle back through the cherry. Tie a knot at the top; then, thread the needle though one end of the leaf and around the key ring. Tie a knot just below the ring and run the needle back through the leaf and attach the remaining cherry. Trim the ends close to the knots on each cherry.

Scottie Key Fob

Pattern, page 34
Basic Instructions, pages 21-22

Supplies
- tissue paper
- freezer paper
- red, white, and black felt scraps
- fabric glue
- 2 black seed beads
- 2 white flat sequins
- 2" length of 1/8"w red corded ribbon
- small and large key ring

Cut 2 of each pattern piece from felt. Glue the Scottie shapes together. Sew a bead and sequin eye on each side of the dog. Glue a collar, cuffs, and dots to each jacket. Fold the red ribbon in half and loop it over the small key ring. Glue one ribbon end on each side of the Scottie at the center back. Glue the jacket pieces to the Scottie, covering the ribbon ends. Slip the small key ring on the large ring.

Cherry Eyeglass Case

Patterns, page 34
Basic Instructions, pages 21-22

Supplies
- two 5" x 7¾" pieces of black wool felt
- two 5" x 7¾" pieces of lining fabric
- tissue paper
- mesh transfer canvas
- white colored pencil
- felting needle tool and mat
- red, brown, light green, and dark green wool roving
- white seed beads
- white thread
- brown embroidery floss
- paper-backed fusible web

Our finished case is 3" x 5¾". Enlarge pattern if necessary.

1. For the case front and back, transfer the outline and cherry patterns to one felt piece and the outline pattern only to the remaining felt piece. Needle felt with wool roving in the cherry pattern areas on the front and press, using a pressing cloth. Sew beads to the background.
2. Use 6 strands of embroidery floss and stem stitch the detail line where the stem meets the cherry.
3. Fuse the felt pieces to the lining pieces and cut out along the outlines. Topstitch the case front and back together where marked along the side and bottom edges. Trim close to the stitching.

Cherry Purse

Patterns, pages 32-33, enlarged to 117%
Basic Instructions, pages 21-22

Supplies
- ½ yd of black wool felt
- tissue paper
- red, green, and brown wool felt
- ½ yd of lining fabric
- freezer paper
- mesh transfer canvas
- white colored pencil
- felting needle tool and mat
- red, light green, dark green, and white wool roving
- 1¾ yd of braided trim and matching thread

Match right sides and use a ½" seam allowance unless otherwise indicated. Use a pressing cloth when ironing.

1. From black wool felt, cut a purse front and back ½" outside the pattern lines and cut a 2½" x 32" side/bottom strip. Cut a flap from green wool felt ½" outside the pattern lines. Using the felt pieces as a pattern, cut each piece from lining fabric.
2. Cut the appliqué pieces from felt.
3. Transfer the patterns to the front of the purse and flap (leaving ½" along the edges for the seam allowance). Needle felt the appliqués to the purse front. Needle felt the shading and highlight areas with wool roving and press.
4. Leaving the top open for turning, sew the flap and flap lining pieces together. Clip curves and turn right side out. Press.
5. Sew the side/bottom strip along the side and bottom edges of the purse front. Repeat to sew the strip to the purse back. Clip the curves and turn the purse right side out. In the same way, sew the lining together, leaving an opening along one side edge for turning. Do not turn the lining right side out.
6. Matching right sides, sew the flap to the top back of the purse. Place the purse inside the lining. Sew the purse to the lining along the top edges. Turn right side out and press. Sew the opening in the lining closed.
7. For the purse strap, beginning and ending at the center bottom of the purse, hand sew the braided trim along the bottom and sides of the purse, wrapping the thread several times around each end of the braid to secure.

Cosmetic Bag & Zipper Pull

Patterns, page 35, enlarged to 118%
Basic Instructions, pages 21-22

Supplies
- tissue paper
- tweed fabric
- lining fabric
- scallop-edged scissors
- teal, yellow, pink, and 2 shades of green wool felt
- freezer paper
- felting needle tool and mat
- red and green embroidery floss
- black seed beads
- teal and pink E beads
- gold bugle beads
- 7" navy zipper
- fabric glue
- 3" length of 1/8"w red corded ribbon

Match right sides and use a 1/2" seam allowance unless otherwise indicated.

1. Using the patterns, cut a bag front and back from tweed, and then from the lining fabric. Cut a trim piece from teal felt, using scalloped scissors on the outer curved edge. Make short clips all along the inner curved edge. Cut the appliqué pieces from felt.
2. Layer the appliqués on the bag front; needle felt the pieces in place and press, using a pressing cloth.
3. Embroider the appliqués, using 3 strands of floss for straight and satin stitches on the flower center and 6 strands of floss for backstitches around the paisley design and for the leaf vein.
4. Sew beads to the appliqués and bag front.
5. With the scalloped edge to the inside, pin the trim to the bag front and baste. With right sides together, pin one flange of the opened zipper to the straight edge of the bag front; sew in place using a zipper foot. Sew the remaining flange to the bag back. Sew the bag front and back together along the curved edges. Turn the bag right side out.
6. Sew the lining pieces together along the curved edges. Do not turn right side out. Press the top edge 1/2" to the wrong side. Slip the lining inside the bag and whipstitch the pressed edge to the bag.
7. For the zipper pull, cut 2 flowers, flower centers, and leaves from felt. Cut an additional pink flower with an attached pink leaf for the base. Fold the ribbon in half, thread one end through the zipper pull, and glue the ends to each side of the base near the leaf. Glue one flower, center, and leaf on each side of the base.

Tote Bag

Pattern, page 36, enlarged to 144%
Basic Instructions, pages 21-22

Supplies
- ¾ yd of tweed fabric
- ½ yd of heavyweight interfacing
- ½ yd of lining fabric
- tissue paper
- mesh transfer canvas
- white colored pencil
- felting needle tool and mat
- red, orange, gold, blue, pink, white, yellow, brown, and 2 shades of green wool roving
- pink, gold, and 2 shades of green wool yarn
- 3⅝ yds of brown cording

Match right sides and raw edges and use a ½" seam allowance unless otherwise indicated. Use a pressing cloth when ironing.

1. From tweed, cut a 13" square tote front and back, a 3½" x 64" strap/boxing strip, and a 3½" x 28" strap backing strip. Cut two 13" squares each from interfacing and lining fabric.
2. Center and transfer the pattern on the tote front. Extend the leaves and stems to ½" from the side edges. Needle felt with wool roving in the pattern areas. Needle felt the detail lines with wool yarn and press.
3. Baste interfacing to the wrong side of each tweed square.
4. Trim the cording seam allowance to ½" and cut the cording into two 64" lengths. Pin a cording length along each long edge of the strap/boxing strip. Starting 1" from one end of the cording, baste each cording length in place, stopping 2" from the other end.
5. Matching the centers and long edges of the strips, sew the strap backing strip to the strap/boxing strip ½" from each long edge (Fig. 1). Turn right side out and press.
6. Being careful not to catch the cording in the stitching, sew the ends of the strap/boxing strip together. For each cording length, remove 1" of sewing from the 2" loose end. Holding the fabric away from the cord, trim the cord ends to meet exactly. Insert one end of the cording fabric into the other, turn the top end under ½" and baste in place (Fig. 2).
7. Centering the strap/boxing strip seam on the bottom of the tote front, pin and sew the boxing strip along the sides and bottom, beginning and ending ½" from the top edge of the tote front. Repeat to sew the strip to the tote back. Trim the corners and turn the tote right side out. Press the top edge of the tote ½" to the wrong side.
8. Sew the lining pieces together along the sides and bottom. To make mock box corners, follow Fig. 3 to pin the side and bottom seams together. Sew across each corner 1" from the point. Press the top edge of the lining ½" to the wrong side. Do not turn the lining right side out.
9. Place the lining inside the tote, whipstitch the lining to the strap backing, and topstitch the remaining pressed edges.

Fig. 1

strap backing

Fig. 2

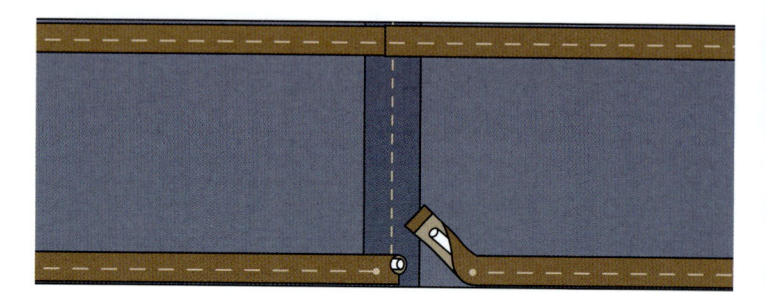

Fig. 3

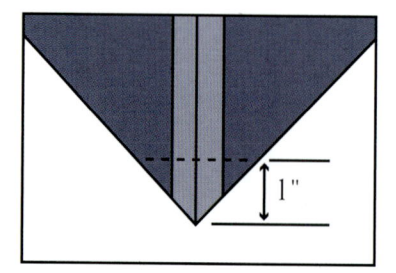

1"

KATRINA: THE NEW GULF COAST COTTAGES page 94
Mary Engelbreit's

Paisley Jeans

Patterns, page 37, enlarged to 114%
Basic Instructions, pages 21-22

Supplies
- red, gold, blue, and 2 shades of green wool roving
- corresponding colors, brown, and yellow embroidery floss
- felting needle tool and mat
- tissue paper
- mesh transfer canvas
- water-soluble pen
- blue jeans

1. To make each appliqué from wool roving, place strips of roving across the felting needle mat and cross them with more strips. Needle felt the pieces together, adding roving as needed to make the felted piece a little larger than the appliqué pattern.
2. Pin patterns cut from tissue paper to the felted roving pieces; cut out the shapes.
3. Transfer the patterns on one jeans leg for the placement of the appliqué pieces. Lightly needle felt the appliqués in place and press, using a pressing cloth.
4. Embroider the design with 3-6 strands of floss, working blanket and stem stitches to outline the flowers, cherry, leaves, and paisley pieces, running stitches for leaf veins, satin stitches for the cherry stem and flower center, and random French knots and stem stitch circles.

Felted Scarf

Pattern, page 38, enlarged to 200%
Basic Instructions, pages 21-22

Supplies
- two 6" x 56" strips of black wool felt
- tissue paper
- mesh transfer canvas
- white colored pencil
- felting needle tool and mat
- red, blue, green, pink, gold, and dark gold wool roving
- clear nylon thread
- gold yarn
- 2" and 4" cardboard squares

1. Transfer the pattern on each end of one wool felt piece. Needle felt with wool roving in the pattern areas and press, using a pressing cloth.
2. Topstitch the scarf front to the scarf back.
3. For each pom-pom, place a 6" piece of yarn along the top edge of a 2" cardboard square. Wrap yarn around and around the square and the yarn piece (the more you wrap, the fluffier the pom-pom). Tie the wound yarn together tightly with the 6" piece. Cut the loops opposite the tie; then fluff and trim the pom-pom into shape (Fig. 1). Sew three pom-poms on each end of the scarf.

Fig. 1

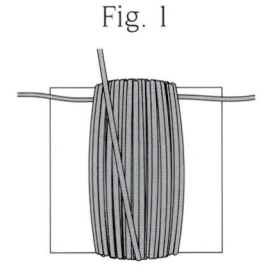

Fig. 2

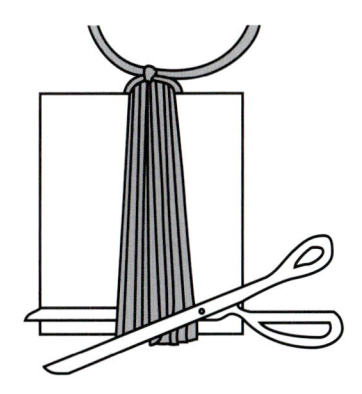

4. For each tassel, place a 6" piece of yarn along the top edge of a 4" cardboard square. Wrap yarn around and around the square and the yarn piece. Knot the yarn piece tightly around the wrapped yarn. Cut the yarn loops at the opposite end of the square (Fig. 2). Tie an 8" yarn length tightly around the tassel, 1" from the top. Tie a tassel to each pom-pom.

Appliquéd Scarf

Patterns, page 38, enlarged to 157%
Basic Instructions, pages 21-22

Supplies
- woven fleece
- red, gold, green, lavender, dark peach, and periwinkle felt
- corresponding embroidery floss colors
- tissue paper
- freezer paper
- fabric glue

1. Cut a 5" w strip of fleece the desired length for the scarf. Use 6 strands of floss to work blanket stitches around the edges of the scarf.
2. Cut the appliqué pieces from felt and place them as you wish on the scarf, dotting the centers with glue to hold them in place.
3. Embroider the appliqués with 2 strands of floss, working blanket stitches or French knots around the flower centers, straight or running stitches for the leaf veins, and stem stitches for the tulip stems.

Basic Instructions

Visit www.leisurearts.com to see a short needle felting Webcast!

Needle Felting Basics

Needle felting is a technique used to apply wool felt appliqués, yarn, or roving to background fabric. We used the Clover Felting Needle Tool and Mat to make our projects. The tool has a locking plastic shield that provides protection from the sharp needles. The brush-like mat allows the needles to easily pierce the fibers. Felt, wool, and woven cotton fabrics all work well as background fabrics.

Follow these easy steps to needle felt your project:
1. Transfer the pattern to the background fabric.
2. Place the background fabric on the felting needle mat.
3. Place the appliqué, yarn, or roving within the pattern lines and follow the manufacturer's instructions to lightly punch the needles through the layers. (Use fewer needles when working with yarn or in small areas.) To adjust the design, simply lift the appliqué or fiber, reposition, and punch.
4. When you are pleased with the design area you are working on, go back over it, punching many times to interlock the fibers for a secure hold. Press with the iron on the wool setting and use a pressing cloth to protect the wool fibers.

TIP: When working with wool roving, punch a thin strip along the outline of the design, twisting it as you go. Overlap the strips for a continuous outline. Fill in the center with thicker pieces of roving. To fit the shape of the design, fold the roving back over itself as needed and keep on punching.

TIP: When adding more yarn to a piece, overlap the ends to give the yarn a seamless look.

TIP: Use an embroidery hoop to keep the background fabric from stretching as you needle felt.

Making Patterns

Half Patterns

When only half a pattern is given (shown by a solid blue line on the pattern), fold tissue paper in half. Place the fold along the blue line and trace the pattern half. Turn the tissue paper over and draw over the traced lines on the remaining side of the paper to form a whole pattern.

Transferring Patterns

- tissue paper
- mesh transfer canvas
- colored pencil or water-soluble pen

Trace the pattern onto tissue paper. Place the transfer canvas over the pattern. Trace the pattern onto the transfer canvas with a colored pencil. Place the marked canvas on the felt or fabric background. Pressing hard and using a back and forth motion, draw over the pattern, leaving a dashed line on the background piece.

TIP: A white colored pencil works best on dark backgrounds and the water-soluble pen works well when transferring appliqué placement onto the background fabric. After the appliqués are secured, dampen any areas where the pen shows, dabbing with a paper towel or cotton swab to remove the marks.

Continued on page 22.

Cutting Appliqué Pieces
- tissue paper
- freezer paper

To cut appliqués from felt, trace the pattern onto tissue paper. Trace each pattern piece onto the dull side of the freezer paper. Iron the shiny side of the freezer paper to the felt with a warm iron. Cut out the pattern and peel off the freezer paper.

Washing Instructions
To guard against shrinkage and color bleed, hand wash or machine wash in cold water, using the gentle cycle. Line dry.

Cutting a Fabric Circle
1. Cut a square of fabric the size indicated in the project instructions.
2. Matching right sides, fold the square in half from top to bottom and again from left to right.
3. Tie one end of a length of string to a colored pencil. Measuring from the pencil, insert the thumbtack through the string at the length indicated in the project instructions. Insert the thumbtack through the folded corner of the fabric. Holding the tack in place and keeping the string taut, mark the cutting line (Fig. 1).

Fig. 1

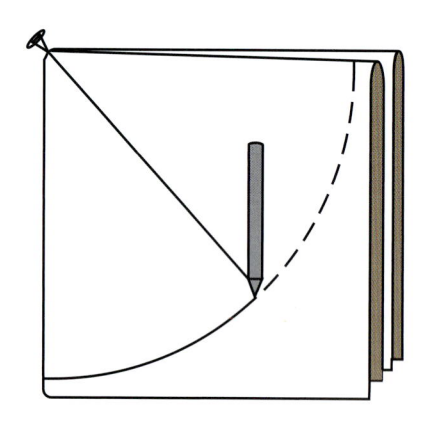

Embroidery
Use 3 strands of embroidery floss for all stitches unless otherwise indicated in the project instructions. Follow the stitch diagrams to bring the needle up at odd numbers and down at even numbers.

Backstitch

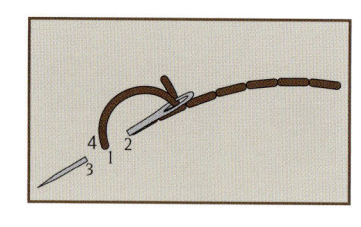

Blanket Stitch

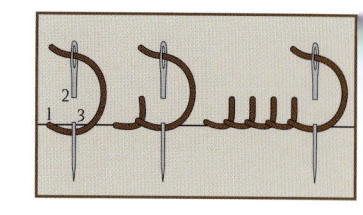

French Knot

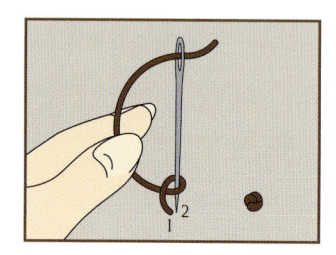

Running Stitch

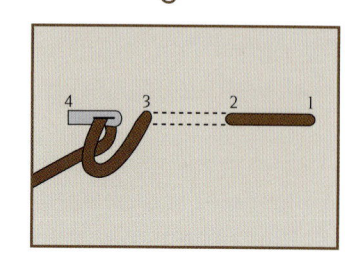

Satin Stitch

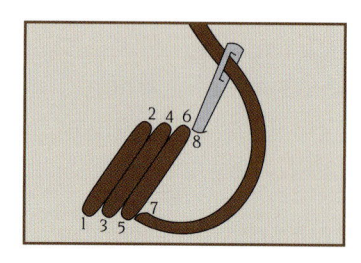

Stem Stitch

Straight Stitch

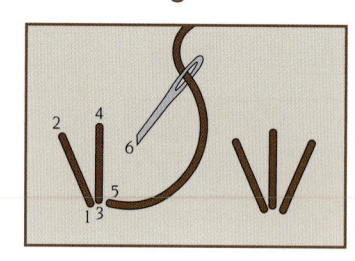

Whipstitch

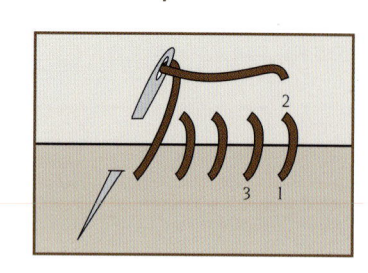

Square Pillow
page 3

Mary Engelbreit Enterprises, Inc., and Leisure Arts, Inc., grant permission to the owner of this book to photocopy the pattern on this page for personal use only.

Round Pillow
page 3

Mary Engelbreit Enterprises, Inc., and Leisure Arts, Inc., grant permission to the owner of this book to photocopy the pattern on this page for personal use only.

Rectangular Pillow
page 4

Mary Engelbreit Enterprises, Inc., and Leisure Arts, Inc., grant permission to the owner of this book to photocopy the pattern on this page for personal use only.

25

Framed Pieces
page 5

Right Frame

Middle Frame

Mary Engelbreit Enterprises, Inc., and Leisure Arts, Inc., grant permission to the owner of this book to photocopy the patterns on this page for personal use only.

Framed Pieces
page 5

Left Frame

Mary Engelbreit Enterprises, Inc., and Leisure Arts, Inc., grant permission to the owner of this book to photocopy the patterns on this page for personal use only.

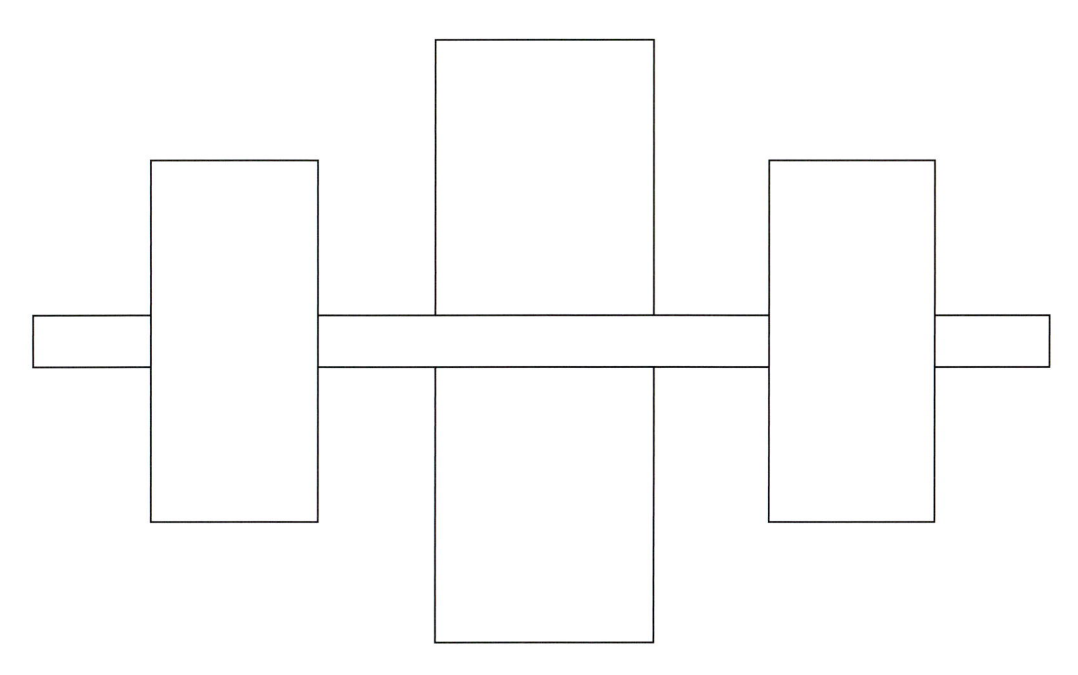

Wall Hanging
page 6

27

Wall Hanging
page 6

Dresser Scarf
page 7

Mary Engelbreit Enterprises, Inc. and Leisure Arts, Inc., grant permission to the owner of this book to photocopy the pattern on this page for personal use only.

Pink & Cream Cover
page 9

Mary Engelbreit Enterprises, Inc., and Leisure Arts, Inc., grant permission to the owner of this book to photocopy the patterns on this page for personal use only.

Scalloped Runner
page 10

Bohemian Cover
page 9

Mary Engelbreit Enterprises, Inc., and Leisure Arts, Inc., grant permission to the owner of this book to photocopy the pattern on this page for personal use only.

31

Cherry Purse
page 14

Flap

Mary Engelbreit Enterprises, Inc., and Leisure Arts, Inc., grant permission to the owner of this book to photocopy the patterns on this page for personal use only.

Cherry Purse Charm
page 11

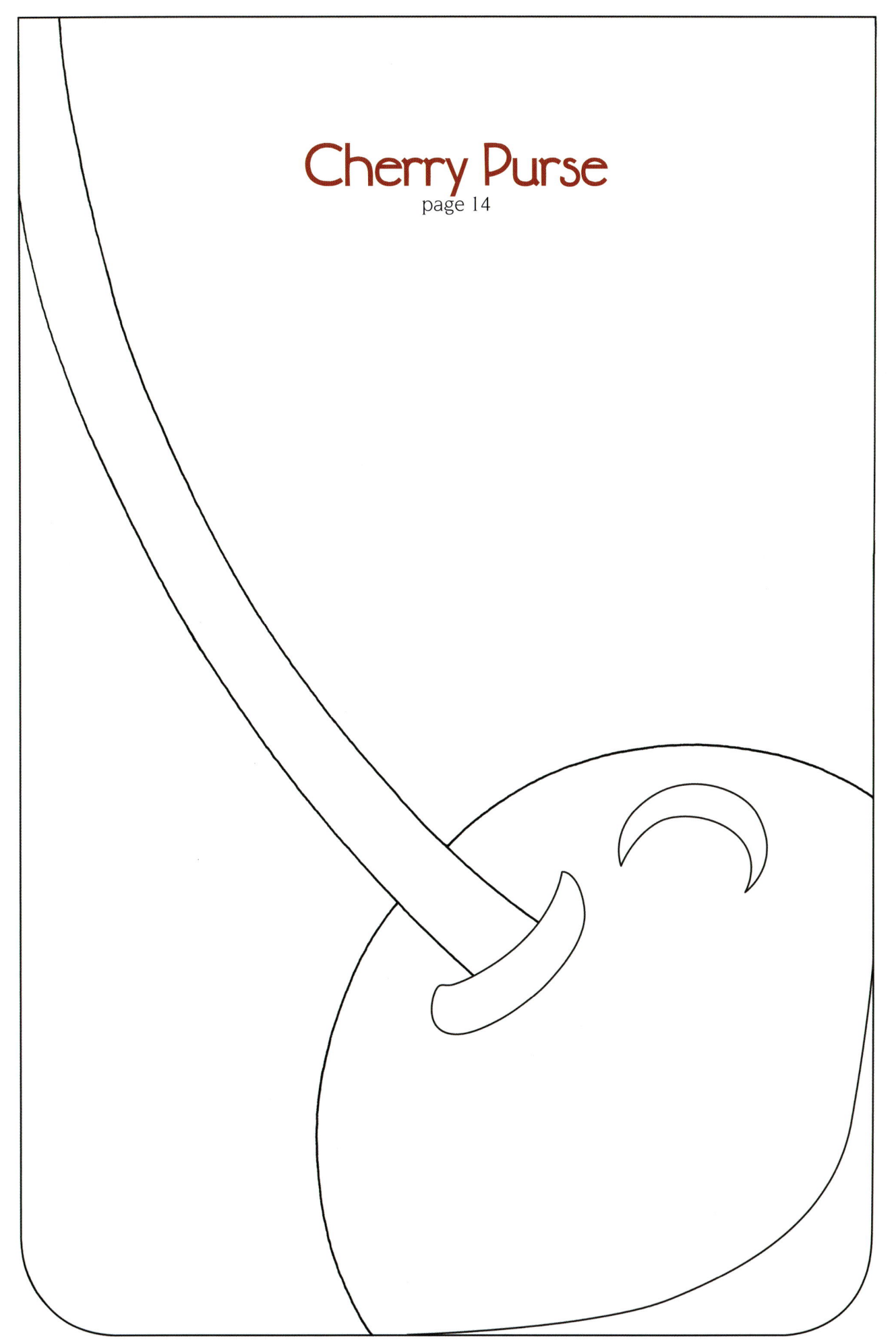

Cherry Purse
page 14

Scottie Key Fob
page 12

Cherry Eyeglass Case
page 13

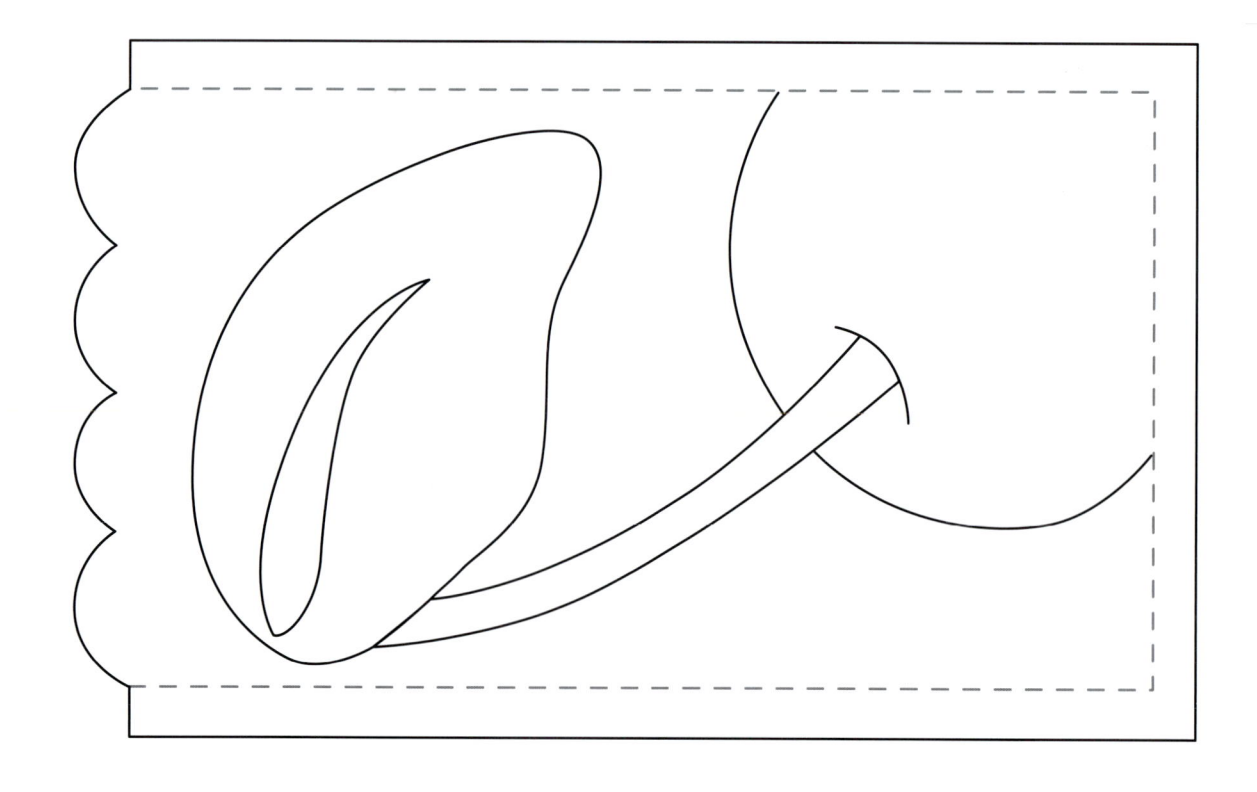

Mary Engelbreit Enterprises, Inc., and Leisure Arts, Inc., grant permission to the owner of this book to photocopy the patterns on this page for personal use only.

Cosmetic Bag & Zipper Pull
page 15

Trim

Mary Engelbreit Enterprises, Inc., and Leisure Arts, Inc., grant permission to the owner of this book to photocopy the patterns on this page for personal use only.

Tote Bag
page 16

Mary Engelbreit Enterprises, Inc., and Leisure Arts, Inc., grant permission to the owner of this book to photocopy the pattern on this page for personal use only.

Paisley Jeans
page 18

37

Felted Scarf
page 19

Appliquéd Scarf
page 20

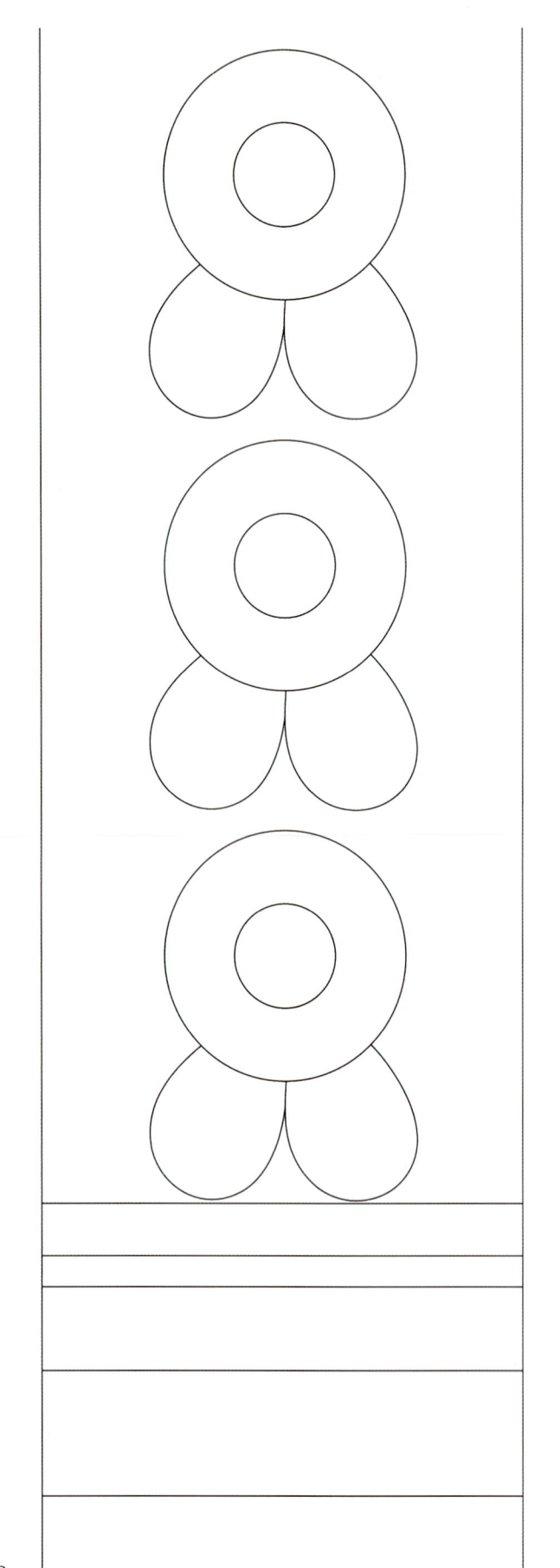

38

Credits

Designers: Kim Kern, Kelly Reider, Anne Pulliam Stocks, Lori Wenger, and Becky Werle
Editorial Writer: Susan McManus Johnson
Project Writers: Laura Siar Holyfield and Christina Kirkendoll
Graphic Artist: Amy Temple
Photo Stylist: Christy Myers
Mary Engelbreit Designer and Artist: Stephanie Barken

We wish to extend a warm thank you to Clover Needlecraft, Inc. for providing the felting needle tool, mat, mesh transfer canvas, and wool roving used in this book, The DMC Corporation for embroidery floss and pearl cotton, Beacon Adhesives™, Inc. for Fabri-Tac™, and National Nonwoven for providing us with felt.

This product is intended solely for non-commercial home use. No license has been granted to apply this product to decorated articles which will thereafter be sold. Any such use is an infringement of the copyright in the designs and artwork portrayed and is specifically prohibited.

All art and designs © Mary Engelbreit Enterprises, Inc. All use of art and designs is intended for personal use only and may not be used for resale purposes.

Mary Engelbreit Enterprises, Inc., and Leisure Arts, Inc., grant permission to the owner of this book to copy the patterns in this book for personal use only.

© 2008 by Mary Engelbreit Enterprises, Inc. Copyright © 2008 by Leisure Arts, Inc., 5701 Ranch Drive, Little Rock, AR 72223-9633, www.leisurearts.com (layout, photography, and crafts). All rights reserved. This publication is protected under federal copyright laws. Reproduction of this publication or any other Leisure Arts publication, including publications which are out of print, is prohibited unless specifically authorized. This includes, but is not limited to, any form of reproduction or distribution on or through the Internet, including posting, scanning, or e-mail transmission.

We have made every effort to ensure that these instructions are accurate and complete. We cannot, however, be responsible for human error, typographical mistakes, or variations in individual work.

Discover the CREATIVE world of Leisure Arts publications, where INSPIRATION lives on every page.

Your next great idea starts here.

Leisure Arts, the Art of Everyday Living

Visit your favorite retailer, or shop online at **leisurearts.com**. For more inspiration, sign up for our free e-newsletter and receive free projects, reviews of our newest books, handy tips and more. Have questions? Call us at 1.800.526.5111.

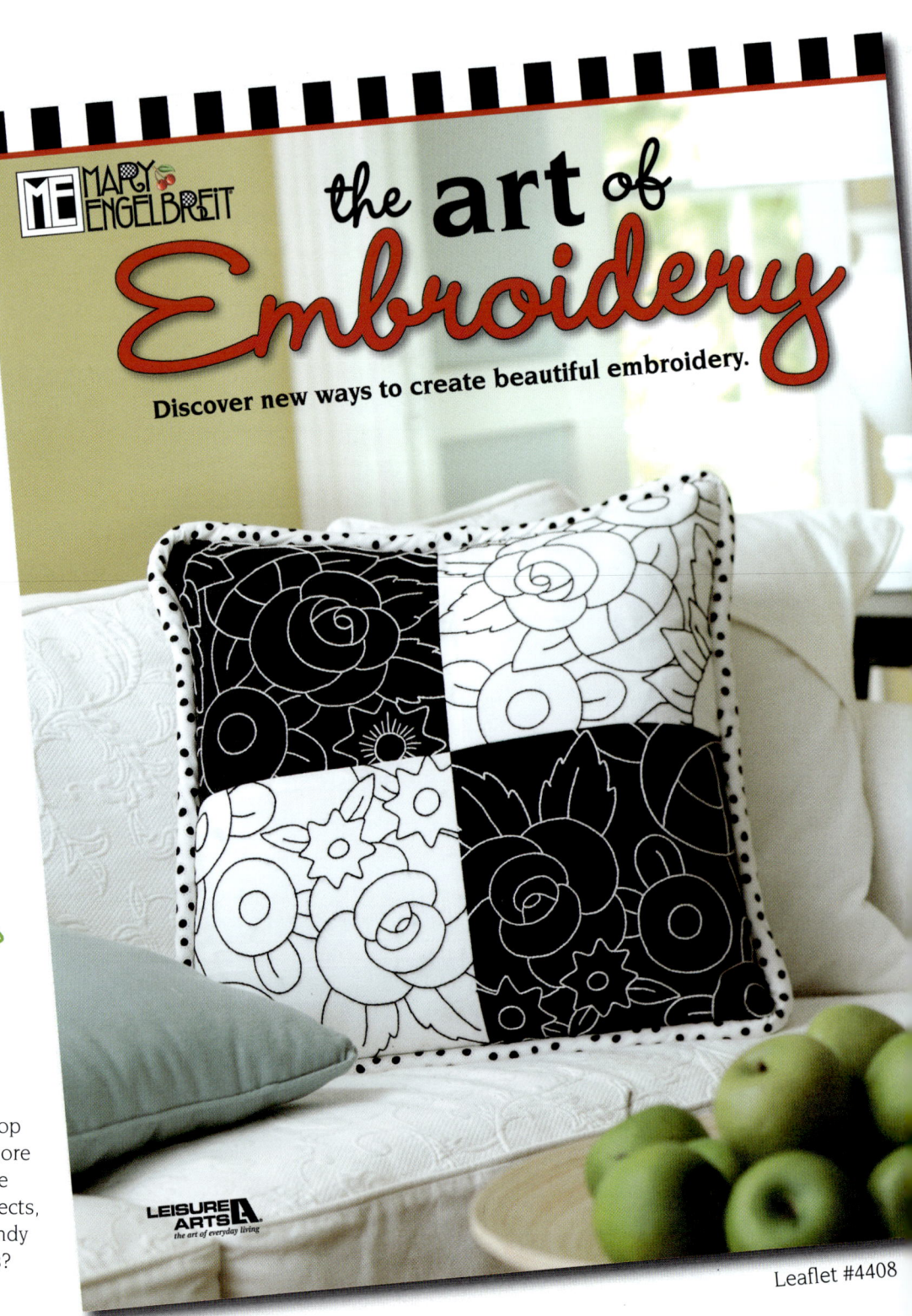

Mary Engelbreit
the art of Embroidery
Discover new ways to create beautiful embroidery.

LEISURE ARTS
the art of everyday living

Leaflet #4408

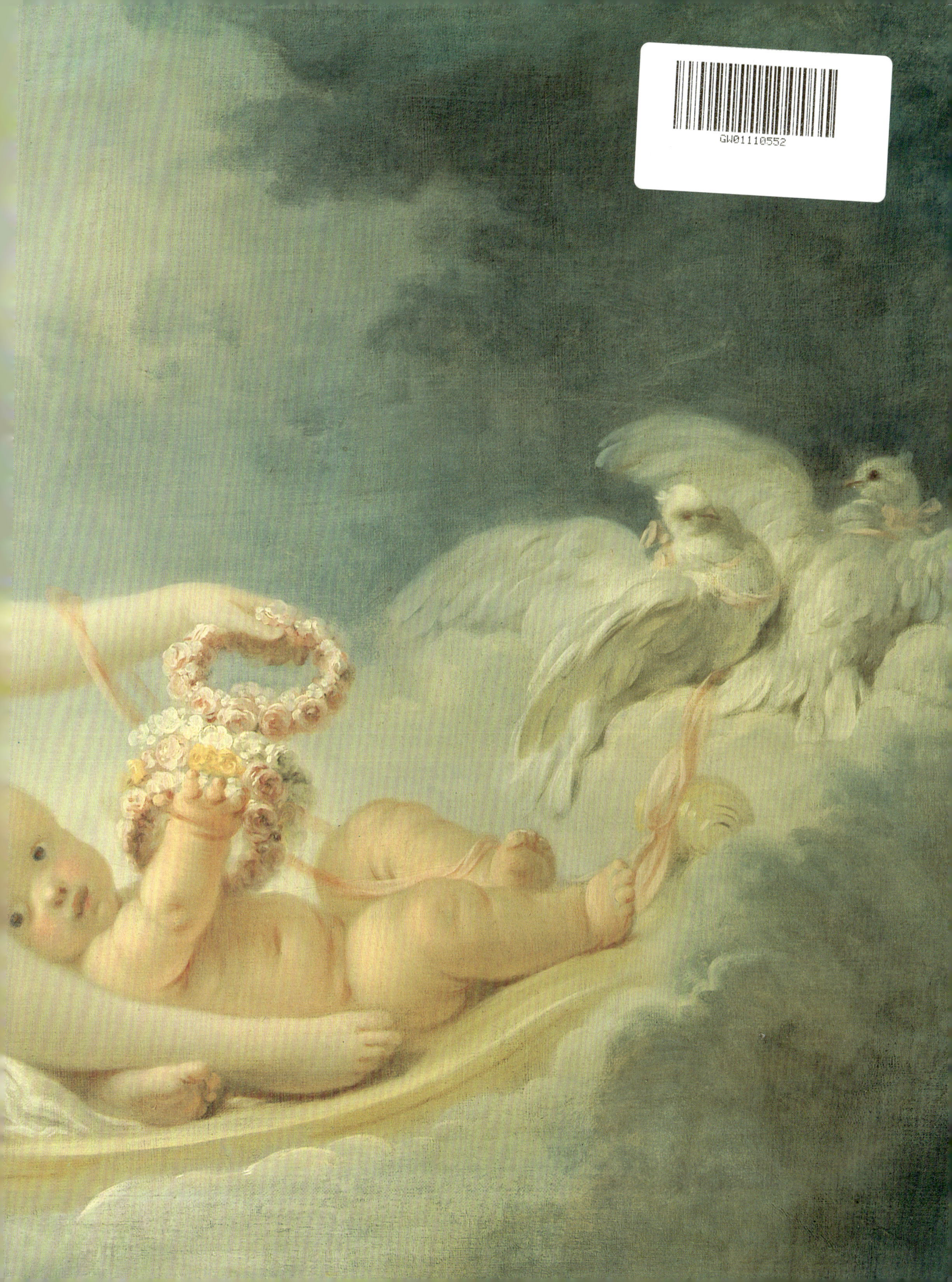

ART IS MY LIFE
A Tribute to JAMES WHITE

THE NATIONAL GALLERY OF IRELAND

Published by The National Gallery of Ireland

© The authors and The National Gallery of Ireland, 1991

All rights reserved. No part of this publication may be reproduced, stored in a system or transmitted in any form or by any means electronic, mechanical, photocopying, recording or otherwise, without the prior permission of the publisher.

British Library Cataloguing in Publication Data

Art is My Life

i. Kennedy, Brian P.
ii. White, James, 1913-
iii. National Gallery of Ireland
709.04

ISBN 0903162601

Edited by Brian P. Kennedy

Produced and designed by Creative Inputs
Colour Reproduction and Printing by Nicholson & Bass

Cover: Nathaniel Hone the Elder *(1718-1784)*
The Conjuror (1775)
NGI. Cat. No. 1790

End papers: Jean Honoré Fragonard *(1732-1806)*
Venus and Cupid (c. 1766)
NGI. Cat. No. 4313

PREFACE

My first memory of James White is of a lecture given by him in the National Gallery of Ireland in the mid-1970s. James was talking about the Renaissance in Italy and his enthusiasm for the subject was infectious. He emphasised the importance of looking at pictures, of studying them and learning from them.

James has always had time for students and, in line with the experience of many others, he has responded generously to my requests for information on various occasions over the past ten years. For me, James White is the archetype Irish cultural administrator. Art is his life. His self-professed aim has been to bring art to the people and in this he has succeeded brilliantly. Many thousands of people have been enriched by his dynamic contribution to Irish cultural life. He has never been shy of work and was always willing to take on the difficult, often thankless role of Honorary Secretary. His reward has been to find himself proposed as the unanimous choice for President, Chairman, or Director of many cultural organisations.

It is fitting that the National Gallery of Ireland should honour one of its most illustrious Directors by publishing this volume. It is offered to James White, a distinguished, cultured gentleman, as a modest tribute in celebration of his life-long commitment to art.

Dr. Brian P. Kennedy

ACKNOWLEDGEMENTS

The editing of this book was made easy by the generous cooperation of the contributors. I am sincerely grateful for their willingness to participate in this volume. The enthusiastic manner in which the contributors dedicated valuable time to writing these essays was due to their great respect for James White.

I wish to thank Michael Olohan for his photographs of works in the collection of the National Gallery of Ireland. I also acknowledge the following photographers who contributed to the volume, Pieterse Davison, Brendan Dempsey and Kevin Wallace. Ms. Paula Hicks, Rights and Reproductions Officer at the National Gallery of Ireland, was diligent and good-humoured in response to my requests for illustrations. The support of the photographic departments of the following institutions is acknowledged: The Hugh Lane Municipal Gallery of Modern Art, Dublin; Trinity College, Dublin; The Limerick City Art Gallery; The British Museum, London; The Tate Gallery, London; The Groeningemuseum, Bruges; The Calouste Gulbenkian Foundation, Lisbon; The Henry and Rose Pearlman Foundation, Inc., The Art Museum, Princeton University, New Jersey; The Metropolitan Museum of Art, New York; The Ashmolean Museum, Oxford; The Bibliothèque Nationale, Paris; The Musée d'Orsay, Paris; The Galleria Sabauda, Turin; The Hirshorn Museum and Sculpture Garden, Smithsonian Institution, Washington; The National Portrait Gallery, Smithsonian Institution, Washington.

Ms. Mary Corcoran of R.T.E. was most helpful in providing tape recordings of interviews with James White. I wish to thank Faber & Faber Ltd. for permission to reproduce the poem, 'The Biretta' from *Seeing Things* by Seamus Heaney. The poem 'Coming Events' by John Montague was published in his collection, *Tides* (The Dolmen Press, 1970). I acknowledge the following institutions for permission to publish copyright material: The Chester Beatty Library, Dublin; Trinity College, Dublin; The British Museum, London; The New York Public Library.

The index was prepared by Mr. Adrian Le Harivel and the production of the book was facilitated by the support of Mr. Raymond Keaveney, Director, National Gallery of Ireland; Ms. Mary Gallery, Manager, National Gallery of Ireland Shop; the book designers, Creative Inputs Ltd.; and the printers, Nicholson & Bass Ltd.

B.P.K.

CONTENTS

JAMES WHITE: A BRIEF BIOGRAPHY
Brian P. Kennedy

ix

THE TURNING POINT FOR IRISH MODERNISM
Bruce Arnold

3

THE FRIENDS OF THE NATIONAL COLLECTIONS OF IRELAND
Nicola Gordon Bowe

15

FROM DUBLIN TO NEW YORK, WITH A DETOUR TO
LENINGRAD: AN ART-HISTORICAL ODYSSEY
Marian Burleigh-Motley

31

W.J. LEECH AND THE CONVENT GARDEN
Julian Campbell

37

LOSING SIGHT OF ART
Ciarán Carty

47

NOTES ON THE CLEANING AND FRAMING OF PICTURES IN
TRINITY COLLEGE, DUBLIN
Anne Crookshank

57

THE CRUCIFIXION
Paul Durcan

67

IRISH ART AND THE POSTWAR ERA
Brian Fallon

69

THE CURIOUS CRAFT OF ART CRITICISM: WITH
DR JAMES WHITE IN PARIS AND OXFORD
Tony Gray

75

THE BIRETTA
Seamus Heaney

83

THE AVIGNON ANNUNCIATION
Eileen Kane

85

PIERRE THOMAS LE CLERC'S ILLUSTRATIONS FOR
DESMARAIS' POEM JÉRÉMIE
Raymond Keaveney

97

THE COLLECTING TECHNIQUE OF
SIR ALFRED CHESTER BEATTY
Brian P. Kennedy

107

FATHER SENAN O.F.M., CAP.:
THE CORPULENT CAPUCHIN OF CAPEL STREET
Benedict Kiely

121

JAMES WHITE
Louis le Brocquy

127

COMING EVENTS
John Montague

131

NATHANIEL HONE AND JOHN QUINN : A CORRESPONDENCE
Homan Potterton

133

THE NATIONAL GALLERY OF IRELAND'S COLLECTION OF
PAINTINGS BY JACK B. YEATS
Hilary Pyle

155

THE FALL AND RISE OF JACQUES LOUIS DAVID IN DUBLIN
Robert Rosenblum

167

THE IRISH CLAUDES
Alistair Rowan

173

GEORGE MOORE AND DEGAS
Denys Sutton

185

ACQUIRING IRISH PAINTINGS
1964-1980
Michael Wynne

197

NOTES ON THE CONTRIBUTORS

206

INDEX

209

James White
standing before the
full-length sculpture of
George Bernard Shaw
(1856-1950) by
Prince Paul Troubetzkoy
(1866-1938) outside the
National Gallery of
Ireland

JAMES WHITE: A BRIEF BIOGRAPHY

Brian P. Kennedy

James White was born in Dublin on 16 September 1913, the son of Thomas White and Florence Coffey. His father, from Tulla in County Clare, had moved to Dublin and had taken up an accounts job but his passion in life was the sporting world of race horses and dogs. He wrote a column for *The Irish Field* under the pseudonym 'Danny Boy' and was a member of the Irish Kennel Club and President of the Irish Kerry Blue Terrier Association. Thomas White sent his son, James, to the Jesuit-run Belvedere College in Dublin as a day pupil. This education was ideal for a boy of James's interests. There were many school clubs which promoted cultural interests, for example, photography, musicals and dramas. In sports, James played tennis, rugby and enjoyed cycling. He also liked languages, Irish, Latin, French and German. His father was an enthusiastic reader and a regular theatre-goer. He took his children to the Abbey Theatre often and to the operas in the Gaiety Theatre.

At the age of sixteen, after James had passed his Intermediate Certificate examination, he had to leave school in order to assist the modest family finances. He got a job, 'a good pensionable post', as a clerk in the John Player Tobacco Company. His first pay was thirty-two shillings and sixpence per week.

While at school, James won the Junior House Medal for Debating. This was a portend of his future reputation as a noted lecturer. He was good at writing too, a quality he attributes to his father's influence. He was especially friendly with one of his classmates, Jack Hanlon, who later became a priest and a distinguished artist. Jack Hanlon was a pupil of Mainie Jellett, the leading Irish modern artist, and he brought James to her for lessons. Mainie, a very decisive personality, took James aside after his second painting lesson and said: 'We have no art critic in this country. We want you to become an art critic'. She did not say that James could not paint but he understood the message.[1]

During the 1930s, there were few exhibition venues in Dublin where new trends in painting could be viewed. Victor Waddington had opened his Gallery in the 1920s but the galleries which most influenced James White were the Contemporary Picture Galleries and the exhibitions of the Society of Dublin Painters. The Contemporary Picture Galleries had its first premises in Leinster Street and showed the work of painters like Mainie Jellett, Evie Hone and Jack Yeats. The Society of Dublin Painters, founded by Paul Henry, Jack Yeats and others, held a few exhibitions each year at 7 St. Stephen's Green. But there was really very little artistic activity outside the formidable institution of the Royal Hibernian Academy. Its annual show was a great social event in Dublin.

Mainie Jellett gave practical encouragement to James White by asking the Contemporary Picture Galleries to host a lecture to be given by him one Saturday afternoon. In this talk, James criticised the Royal Hibernian Academy for its lack of figurative and religious painting. Landscape was then the favoured subject matter and the Academy tended to ignore modernist trends such as those promoted by Mainie Jellett and Evie Hone. The lecture received some notoriety because Alec Newman, who wrote 'Dubliner's Diary' for the the *Irish Times*, reported its contents and agreed with the young lecturer's assessment of the arts scene in Dublin.

Besides painting, the other area into which James White poured his energies was the art of ballet. He helped to found the Irish Ballet Club in 1937 and served as its Honorary Secretary. The other founders included the choreographer, Cepta Cullen, and Maureen Newman who became the Honorary Treasurer. The first Club President was F.R. Higgins and other key figures were R.C. Fergusson, Ernest Little and Arthur Power. James White had met Marie Rambert and Ninette de Valois in London and, from them, he learned that in ballet, the script comes first, then the music followed by the set and costume designs, and finally the choreography. The first big production staged by the Club was 'Puck Fair' by F.R. Higgins, with stage sets by Mainie Jellett, choreography by Cepta Cullen and music by Elizabeth Maconchy. James White considers that: 'Through ballet, I saw the meaning of painting as a background to movement and music. I owe more to this than perhaps anything else. I was never educated formally for the career I was to follow'.[2]

Each year, James visited the galleries and museums of London and it was there that he learned about paintings by studying them carefully. Later he travelled to many European countries including France, Italy and Greece, fulfilling his appetite for a deeper knowledge of art. In 1938, James persuaded Peadar O'Curry, editor of *The Standard*, to take him on as an art critic. He reviewed mainly religious work by artists like Mainie Jellett, Evie Hone and Seamus Murphy. The late 1930s and the early 1940s saw many cultural changes in Ireland. Much of this change was stimulated by the forced isolation resulting from Irish neutrality during the Second World War. The most significant artistic event in Ireland at this time was the establishment in 1943 of the Irish Exhibition of Living Art. Its annual exhibition provided a platform for a new generation of Irish artists and acted as a stimulating counterpoint to the Royal Hibernian Academy's annual show. James White was closely involved with most of the changes occurring in the arts scene. He was, however, still a full-time employee of John Player & Sons. He tried to conceal his arts writing by using the name James White for his work as a critic and Patrick or Paddy White for his career with John Player's. He led a dual life, using his lunch hours to review exhibitions and his evenings to deliver talks about art.

When Mrs. George Bernard Shaw died, she left some money to be used for the education of Irish girls. The fund was administered by *Foras Eireann*, an umbrella group of voluntary organisations, founded in 1949, and it was decided that one of the activities financed by Mrs. Shaw's money should be lectures on art. Hugh Fitzpatrick, an accountant by profession, who helped run *Foras Eireann*, asked

James White to travel around Ireland giving art lectures. These were usually held at 8 p.m. in a small public hall or school room. James would leave Dublin after work at 5 p.m. and drive down to the venue where he would set up his own slide projector and screen. The groups were small, about twelve or fifteen people. Many of these people later told James that these lectures gave them their first exposure to fine paintings. James himself thinks that the missionary nature of these lecture trips gave him his main aim in life: 'to bring art to the people'.[3]

In 1950 the *Irish Press* decided to match its rival daily newspapers by appointing an art critic and James White was offered the job. He was delighted to join the other critics, David Sears of the *Irish Independent* and Tony Gray of the *Irish Times*, because, like them, he could now review all types of exhibitions, featuring both secular and religious work. He also extended his experience as a broadcaster. He had been employed by *Radio Eireann* to present a programme 'Records and Recollections' which was transmitted from the studio at Henry Street, Dublin, from 11 to 11.30 p.m. This programme offered stories about the lives of composers along with recordings of their music. The B.B.C. in Belfast, under the inspired guidance of the poet, Robert Greacen, began to ask James to travel there to contribute to arts programmes and he was also invited frequently to deliver lectures at the Ulster Museum by its Director, the poet John Hewitt.

When the Cultural Relations Committee of the Department of External Affairs was established in 1949, James White was invited to select exhibitions which would travel abroad with the Committee's financial support. The Arts Council, *An Chomhairle Ealaíon*, founded in 1951, was similarly eager to involve James in its activities. He was asked to deliver lectures throughout the country to coincide with a touring exhibition of prints of Impressionist and Post-Impressionist paintings. Fr. Edward Coyne, who organised the extra-mural lectures at University College, Dublin, heard of James's reputation as a lecturer and asked him to present talks to U.C.D. students. Not to be out done, Trinity College, which hoped to establish a course in the history of art, asked James to give lecturers to Bachelor of Arts students and to set their examination papers. Thus, despite the fact that he had no university degrees, James found himself in the enviable position of part-time lecturer in both Dublin universities.

Through his many and varied activities in the arts, James met nearly all of Ireland's distinguished artists, writers, dramatists, architects, musicians, dancers, actors and arts administrators. He knew three Directors of the National Gallery of Ireland, Thomas Bodkin (1928-35), George Furlong (1935-50) and Thomas MacGreevy (1950-64). He supported Bodkin in his tireless efforts to retrieve the Lane Pictures for Ireland, in fulfilment of the signed but unwitnessed codicil to Sir Hugh Lane's last will and testament.[4] Thomas MacGreevy was a particular friend. They both shared a profound admiration for the work of a number of Irish artists, especially Jack Yeats. In 1949, Thomas MacGreevy told James that he would like Ireland to be represented as a member country of the International Association of Art Critics. James made the necessary arrangements and he and MacGreevy went to Paris for the Congress of International Art Critics. James proposed that the 1953 Congress should be held in Dublin. This was a big undertaking but the week of events, held in Dublin in 1953 to coincide with the Congress at Newman House, was an outstanding success. Many leading international critics attended the Congress and the Irish Government supported it.

The Art Critics Congress was the first of two major events in the 1950s which helped to raise Ireland's profile in the international art world. The second was Louis le Brocquy's achievement in winning an international prize at the Venice Biennale in 1956 for his painting 'A Family' (1951, Private Collection, Milan). James White was among the first art critics to appreciate the quality of Louis le Brocquy's work and he wrote the catalogue accompanying the artist's show at the Venice Biennale.[5]

Throughout the 1950s, James organised a series of exhibitions which helped to expand the interest of the Irish public in the arts. For example, in 1954, as part of the cultural festival known as *An Tóstal*, he organised an exhibition of 'Early Bronze Crucifixes and Bronze Statuettes of the Renaissance', mainly from the collection of Sir Alfred Beit. In 1957, James organised an exhibition at Dublin's Municipal Gallery of Modern Art entitled 'Paintings from Irish Collections'. Few people had realised the depth, range and excellence of the paintings in private collections in Ireland and there was an enthusiastic response to the exhibition. The Chairman of the Exhibition Committee was Senator E.A. McGuire, James White was Honorary Secretary, and the committee included noted private owners like Sir Alfred Beit. This exhibition marked a decisive turning point for James because he now changed from a concentration on modern art to close involvement with old master paintings. He was soon to make the most significant career-move of his life.

When the Curator of the Dublin Municipal Gallery, Patrick O'Connor, retired in 1960, James decided to apply for the job. He was delighted and surprised when it was offered to him. He had been working in John Player & Sons for thirty years and had become an Assistant Manager. The move to the Municipal Gallery was a great adventure. It involved bringing his wife, Agnes ('Aggie'), whom he had married in 1941, and their three sons and two daughters, to live in a spacious flat at the top of the Municipal Gallery. It was a magnificent eighteenth century Georgian building but it had one negative point, no garden. James developed the habit of taking his youngest son, Mark, to the Phoenix Park every day. For four years, the Park was his back garden.

The Municipal Gallery was elegant and housed a fine collection of pictures, but it lacked publicity. James's enthusiastic personality was well-suited to the task of attracting publicity. He also had experience of practical business management, such as dealing with unions. His basic aim was to popularise the Gallery and he began by inviting the staff of selected business firms to visit the Gallery on Sunday mornings. He organised numerous temporary exhibitions but his greatest success was the Children's Art Holiday which was held for the first time in 1962, just after Christmas. Artists were brought in to offer classes in drawing and painting to children. Parents had to collect their children and they were, consequently, obliged to visit the Gallery themselves. They were enthused and attracted by the sight of children creating their own art works, as indeed were newspaper photographers and the recently established national television service.

On 1 June 1964, James White was appointed as the Director of the National Gallery of Ireland, in succession to Thomas MacGreevy. James's appointment occurred in the Gallery's centenary year so the first task at hand was the organisation of a 'Centenary Exhibition'. From October to December 1964, the Gallery hosted a splendid show of old master paintings. There were 205 works in the exhibition, most from the Gallery's own collections but including loans from museums in many cities, Amsterdam, Berlin, Brussels, Florence, The Hague, Milan, New York, Oslo, Ottawa, Rome, Stockholm and Venice. In his introduction to the exhibition catalogue, James White declared his intentions for the National Gallery of Ireland: 'Our only thought is to find a means of extending the service and of making the Gallery more attractive to the public'.[6]

James has always said that he was born lucky: 'People play games and speculate about what country and what period they'd have been from, and whom they'd have been if they had the choice. On reflection I think I was born just when I would like to have been born. I've been an enormously lucky man'.[7] Luck is, of course, what one makes of it and James White seized his chances vigorously. His arrival at the National Gallery coincided with increased capital funding. In 1951, Thomas MacGreevy had begun a campaign for Government support for the construction of a Gallery extension. He finally received a funding commitment in 1962 but the construction of the new wing took place during the first few years of James White's Directorship. The extension, designed by Frank Du Berry of the Office of Public Works, was completed in May 1968 at a cost of £420,000. The public response was quite phenomenal. From 25 September 1968, when the new Gallery was opened officially, until 31 December 1968, there were 96,061 visitors, an average of one thousand per day. The annual attendance figure at the Gallery increased form 93,179 in 1967 to 324,573 in 1969.[8] But the new wing was only part of the reason for the increase. If we take a longer period of time, we find that from 1963 to 1971, the annual attendance increased from 55,125 to 359,102.[9] In 1980, the year James White retired as Director, the annual attendance was 426,416.[10]

Much of this increase in visitor numbers can be attributed to the dynamic leadership of James White, and the dedicated support of the Gallery staff. He foresaw the huge rise in leisure-time interest in painting and sculpture. He recognised that there was a large audience eager to interest itself in art. Exhibitions were organised, lecture programmes established, concerts held, seminars arranged; in short, the Gallery became a hive of cultural activity. The Children's Art Holiday was moved from the Municipal Gallery to the National Gallery and the numbers of children in attendance increased annually.

Remedial legislation assisted the Gallery when, in 1963, the Oireachtas passed a National Gallery of Ireland Act to allow the Gallery's Board of Governors and Guardians to lend works to any institution approved by them. Previously, the Gallery could lend to public exhibitions only. James was especially keen to lend pictures to provincial galleries because he knew them well from his days as a touring lecturer. Facilities at the National Gallery itself were improved, especially with the establishment of an art reference library, a lecture theatre and a fully-equipped restoration studio. In the summers of 1967 and 1968, with the cooperation of the Istituto Centrale del Restauro in Rome, a team of fourteen Italian restorers came to Dublin to carry out canvas relining, panel repairs and painting restoration on 120 works from the collection of the National Gallery of Ireland.[11] As a direct result of the success of this initiative, the Gallery was authorised to employ its own restorers. Another new facility which was well-received was the Gallery restaurant. Many visitors came to enjoy a meal at the Gallery and left under the gentle spell of the picture collection.

The attraction of temporary exhibitions stimulated public interest. These ranged from home-generated shows to international touring exhibitions. A special effort was made to increase interest in Irish art with shows like *W.B. Yeats: A Centenary Exhibition* (1965), *Cuimhneacháin 1916* (1966), *Irish Portraits 1660-1860* (1969), *Jack B. Yeats* (1971), *John Butler Yeats and the Irish Renaissance* (1972), *The Irish 1870-1970* (1974), *The Architecture of Ireland in Drawings and Paintings* (1975), *William Orpen: A Centenary Exhibition* (1978) and *The Abbey Theatre 1904-1979* (1980). Exhibitions from the National Gallery of Ireland which were sent abroad included *Drawings from the National Gallery of Ireland* (1967, London), *Aspects of Irish Art* (1974, Columbus, Ohio; Toledo, Ohio; St. Louis, Missouri), *Irish Watercolours* (1976, Dallas, Texas) and *Ireland's Literary Renaissance* (1980, Chicago). The catalogues accompanying many of these exhibitions were written, either wholly or in part, by James White. There were also exhibitions from abroad which were shown in Dublin, examples include: *The Armand Hammer Collection* (1972), *Ferdinand Howald: Avant-Garde Collector* (1973), *Nineteenth Century German Drawings and Watercolours* (1976), *100 American Drawings from the J.D. Hatch Collection* (1976) and *Paul Klee* (1980).

James White's arrival at the National Gallery of Ireland coincided not only with increased Government funding but also with the large-scale accrual of moneys to the Shaw Fund. George Bernard Shaw (1856-1950), in tribute to the National Gallery of Ireland for the part it played in his education, left to it one third of his estate. Due to the commercial success of the film, *My Fair Lady*, which was based on Shaw's *Pygmalion*, the National Gallery of Ireland had the funding necessary to acquire major old master paintings. Among those purchased by the Gallery Board, on the advice of James White, were the following: Giovanni di Paolo, *Crucifixion* (1964, £79,000); Jacques Yverni, *Annunciation* (1965, £220,000), Francisco de Goya, *El Sueno* (1969, £225,000), Baron Gérard, *Julie Bonaparte with her Daughters* (1972, £40,000), Jacques Louis David, *The Funeral of Patroclus* (1973, £250,000) and Jean Honoré Fragonard, *Venus and Cupid* (1978, £375,000).

The purchase of Irish paintings was also an important feature of James White's Directorship. Those acquired included: Nathaniel Hone the Elder, *The Conjuror* (1966, £2,500), Thomas Roberts, *An Ideal Landscape* (1972, £8,000), Robert Carver, *A Landscape with Peasants and a Dog* (1973, £4,500) and William Ashford, *A View of Dublin from Clontarf* (1976, £6,000). Dr. Michael Wynne, whose expertise was invaluable, especially on Irish paintings, compiled a concise catalogue of the Gallery's entire collection of paintings. This catalogue, published in 1971, was the first complete list of the Gallery's paintings to be produced since the nineteenth century. A catalogue of the Gallery's sculptures, also compiled by Dr. Wynne, was published in 1975.

James White retired as Director of the National Gallery of Ireland on 31 May 1980. During the fifteen years of his Directorship, he brought about a gentle revolution at the Gallery. Denys Sutton, editor of the fine art magazine, *Apollo*, wrote this assessment of James's achievement to mark his retirement: 'The National Gallery of Ireland has now become a leading museum in Europe. That this is so is due to the drive of James White... The transformation that has occurred in the Gallery is remarkable; it shows that effort can win rewards... James White's achievement has been to transform an old-fashioned gallery into a modern one, yet at the same time, its former charm has been retained. It is a gallery with a human character'.[12]

The list of major honours awarded to James White is indicative of the high esteem in which he is held: an Honorary Doctorate from the National University of Ireland, 1970; Chevalier of the Légion d'Honneur, 1974; Order of Merit, Government of Italy, 1977; and Commander of the Order of Merit, Government of the Federal Republic of Germany, 1983. He has served as President of the Friends of the National Collections of Ireland, Chairman of the Irish Museums Association, Chairman of the International Council of Museums (Ireland), Chairman of the Association of Irish Art Historians, Trustee of the Chester Beatty Library and Trustee of the Alfred Beit Foundation. He has also served as a courageous, outspoken and independent Chairman of the Arts Council (1978-83).[13] His list of publications is long and wide-ranging. It includes monographs on the painters Louis le Brocquy, George Campbell and Brian Bourke; numerous catalogues including *Evie Hone* (1958), *Irish Stained Glass* (1963, with Michael Wynne), *Jack B. Yeats* (1971, with Hilary Pyle), *John Butler Yeats* (1972), and an impressive survey book, *The National Gallery of Ireland* (1968).

James White discovered that a love of art can be a recipe for a happy life. He succeeded in making the National Gallery of Ireland available to everyone. Art has been his life and it is to his great credit that, by virtue of his dedication, enthusiasm and good humour, he has encouraged many thousands of people to share his passion. Ireland owes him a considerable debt.

Notes

1. R.T.E. radio interview with Pádraig O'Raghallaigh, 1989. I am most grateful to Ms. Mary Corcoran, the producer of this series of six interviews with James White, for providing me with tape recordings of the programmes.

2. Ibid.

3. Ibid.

4. It was during a discussion following a lecture given by James White in 1975, marking sixty years since the death of Sir Hugh Lane, that Cearbhall O'Dálaigh made the suggestion that the Municipal Gallery of Modern Art should be renamed the Hugh Lane Municipal Gallery of Modern Art. The suggestion was adopted by Dublin Corporation.

5. James White, *Louis le Brocquy*, Venice Biennale Catalogue, June 1956.

6. *National Gallery of Ireland Centenary Exhibition 1864-1964*, Oct.-Dec. 1964.

7. Ciarán Carty, Interview with James White, *Sunday Independent*, 4 Feb. 1979.

8. National Gallery of Ireland, unpublished annual reports, 1967-9.

9. Ibid., 1963-71.

10. Ibid., 1980.

11. *Catalogue of Paintings restored in the National Gallery of Ireland to December 1971*, 2nd ed., 1972.

12. *Apollo*, June 1980, editorial, p. 416.

13. For an account of James White's Chairmanship of the Arts Council, see Brian P. Kennedy, *Dreams and Responsibilities: The State and the Arts in Independent Ireland* (Dublin, 1990), pp 193-214.

Principal Shaw Fund Purchases during James White's Directorship

(I am grateful to Dr. Michael Wynne and Mr. Adrian Le Harivel for assistance in the compilation of this list).

N.G.I. Cat. No.	Artist's Name	Title of Work	Year Purchased
1766	Jack Yeats	About to write a letter	1964
1768	Giovanni di Paolo	Crucifixion	1964
1769	Jack Yeats	Grief	1965
1780	Jacques Yverni	The Annunciation	1965
1790	Nathaniel Hone the Elder	The Conjuror	1966
8011	Auguste Renoir	Hymn to Life Clock	1966
1812	Ludovico Cigoli	Siege of Jerusalem	1967
8030	François Duquesnoy	Cardinal Bentivoglio	1967
8031	Attributed to Juan Alonso Villabrille y Ron	Elias overthrowing the false prophets of Baal	1967
8049	Workshop of Lorenzo Ghiberti	Virgin and Child	1967
1822	Albert Marquet	Porquerolles	1967
1824	Alexander Roslin	Le Marquis de Vaudreuil	1967
8050	Gustave Courbet	Madam Buchon	1968
1867	Etienne de La Tour	The Image of St. Alexis	1968
1835-58	Icon Collection	24 Greek and Russian Icons	1968
1928	Francisco de Goya	El Sueno	1969
8081	Ferdinand Dietz	Cronos eating one of his children	1970
1982	Simon Vouet	The Four Seasons	1970
4038	Roderic O'Conor	Reclining Nude	1971
4025-6	Valencian School	Life of St. James the Greater	1971
4055	Baron Gérard	Julie Bonaparte with her daughters	1972
4050	Eva Gonzales	Two children playing on sand dunes	1972
7517-33	Francis Place	Drawings from Irish visit	1972
4060	Jacques Louis David	The Funeral of Patroclus	1973
4074	Nathaniel Grogan	Tivoli, near Cork	1973
4304	Philip Hussey	Interior with a family	1973
4089	Giovanni Sogliani	The Virgin and Child with St. John the Baptist	1974
4134	Roderic O'Conor	La Jeune Bretonne	1975
4137	William Ashford	A view of Dublin from Clontarf	1976
4138	William Ashford	A view of Dublin from Chapelizod	1976
4170-1	French School	Large and Small Apse from the Chapel of St. Pierre de Campublic, Beaucaire, France	1976
4186	Juan Fernández	A still life	1976
4303	Nathaniel Grogan	A harbour in County Cork	1978
4313	Jean Honoré Fragonard	Venus and Cupid	1978
8246	Ligier Richier	The Virgin	1978
8247	Ligier Richier	St. John the Evangelist	1978
4315	Jan Provoost	Triptych: Virgin and Child with Saints	1979
4339	Joshua Reynolds	The Right Honourable John Hely-Hutchinson	1979

ESSAYS AND POEMS IN TRIBUTE TO JAMES WHITE

Mainie Jellett,
(1897-1944)
Decoration (1923)
NGI. Cat. No. 1326

THE TURNING POINT FOR IRISH MODERNISM

Bruce Arnold

James White first met Mainie Jellett in the early 1930s, and remained her friend and associate until her death. He was introduced to her by Jack Hanlon, with whom he had been at school at Belvedere College. Hanlon, who later became a priest but never relinquished his work as a painter, was a pupil for a time of André Lhote, in Paris, and a convinced Cubist, though not an abstract one. He persuaded James White to go to Mainie and explore the possibility of becoming a painter. Mainie's advice, sensibly and gently put to the young art lover, was that Ireland needed an art critic. And this defined his future career, though he was not able to take it up until much later.

No particular year, out of the ten during which James White was associated with Mainie Jellett, can be picked out as of special importance, though their closest working relationship was during the period when she was involved in stage sets for the ballet production choreographed by Cepta Cullen, written by F.R. Higgins, and set to music by Elizabeth Maconchy. This was *Puck Fair*, produced at the Gaiety Theatre in February 1941. I choose a different year, of great importance for Mainie herself, and significant in a broader, national context, and for the Modernist Movement.

1938 saw the opening of the group show of the Society of Dublin Painters in early February. The ceremony was performed by Seán T. O'Kelly, the first time a major politician had officiated at such a function. A leading member of the Fianna Fáil Government, O'Kelly was then Tánaiste and was later to become President of Ireland in succession to the eminent Gaelic scholar, Douglas Hyde. He was also Minister for Local Government and Public Health.

In his speech at the opening he stressed the independence of the group of artists who made up the Dublin Painters and their determination to provide a forum for those who were out of sympathy with the academic tradition. And he spoke also of the benefits of the artist to the community 'which enhanced the national culture and enriched the national life.' Though not untypical of such speeches on such occasions, the presence at the opening of the show of a senior member of the Fianna Fáil Government represented a significant degree of acceptance of the Modern Movement in art in Ireland which was publicly endorsed shortly afterwards with the choice of Mainie Jellett as the artist responsible for the decorations of Ireland's pavilion at the Glasgow World Fair.

Mainie herself presided at the opening and guests included another Fianna Fáil politician, Erskine Childers, who was later to become a government minister, and, at the end of his life, President of Ireland. Senior diplomats from the French, German, Swiss and Dutch missions were also present, as were leading literary and society figures - Oliver Gogarty, Con Curran - and of course the painters themselves.

The artistic 'discovery' of the show was E.A. McGuire. Already well-known as a sportsman - he played polo and was a Davis Cup tennis player - he had taken up painting at the suggestion of Harriet Kirkwood, a leading member of the Dublin Painters, and this 'news story' aspect of his first venture as a painter was predictably seized on by the newspapers, and not without subsequent justification, since McGuire became a leading figure in artistic circles, a Senator, a Governor and Guardian of the National Gallery, and father of the distinguished portrait painter, Edward McGuire.

The Dublin Painters had expanded their membership to eighteen, with Dolly Robinson (Lennox Robinson's wife), Margaret Clarke and Mabel Annesley the most recent recruits. Among Mainie's exhibits was 'Study: Waterfall', of which she did several versions, all based on the waterfall at Powerscourt, 'Wood in August', another naturalistic subject, and a large abstract in oil.

Rivalry between the two traditions still existed. At one level there was good-natured co-operation. Several of the Dublin Painters - Charles Lamb, Margaret Clarke, Letitia Hamilton - were members of the Royal Hibernian Academy. Jack Hanlon painted a portrait of Maurice MacGonigal and exhibited it in the February show, and MacGonigal himself, who was in due course to succeed Seán Keating as P.R.H.A., showed with the Dublin Painters. Keating himself was at the opening of the exhibition.

But behind the scenes there were still bruised feelings. Both Mainie and Evie Hone had work rejected by the Royal Hibernian Academy in 1938, as did Nano Reid, and it echoed the much larger controversy provoked in Britain, in April 1938, when Wyndham Lewis's portrait of T.S. Eliot, (now in Durban, South Africa), was rejected by the Royal Academy. Augustus John resigned in protest. Lewis himself described John's supportive action as 'a mortal blow to the Academy, if it is possible to use the expression, "mortal blow" with reference to a corpse.'

In Dublin the point was made that the Royal Hibernian Academy lacked the substance in its academic tradition which would allow for rejection on grounds of offensive modernism. So what were the standards by which these three established painters - all with international reputations or exhibitions to their credit - were refused by the R.H.A.? Press comments on the Irish controversy referred to the fact that both Mainie and Evie Hone had won gold and silver medals respectively from the Tailteann adjudicator and that Mainie Jellett had been chosen to decorate the Irish Pavilion at the Glasgow International Exhibition.

The new figure in the Dublin Painters' Exhibition, E.A. McGuire, was well-off and influential, and he organised in April an exhibition for the group at the premises in Bedford Square, London, of the British Architectural Association. And this was followed by another exhibition at the Irish High Commission, in Piccadilly House, Regent Street, in June. The *Irish Press* reporter wrote: 'Miss Maimie [sic] Jellett has a number of works, ranging from Cubist design through objective transcription to ancient themes.'

But the biggest international event in which Mainie Jellett was involved in 1938 was the Glasgow British Empire Exhibition, which opened in May. Her two murals for the Irish Pavilion, which depicted various aspects of Irish rural, industrial and cultural life, measured ten feet by eighty feet each. The Pavilion itself, which was built by a Greenock firm, was of Modernist, Art Deco design, described in one report as 'the only one of its kind in the Exhibition', and it stood between the Canadian and Australian pavilions on what was called 'Dominion Avenue'. Mainie had already exhibited her small gouache studies for the murals at the summer exhibition of the Irish Water-Colour Society, and sketches and squared-up drawings have survived, showing the extent of preparatory work for the final panels.

Ireland's social and industrial development, its marketable produce, its history and tradition, its contribution through Shannon Airport to world travel by air, its theatrical, literary and horse-racing traditions, were all encompassed in the exhibition, which was a triumph of organisation and diversity. And even before it was over the decision was made by the Irish Government that Mainie's murals would be shipped to New York and used for the Irish Pavilion at the World Fair planned for 1939.

There were two slightly negative aspects to the Glasgow Exhibition. The first was that it underlined Ireland's divided political state; there were in fact two Irish pavilions, the second one for the Six Counties, and this meant the separate assertion of things like butter coming from the Twenty-Six Counties, while linen came from the North. The second was the somewhat negative response of Dublin Corporation to the idea that the city should follow New York's example, and hold the third successive world fair in 1940. While international events would probably have intervened, the lukewarm civic response to the various proposals based on the need to persuade the people of other countries to take an intelligent interest in Ireland was much criticised. At that time - and indeed for many years to come - the only really international focus upon Ireland was achieved by the Royal Dublin Society through its two annual shows, and particularly the second of these, the Horse Show in early August each year.

Mainie did not have a solo exhibition during 1938, though she participated in at least three group exhibitions. Her Glasgow murals went to New York early in 1939, for the New York World Fair. Additionally, her painting *Achill Horses* (now in the National Gallery of Ireland) was requested for New York by the Department of Industry and Commerce, who undertook responsibility for insurance and shipping in a letter dated 14 April 1938. She received an inscribed certificate from the Board of Directors of the New York World's Fair, in appreciation of her 'substantial contribution'. In his letter thanking her for the loan, on the Minister's behalf, Philip Dempsey, of the Department of Industry and Commerce, referred to 'a condition of the arrangement, that the picture would not be removed from the Irish Pavilion before the termination of the Fair on the 31st October next.'

It was an ironic stipulation; by the time that date came the world was at war. Indeed, from the previous autumn the inevitability of war in Europe had been signalled by a sorry tide of events, beginning with Neville Chamberlain's return from Munich guaranteeing 'peace in our time' as a result of the agreement signed with Hitler over the Sudetenland. German occupation of this territory was followed in the spring of 1939 by the complete annexation of Czechoslovakia. The

Mainie Jellett,
(1897-1944)
Achill Horses (1944)
NGI. Cat. No. 4320

civil war in Spain ended, with Franco victorious. Italy invaded and occupied Albania, and a 'Pact of Steel' was signed between Mussolini and Hitler, with the two leaders declaring that they would act together, with force, to secure their *lebensraum*. This agreement was followed, in August, by the secret Non-Aggression Pact between Hitler and Stalin, and a week later Russian and German troops entered Poland. War was declared by Britain and France on 3 September.

Ireland's position was officially that of a neutral nation. This was in keeping with the traditional policy of small European nations, yet was somehow pretentious, in that Ireland was in no position whatever to back up its neutrality and had arrived at it in confused circumstances. The unofficial position - 'the Irish solution' which always seems to emerge to resolve difficult national questions - was that Ireland's neutrality was essentially pro-British. And it became more so as the war progressed, though with no serious economic expenditure in order to maintain it. Neutrality was an impressive, statesmanlike stance to adopt in 1939, and twenty nations, including the United States, did so. Only five preserved it for the duration, and in the short space of six months from April 1940 the Axis Powers swept into eight 'neutral' countries, taking them over. Mild consideration was given to treating Ireland in the same way, but Hitler abandoned at a very early stage anything beyond a perfunctory use of the country for espionage purposes. With one notable exception even this proved futile. All German agents were captured and interrogated, such information as they had was passed on to British Intelligence interests. All German pilots and other military personnel arrested or captured in Ireland were interned; their British, American, or other allied opposite numbers were repatriated. And considerable additional help was given in different ways.

Among other things this meant that the Irish economy suffered less during the war years than might have been the case. It must also be said that the Irish economy during the 1930s had survived in ways that were markedly in contrast with the baleful fate of many European societies, whose miseries had strongly contributed to the rise of Fascism and the holocaust which followed. Eamon de Valera had successfully negotiated an end to the Economic War in 1938, the return of the Ports, and a once-off payment settling all long-standing debts to the British. It was a triumph, and it cemented him in position politically. And we have the subsequent remarkable achievement of a country able to reduce its public expenditure, as a proportion of its gross national product, throughout the period of the war.

What did all this mean to Mainie Jellett, her family, her friends, and the arts generally? Throughout the 1930s there was a consistent growth in her output, the confidence of her work and her views, and the stature of her influence on others. She was restricted somewhat, in financial terms, by the responsibilities which had descended on herself and her sister Bay after their father's death in 1936. Foreign travel, which had been made more difficult by the devaluation of the pound, had lessened but in no sense stopped entirely, and the decade had been punctuated by visits to various places, including Lithuania, Amsterdam and of course, on several occasions, France. What the outbreak of war and Ireland's declaration of neutrality also brought was an influx of foreigners and a heightened interest in the life of the country among diplomats stationed in Dublin. Among those who came were a number of artists, among them Basil Rákóczi and Kenneth Hall, two young painters who were to have a considerable influence on Irish art in the 1940s, and to provide Mainie with new allies and a new platform for her work and ideas.

It was not, then, a black period into which the artistic community entered, with the coming of 'the Emergency'. It was, on the contrary, an exciting phase for the arts generally, with a great deal happening, much controversy, and even the phenomenon of buyers for works of art. Though Mainie, regrettably, kept no consistent records of the sales and ownership of her own works, her rough notes for the 1939 solo exhibition show an impressive number of works sold. Her fellow artists, Ralph Cusack and Jack Hanlon, both bought from her show. So did the head of the German Mission in Dublin. J.J. Holloway, the diarist and veteran supporter of art in Dublin, bought a gouache entitled 'Meadows'. And the names of other buyers included Boydell, Meredith, Gavan Duffy, Geoghegan, McCarron, Moore, Stevenson, and Mainie's sister, Bay, who acquired for ten shillings a sketch of Croagh Patrick which had been listed in the catalogue at £2.10s.

The main paintings in the 1939 solo exhibitions included *Descent from the Cross*, *'Let There be Light'*, a *Madonna* and *Madonna of the Spring*, two *Abstracts* and *Achill Horses 11*. Further studies for the Glasgow Murals, and her gouaches of the *Elements* were included.

One reviewer claimed: 'This artist has won her struggle to educate her public in the most modern methods and her Cubist work is now familiar ... The exhibition brought many visitors during the month, and was regarded as the best Miss Jellett has ever held.'

The Irish Times described the exhibition as the most interesting she had ever given. Bewilderment is there as well, however, though concealed now by attempts to praise and endorse. The same critic suggests, a little puzzlingly, 'Her Cubistic conceptions stir imagination in the endeavour to relate them to the inspiration as described in the titles of the pictures. Sometimes the painting in the splendour of its colour occasions sensuous excitement in vision, while one's understanding is wholly absorbed in apprehending the idea involved. The canvases show a glorious conglomeration of intense tones in which an undefined atmosphere unifies the composition, but truth to tell meaning sometimes is far to seek.'

It would be a fruitless exercise to demonstrate the continued fumblings of the art critics of the time, as they searched their minds for 'meaning', still blissfully unaware of the basic principles of Cubist abstraction, were it not important from Mainie's own point of view. She had clearly triumphed in terms of her acceptance at every level, including the most difficult, technical one, of having pupils, followers and collectors of her work who did understand what she was doing. But she still had not *educated* her own critics. Their grasp upon the realities of non-representational art was almost universally frail or faulty. What Seamus O'Sullivan, in *The Dublin Magazine*, back in the early 1920s, had grappled with and overcome, still seemed to be eluding the majority of art critics writing for Dublin newspapers and periodicals. They all seem to be *frightened* of her. At the end of the 1930s perhaps the two most determined and self-confident voices in art criticism were Stephen Rynne, who wrote regularly for *The Leader*, and John Dowling, who wrote for *Ireland Today*. Rynne, in the November 18 issue of *The Leader*, referred to Mainie's 'technique, medium, pigments, and the instruments of the painter's craft' as being 'accidents which lay far behind her intellectual invention. One gets the feeling that Mainie Jellett only paints a fraction of the pictorial images which form themselves in her mind ... Occasionally she is rather more abstract than her very concrete subjects permit of. Yet it is seldom her "metre" breaks down when she ventures to rhyme in paint as in her interpretation of Fire, Air, Earth, and Water.' And Rynne concludes: 'but she does *not* paint in the style which she is most frequently said to, the Cubist.'

Criticism of her work had by this stage fallen into two definite groupings. The regular newspaper critics indulged in little more than descriptive reporting, generally in respectful and admiring language. The more serious criticism - confined to weeklies and monthlies - endeavoured to argue and confront her intentions, and the shift or otherwise with which she solved problems.

At a more practical level, as Mainie's mother repeated to her daughter, Betty, in Glasgow, 'Unfortunately Paul Henry & another popular Belfast painter [this was William Conor] have just had shows & sold a lot.' Mainie was always helped in hanging her shows by Maude Ball, whose faithful support since the first great abstract art controversy in Dublin in 1923 had been so valuable. But for the 1939 exhibition 'Maw Baw', as she was known in the Jellett family, 'was so submerged in new pipes in her house & a new maid' that she could not assist. The exhibition included more flower paintings; these were arranged on tables, on white paper under sheets of glass, and in Bay's opinion 'the little exhibition looks lovely!' Speaking for herself, Janet Jellett, who seems never to have greatly understood or sympathised with the pure abstract work, and certainly preferred, and had hanging in her own home, paintings and watercolours from the Sickert and pre-Sickert period, wrote: 'She certainly has far more interesting and varied work this time'.

Towards the end of 1939 a new figure emerged in Irish art who was to have a significant if eventually rather brief impact. This was Jack Longford who came to public attention when he opened a gallery in South Leinster Street in October with what he described as 'A Loan and Cross-Section Exhibition of Contemporary Paintings'.

The opening ceremony was performed by Dermod O'Brien who stressed the importance of 'carrying on work in the arts' in spite of the international crisis. He referred to works of art elsewhere in Europe being consigned to the safety of cellars and storerooms because of the war, and how this had led to gloomy predictions about the immediate fate of the arts. And he endorsed warmly the organisers of the show which was held in the Contemporary Picture Galleries. This modern commercial gallery had been opened in 1938 by 'Deirdre McDonogh', a pseudonym for Moira Pilkington, who had married Kathleen Tynan's son, a marriage which later failed. Deirdre McDonogh was joined in the running of the business a year later by Jack Longford. He had studied medicine at Trinity College and then in Edinburgh, but had given up these studies in favour of literature and art.

The partnership had a distinct policy, represented in the 1939 Loan and Cross-Section Exhibition, by the inclusion of works of art by international painters of some repute in a loan section, side by side with paintings for sale, mainly though not exclusively the work of Irish artists. The approach was not exclusively Modernist. Maurice MacGonigal, Seán Keating and Harry Kernoff, all full members of the Royal Hibernian Academy, were included, as was Jack Yeats, also a full academician. Duncan Grant was one of several English painters. Others who exhibited works then and later, and were indeed introduced to Ireland by Jack Longford, included Graham and Vanessa Bell, William Coldstream, John Piper and Edward Ardizzone. Mainie Jellett was an exhibitor, but also gave one of four lectures which were part of the October programme for the gallery, on French Painting. Again, the lectures reflected a catholicity of taste. Louis MacNeice spoke on 'English Painting Today', the Director of the National Gallery of Ireland, Dr. George Furlong, gave a lecture entitled 'Why Landscape?' and Edward A. MacGuire spoke on 'Irish Painting Today'.

Edward McGuire, who, as already noted, was a Davis Cup tennis star, and had the benefit of the business venture, Brown Thomas, behind him. He was making a reputation both as a painter and collector. Late in 1939 he lectured on eighteenth century painting in Dublin, which he also collected at this time, but for the loan exhibition his contribution was a spirited defence of Modernism, with particular reference to the two artists he regarded as the leading figures in art in Dublin at the time - Jack Yeats and Mainie Jellett. 'Her treatment was a highly intellectual one, whereas Jack Yeats's treatment was romantic. Miss Jellett by her lectures and in her work had shown that a deep purpose and high significance existed in the work of the good moderns.' McGuire was also an exhibitor. In the slightly acid words of Stephen Rynne, writing about the exhibition in *The Leader*, McGuire's 'paint is laid on regardless of expense'.

Jack Longford, in this and subsequent exhibitions, made a real contribution to Irish art until his unfortunately early death in 1944, after a fall, and at the age of only 33. He was one of the earliest champions of Jack Yeats, giving him one-man exhibitions, immediately after the Loan and Cross-Section Exhibition, in November 1939, and then again in 1940 and 1941. Many years later Stephen Rynne wrote of Yeats's relationship with Longford: 'The old man and young Longford were warm

Mainie Jellett,
(1897-1944)
**The Virgin of Éire
(1943)**
NGI. Cat. No. 4319

friends; there was something of a father and son affinity between them.'

For its time the loan side of the exhibition was very distinguished indeed. Bonnard, Braque, Picasso, Vlaminck, Marquet, Derain, Dufy, de Chirico, Gris and Gleizes were all represented, and by significant works, several of which are now in the National Gallery of Ireland. English painters included Tonks, Sickert, Steer, Christopher Richard Wynne Nevinson and Mark Gertler, with his painting *S.S. Koteliansky*. Many members of the Society of Dublin Painters had pictures for sale.

Mainie's own lecture, entitled 'The Influence of Contemporary French Painting', began with advice on how to look at pictures and employed the witty and elegant quotation from Schopenhauer: 'A work of art should be treated like a prince - It must speak to you first.' She developed this idea that one might have to wait in silence for some time, also that the 'words' may be quite unfamiliar and convey nothing. The fault, she went on, could be in the beholder. 'Remember that the artist if he is worthy of the name is someone whose business it is to have a wider vision in several senses of the word, than his fellows - It is nothing for the artist to boast about, it should be simply a result of his work which is contemplative and directed towards universal truths, which others can not give time from their more material occupations to consider. Therefore the creative artist's vision is often ahead of his time & on that account the onlooker must realise that the artist is very often a forerunner of new ideas, not yet sensed in the material world, & again not condemn without a few moments thought as to what the new idea may be.'

Though the basic argument of her lecture is the relatively familiar one, in which she takes up the distinctions between academic and materialist painting on the one hand - the dead representation of the material world 'where a picture is expected to do only slightly better what the coloured photograph is already doing'

Mainie Jellett, *(1897-1944)* **A Composition (c. 1933)** *NGI. Cat. No. 1874*

- and on the other hand the modern adventure of research and analysis represented particularly by Post-Impressionism and by the Cubists, there are still new elements in what she has to say. She develops, for example, the argument, central to her own work, of the divisions within Cubist and Post-Cubist art which led to the emergence of pure abstract and what was then referred to, with a combination of ambiguity and common-sense, as 'semi-abstract'. 'By degrees,' she told her audience, 'the Cubist abstract movement divided itself into two main groups - those who created with natural forms as a basis for their researches, of whom Lhote was one, and those who created on geometric principles and rhythmic harmonies evolved from the particular shape of the two-dimensional surfaces they were filling. Of the first group Braque I would consider the finest example - And of the second Albert Gleizes from the theoretical standpoint is the purest example.' She then turns to the vexed question of Picasso, 'a brilliant genius', but one who fluctuates between the two extremes 'always pushing out at a tangent, restless, a product of the times.' She expressed her admiration for his Spanish Civil War painting, *'Guernica'*, 'that great human document in art', but is otherwise unable to place him clearly in a position that related to herself or to what she believed modernism had achieved. Among a number of quotations culled from the artists she admired she included this from Picasso himself: 'They speak of naturalism in opposition to Modern Painting. I would like to know if anyone has ever seen a natural work of art. Nature and art, being too [sic] different things, cannot be the same thing. Through art we express our conception of what nature is not.'

From Braque she quoted the following: 'the aim is not a wish to reconstitute an anecdotal fact, but to constitute a pictorial fact.' 'To work from nature is to improvise.' 'The senses deform, the spirit forms. Work towards the perfection of the spirit. There is no certitude except in spiritual conceptions.' 'Nobility comes from controlled emotion.' 'I like the will that controls the emotion.'

She quoted also from Juan Gris: 'I work with the elements of the spirit, with imagination; I try to make concrete that which is abstract, I go from the general to the particular, which implies I go from an abstract to arrive at reality. My art is an art of synthesis and deduction.'

And she quoted Gleizes: 'In the reality of the outside world it is the physical aspect at first which strikes the senses exclusively - the spirit is hidden, mysterious and it takes an effort to reveal it. In the truth of a work of art it is the spirit which first demands exclusive attention. Painting is therefore not an imitation of objects. The reality of the exterior world serves as a departure, but that reality is purified so as to attain the spirit. Painting starting from the temporal tends towards the eternal.'

Mainie expressed in this lecture a view already contained in earlier talks on art, that Matisse was 'perhaps France's greatest colourist' and she linked this to a discussion about the Fauves and about the working relationship between Vlaminck and Derain, as well as an expression of her great admiration for Bonnard and Vuillard.

In much of what she said there was a broad examination of French art as it was reflected by the paintings included in the loan section of this exhibition. While it is likely that this exhibition included works owned by Mainie, among which was at least one major oil by Albert Gleizes, noticed in the Fitzwilliam Square house only a few months later by Hélène de St. Pierre, works came also from the collections of Sarah Purser, R.R. ('Bobs') Figgis, Evie Hone and May Guinness.

Mainie was also at pains to suggest that, while the movements in French painting about which she was lecturing were international, with a world-wide following which included herself and other artists, there were countries which were exceptions 'like the U.S.S.R. and Germany under Hitler, where these movements have been put down by the State and propaganda art set up in their place - ' She ended unequivocally: 'An artist who has the creative instinct and advances beyond the picture postcard type of painting must face these facts - they are born of his time, he *can not* escape them and they are not only a product of France - they resolve themselves into a very simple question - do you stand for the creative universal spiritual qualities in art, or do you stand for the materialistic photographic picture postcard standard of so called art - The creative spirit in opposition to the machine.'

That simple conflict, so clear then, so redolent for her of the campaigning years through which she had struggled and suffered, seems simplistic now. The divisions have been overtaken and changed. Those battles and the territory over which they were fought lie mostly in the past. But the clear light in which she saw things, and the firm determination of spirit with which she addressed the main issue as she conceived it to be, had about it the flash and surge of her courage. She was still, then, a solitary figure, at least in the campaigning sense. She was still the only person speaking out unequivocally in defence of abstract cubism.

Evie Hone was a caller at the Jellett house fairly regularly. She had not been well, and her sister, Mrs. Connell, whose life was dedicated to the horse, had suffered one of many accidents while out riding. It was in 1939 that Evie entered the Catholic Church, though with what seems to have been further spiritual indecision. In a letter which Mainie wrote to the painter Margaret Clarke, who had been William Orpen's pupil, and was a mutual friend, she said, 'I am very distressed over Evie. She has changed her plans so often that I will be away now when she makes the final step. I do wish she could find the *peace* of Christianity and trust she will find it in your Church and I wish she had made the move sooner.'

James White makes a perceptive comment about both women, and their intense Christian faith, in which much of their passion and emotion found its focus. In the case of Mainie he was astonished, in the first place, to discover that she felt deeply about her beliefs. On one occasion, on a Good Friday, when he was free from his work and able to paint scenery with her for a ballet production, she announced her intention to depart for the three-hour service of Passiontide devotion in St Patrick's Cathedral. It had never occurred to him, he says, that Protestants went to such religious extremes.

To Mainie he gives credit for directing the early course of his life. Perhaps more importantly, he attaches to her a pre-eminence in twentieth century art, in the field of educating and leading his contemporaries and followers with a clear-sightedness and dedication for which he maintains to this day the greatest admiration.

Sarah Cecilia Harrison
(1863-1941)
Sir Hugh Lane
NGI. Cat. No. 1280

THE FRIENDS OF
THE NATIONAL COLLECTIONS
OF IRELAND

Nicola Gordon Bowe

The Society of the Friends of the National Collections of Ireland was founded by Sarah Purser on Thursday February 14th, 1924, at an inaugural meeting held at the Royal Irish Academy in Dublin. Purser (1848-1943),[1] an established painter and leading figure in Dublin's cultural revival in the first thirty or so years of this century, had already founded *An Túr Gloine* (The Tower of Glass),[2] the pioneering stained glass co-operative workshop, in 1903. Their initial stated purpose was "to secure works of art and objects of historic interest or importance for the national or public collections of Ireland by purchase, gift or bequest, and to further their interest in other analogous or incidental ways".[3] They were only too aware that "Public collections do not thrive in modern conditions if supported only by the State" and that at this crucial stage in the emergence of the new Free State "to buy successfully requires ample resources and great freedom of action. The modern State is not in a position to concede either, and the great European and American Collections depend for their development in growing measure upon the collaboration of the private citizen ... [whose] taste and generosity" have resulted in collections "eminent precisely in the degree in which they attract ... enlightened benefactors. The names of William Dargan and Sir Hugh Lane forbid one thinking that such princely benefactors are impossible in modern Ireland; but they are of necessity rare, and even if they are less infrequent, the needs of our National Collections, like others abroad, make continuous corporate assistance desirable". This, they felt, was a propitious moment "to group into a Society" similar to those already established in Paris, Amsterdam, Berlin and Britain, Irish citizens "who have a care for our public collections and value the prestige which they confer upon our country".[4]

In 1907 Sir Hugh Lane had written in his Preface to the first (and only) *Illustrated Catalogue* to the collection of the Municipal Gallery of Modern Art in its original home in Harcourt Street,[5] "Till to-day Ireland was the only country in Europe that had no Gallery of Modern Art. There is not even a single accessible private collection of Modern Pictures in this country. That reproach is now removed" - namely by his magnificent bequest to the City of Dublin. He added, "The National Gallery of Ireland has a fine collection of works by the old masters, yet Sir Walter Armstrong himself says: "I would place the importance of a modern Gallery even before that of a National Gallery". To those actively engaged in Art this must be so, as it is his contemporaries that teach the student most, their successes that inspire him, for their problems are akin."

John Butler Yeats
(1839-1922)
Portrait of Sarah Purser
Limerick City Gallery of Art, gift of J.E. Geoghegan, 1950

At an adjourned meeting two weeks after the Society's formation, the Rules of the Society were adopted and its first Council and Officers elected. The Earl of Granard was elected its first President and its Vice Presidents were Sarah Purser R.H.A., Dermod O'Brien P.R.H.A., W.G. Strickland M.R.I.A., the art historian, George 'AE' Russell, painter, writer and visionary reformer, Sir Robert Woods F.R.C.I., the surgeon and Sir John Leslie, Bart. The original list of members represented distinguished men and women from public life in Ireland, including Mr. and Mrs. George Bernard Shaw, Mrs. W.B. Yeats and Oliver St. John Gogarty. By their first A.G.M. on March 25th 1925, held at Dermod O'Brien's house at 65 Fitzwilliam Square, they had secured a small supportive core of 112 members at a guinea a piece, and three bequests: a miniature of a Mrs. Coote by the 18th century Irish miniaturist John Comerford (for the National Gallery), a 19th century flowerpiece by Quost (for the Municipal Gallery) and a 16th century engraved powder-horn (for the National Museum).

Thomas Bodkin,[6] a founder Council member, who became the Director of the National Gallery of Ireland in 1927, wrote that under Sarah Purser's leadership the Society "soon came to the conclusion that they should occupy themselves largely in the endeavour to secure a return of the Lane Conditional Gift of Modern Continental Pictures to Dublin".[7] A British Government Commission Report of 1924 had recently found "that Sir Hugh Lane, when he signed the codicil of the 3rd February 1915, thought he was making a legal disposition" although speculated how he might have destroyed this had he seen London's new Tate Gallery extension.[8] On May 18th 1924, Sarah Cecilia Harrison,[9] the painter, confidante of Lane and annotator of the 1908 Municipal Gallery catalogue, submitted a full statement[10] to the Dublin Municipal Council who were to implement the formal request for the immediate return to Dublin of the 39 pictures known as the Lane Bequest to the English National Gallery.[11] In this, she methodically set out the situation to date, but referred to the dubious authenticity of the 1915 unattested codicil to what she saw as Sir Hugh Lane's earlier equally questionable will of 1913, which would revoke his bequest of these pictures to London in favour of Dublin. This, perversely, she refuted, documenting Lane's pressing last wishes expressed to her and Alderman Kelly in February 1915 before his ill-fated departure on the *Lusitania* to America: "If Dublin would build a gallery for them, they had the first claim, if not, the Gallery of a Modern Continental Art in London." The raging controversy was brought to a head when Lord Duveen's extension to the Tate Gallery, opened by the King on June 26th 1926, featured (but never referred by name to the benefaction of Lane, only to that of Samuel Courtauld) Lane's thirty nine treasures as among the best of their collection of "modern Continental pictures". The Friends canvassed national opinion and passed a resolution urging the Free State to act on growing public support and press for the pictures' return. At the same time, they pressurized the County Borough Commissioners of Dublin to proceed with "the suitable and safe housing" of the part of Lane's collection currently housed in the Municipal Gallery's premises at 16/17 Harcourt Street; also "to form a sort of voluntary endowment for it and to keep it up to date with modern art".[12]

At the 1926 A.G.M., W.B. Yeats had urged the importance of buying "works of art before the reputations of the painters are established, or [a Gallery] will never be able to afford their price". He also lamented the "muddled" displays of the National Museum, squeezed out by the Dáil and Senate's recent occupation of part of the building hitherto theirs.[13]

In 1927, Thomas Bodkin conveyed to President Cosgrave the Friends' unanimous resolution that Lane's collection be housed in its entirety in accommodation commensurate with its quality and that of a European capital city. Support for an updated estimate for the site proposed on St. Stephen's Green by Lane, using a design by Sir Edwin Lutyens, was sought; the main point was to build a gallery "at the earliest possible moment in order to remove the strongest argument put forward in England for the retention there of the pictures".[14] As it was now fifteen years since Lane's removal of his controversial paintings to London from Dublin, a huge public meeting was held in June 1928 at the Theatre Royal "to give the younger generation a full account" of the matter. Bodkin showed slides of them and summarized the case. Lady Gregory, Lane's aunt, and Major Bryan Cooper spoke and letters of support were read from Eamon de Valera and Seán O'Casey. A few days later, a representative quota of public figures attended a public enquiry at City Hall, resulting in cautious official financial provision.

Sarah Purser then had the brainwave of housing the new gallery on the site of the 20,000 square foot garden behind Lord Charlemont's magnificent 18th century Dublin mansion, designed for him by Sir William Chambers; the house had recently been vacated by the Registrar-General for Ireland. In February 1929, the Government adopted her proposal "that Charlemont House together with the land behind it and as much land behind nos. 23-27 Parnell Square as might be required

... should be offered to the City Commissioners on condition that a suitable Municipal Gallery is to be erected on the site".[15] In return for a 99 year lease and a small rent, the City undertook to spend "not less than £20,000 within four years on the conversion and extension of the building for use as a Municipal Gallery of Modern Art".[16] The plans of the city architect, Horace O'Rourke, "for the erection of a new gallery of the most up-to-date kind" of "splendid dimensions"[17] did, unfortunately, involve "drastically" remodelling and extending Chambers' original structure and a number of the building's fine original features[18] but everyone was assured that Lane would have approved the new gallery "of lordly dimensions and scientific construction".[19] At last a special gallery was designated to show his bequest. He had stipulated he wanted the paintings to be seen not necessarily in "a fashionable quarter" but "where there is most traffic" and safe from the dangers of fire.[20] Building began immediately, with the help of a Government loan, and the new gallery was opened by President de Valera on June 19th 1933.

Sarah Purser was relentless in her work to try to increase membership, galvanize support and to secure good modern work by up-and-coming artists. This was apart from canvassing for bequests, gifts, legacies and buying pieces in danger of being lost to the nation. Members like the Belfast Municipal Gallery and the London-based Irish Literary society publicized the aims of the Friends. The implementation of the Haverty Bequest in 1930, with its annual provision of funds for purchasing pictures by Irish artists living in Ireland, led the Council to decide that the Friends should, generally speaking, allot their limited resources to follow Hugh Lane's practice "and keep our collections supplied with examples of the work of modern Continental and British painters".[21]

By December 1930, their acquisitions numbered 36, ranging from a collection of Javanese batiks, a drawing by Pietro da Cortona, a John Comerford miniature, a 14th century French carved ivory leaf, an early 18th century embroidered silk coverlet to contemporary paintings by Meninsky, Nevinson, John Nash and the Irish artists, Albert Power, Sir William Orpen and Sarah Purser. Work followed by Duncan Grant and Selwyn Image and it was hoped some of the major early 20th century modern painters (e.g. Gauguin, Degas, Van Gogh, Cézanne, Picasso, Matisse etc.) might be acquired through "wealthy donors of Irish birth at home and abroad",[22] once the quality of the new purpose-built gallery became apparent.

At its first meeting in March 1934,[23] the new gallery's Advisory Committee duly thanked the Friends for their work and valuable contributions to the collection. However, membership drives were (and still are) a prime concern.

The 12th Annual Report for 1935-6 records 153 members,

"a figure that is slightly above last year's membership but corresponds in no way with our population or the potential usefulness of our Society. A comparison with the National Art Collections Fund of Great Britain is hardly just to this country, but it is nevertheless worth noting that its membership has increased in thirty years from an original figure of five hundred to its present total of ten thousand, while ours in ten years has remained almost stationary. Our usefulness depends on our purchasing power and that depends on our membership. It is our money, changed into Art, that our National Collections want. To improve the position in this respect by increasing its members, we renew our annual appeal for the active co-operation of all old members in the pursuit of new ones without which the Council's propaganda falls short of its full effect.

The Council recognises that our Society offers no inducement to intending members other than an opportunity for the private discharge of a patriotic duty. This austere attitude is the probable explanation of our slow growth. It now proposes to substitute common pleasure for secret virtue and a tentative step was taken in this direction by an At Home in January last at Mr. Egan's Gallery, in the course of the AE Memorial Exhibition.[24] *Members expressed themselves pleased with the function and it is accordingly proposed to take advantage of other exhibitions for similar reunions. The Council has also in consideration the arrangement of visits by the Society to private collections in Dublin and its neighbourhood and to houses of architectural interest."*[25]

(This policy is basically still in operation). As a result, an Entertainment Committee was formed, leading to a series of visits and an 80% increase in membership. The first visit was to Beaulieu, Mr. Montgomery's 17th century house and collection in Co. Louth; then to Castletown, Major Connolly's magnificent 18th century mansion in Co. Kildare and a lecture on it by Mr. Sadleir; to the painter May Guinness in Co. Dublin and what would become an annual reception in November in the new Municipal Gallery. They also mounted a loan exhibition of contemporary painters, which included Bonnard, Chagall, De Chirico, Dufy and Derain. Sarah Purser reiterated the Society's aims and policy as far as the Gallery was concerned:

"We are anxious that this gallery be maintained as a gallery of contemporary art. Familiarity with the art of our own day in Europe is essential to the development and progress of our own. Without this constant familiarity taste is dulled and design stagnates. We are anxious that our chief Irish collection of modern art should provide this necessary contact. No state or municipal endowment is, at the moment, available in the Irish Free State to provide this vital stimulus. The absence of such provision is not creditable to our community and we cannot but regard some provision as at some time certain. But in the meantime, notwithstanding our efforts, the gaps in the gallery become every day wider and more conspicuous. We have no early examples of the first post-impressionist group ... We have no examples of the living art of Central Europe or of Italy. We have no contemporary continental sculpture. Let no one charge us with lack of patriotism if we believe that our funds, as a rule, will be most usefully spent abroad. To place good examples of the best foreign artists before our students and the public is a patriotic duty, and having regard to the splendid generosity of the late Thomas Haverty the duty may be discharged without any searching of heart."

They proposed to pursue an "attempt to forecast taste upon whose success only posterity can securely judge" and felt "a duty to give representation to movements in art with which we may not all, or always be in complete sympathy but which at any rate has powerfully affected its development. These are risks we may not shirk".[26] Their recent bequests included works by Lurçat, Tonks and Stanley Spencer.

In 1937 the Organizing Committee's events included a lecture on "Italian Schools of Painting in the National Gallery" by its director, Dr. George Furlong, a visit to the tapestries and paintings at Mrs. Shelswell-White's Bantry House in Co. Cork, to Derrynane, home of Daniel O'Connell and his descendants, to the Gaisford St. Lawrences' historic Howth Castle, to the Provost's House, Trinity

Georges Rouault
(1871-1958)
Le Christ et le Soldat
*Hugh Lane Municipal
Gallery of Modern Art*

College and to Dr. and Mrs. Cremin's collection in Richard Cassell's masterpiece, 122 St. Stephen's Green. The President attended the gala annual reception, which revived the civic tradition of inviting the presence of the Dublin Fire Brigade. Acquisitions included a rare fragment of 12th/13th century woven patterned Lucchese silk and a 16th century Persian brocade for the National Museum. At the January 1938 A.G.M., Sarah Purser, aged 90, announced her retirement after 13 years as the Hon. Sec. of the Friends, although she continued as one of the four Vice-Presidents. A dinner was given at the Shelbourne Hotel in her honour, with a menu cover designed by Jack Yeats.

In 1938 members of the Society were received by Viscount Powerscourt at Powerscourt, by Thomas Bodkin's brother, the Rev. Matthew Bodkin, S.J. at Belvedere House, at Drumcondra House, built for the Coghills in 1720, at the restored Casino at Marino, led by Harold Leask, Inspector of National Monuments, at the Norman Pale castles of Killeen and Dunsany, and they attended a lecture at the College of Surgeons on "The French Mind in Art" by a conservateur from the Louvre. At the annual reception, attended by the Taoiseach, the Society's president, the Earl of Granard, received over 300 members, Dermod O'Brien and Sir John Leslie, Vice Presidents, and the painter, Eva Hamilton, representing the Council. Because Dublin's Gallery of Modern Art still had "no public endowment, national or municipal, for the purchase of pictures",[27] resulting in its being "precariously dependent upon casual gifts" for its "modern character", the Society had decided to spend a "substantial portion of its funds" on paintings by two major artists, Picasso and Utrillo. They also bought for the National Museum a set of Uileann Pipes by the Dunhallow piper, Donnchadh O'Laoghaire and, mystifyingly, 16 colour reproductions of well-known contemporary European painters. A Nathaniel Hone self-portrait and Nicholas Crowley portrait were among several fine Irish works presented through the Society in what was their busiest year yet. Partly because of the War, 1940 saw a decline in membership and social activities, although a Bonnard oil, *Boulevard Clichy, Paris* (1895) and a Matisse lithograph were purchased, a lecture on contemporary French painting was organised and visits were made to Slane Castle and Piltown.

In 1942, Dermod O'Brien assumed the Presidency of the Friends from the Earl of Granard, who had held the office since the Society's inception; this office O'Brien, who was still also the President of the R.H.A., held until 1945, when he was succeeded by the Earl of Rosse, newly elected as a Vice-President. It is interesting to note that on the Council there were three further painters: May Guinness, Eva Hamilton and Mainie Jellett, as well as eminent art historians: C.P. Curran, George Furlong, Françoise Henry, Ada Leask and Dudley Westropp. Despite the War and a drop in membership and activities, Sir Kenneth Clark, then Director of the London National Gallery, lectured "brilliantly" on "The Still Life" in the Abbey Theatre; C.P. Curran, the distinguished architectural historian of Dublin's 18th century plasterwork and a founder Council member and later Vice-President of the Friends, gave detailed talks to members during visits to 18th century Dublin townhouses, and the Society organized its first exhibition, a centenary show of James Arthur O'Connor, at the Municipal Gallery. New members included the painter Lady Glenavy, the historian Constantia Maxwell and the art historian Thomas MacGreevy. That year, the Municipal Gallery's Art Advisory Committee was too scandalized to accept an offer of the loan of Georges Rouault's powerful *Le Christ et le Soldat* ("I go into a gallery for the relaxation and sense of peace and enjoyment one gets from being among things of beauty", wrote one outraged member, suspending his subscription. "Pictures like this induce only a feeling of depression, disgust and anger so far as I personally am concerned"). Ironically, the President of Maynooth College accepted its loan "with the greatest pleasure" and promised to ensure its accessibility to students, visitors and "even Bishops!".[27] The publicity which attended the Gallery's scandalous rejection of the picture and its subsequent exhibition in the College of Surgeons, drew the open support of existing members like Evie Hone and Mainie Jellett as well as new members. The latter gave a thought-provoking lecture on "Painting and Understanding", a sequel to the art critic Eric Newton's lecture on the "Meaning of Modern Art".

The 1944 A.G.M, was overshadowed by the deaths of key members of the Society: Sarah Purser, Sir John Leslie, Mainie Jellett and Mrs. G.B. Shaw. A Berthe Morisot watercolour, a Vlaminck cubist composition and a Mary Swanzy portrait were among pictures from Sarah Purser's collection presented through the Society from her estate. Although these should be seen as major investments, funds were still short, particularly as the last two years had seen a substantial rise in European market prices. It seemed impossible to secure more than 300 members; meanwhile "the work of the great European Masters of the last 60 years is conspicuously unrepresented".[28] In an attempt to represent the "developments that have taken place in the various schools of painting on the Continent ... from ... the French Impressionists ... to our own day," the Society planned a Loan

Exhibition of over 90 major paintings and drawings that summer, in the National College of Art and Design; this, at a time of "marked increase of interest in painting in this country". Its success resulted in the subsequent acquisition of a good Dunoyer de Segonzac watercolour for Charlemont House, skilfully engineered by the Society's Hon. Sec., R.R. Figgis. Among the 32 new members for that year were Louis le Brocquy and James White.

It was still a matter of grave concern to the Friends that

"Of our metropolitan collections, the Municipal Gallery alone remains totally inadequate in fulfilling the function for which it was founded. In attempting to deal with this lamentable state of affairs this Society is up against a depressing problem. The few hundreds annually at its disposal are wholly insufficient for any scheme of systematic purchasing of contemporary work, much less for any determined effort to secure examples of the art of those earlier painters who though still classed as "moderns" have long since in monetary value and international prestige, joined the ranks of the Old Masters. We all look forward to an expanding tourist traffic and it is of paramount importance that our National Collections should be a source not only of inspiration to ourselves, but of interest to others... If public funds were available for this purpose, we should feel its achievement to be still nearer realisation."[29]

The Hon. Secs. recorded a Mainie Jellett bequest to the National Gallery, as well as a collection of china to the National Museum; lectures by Bodkin (in his capacity as Director of the Barber Institute of Fine Arts in Birmingham) and Sir John Rothenstein (Director of the Tate Gallery) had had to be postponed. The 22nd A.G.M. in 1946 marked the death after illness of the Society's firm supporter and President, Dermod O'Brien, and the first year of Lord Rosse's long and active Presidency and Chairmanship of the Friends. It also saw the post-war restoration of the Annual Reception, Rothenstein's lecture on "Recent Developments in English Painting" and plans for sponsoring and organizing two exhibitions at the Municipal Gallery the following year: one to show *Modern Czechoslovakian Painting and Sculpture*, the next the development of *Twentieth Century French Painting*. C.P. Curran's extensive knowledge of 18th century Dublin plasterwork was once more appreciated on visits to the Rotunda Hospital and to St. Saviour's Orphanage in Dominick Street, while the collection of Edward McGuire, another Council member, was the focus of another visit. Victor Waddington was among the new members.

As the 101 acquisitions listed in the 24th Annual Report of 1948 demonstrate, the Friends were not exclusively concerned with trying to establish the capital city's Gallery of Modern Art, partly because of the successful activities of artists (and Council members of the Friends) like Norah McGuinness, a founder member of the now thriving Living Art exhibition (founded 1943).[30] That year they acquired a superb 18th century Irish carved wood gilt couch that had belonged to Lord Charlemont, and William Turner de Lond's painting of *The Ceremonial Entry of George IV into Dublin* (1821) for the National Gallery. Through them public galleries outside Dublin and Belfast - Cork, Galway, Clonmel, Kilkenny, Maynooth, Limerick - were included in bequests, as well as the National Museum, the R.H.A., the Royal Society of Antiquaries of Ireland and the National Library, and that venues for receptions and lectures (e.g. the Director of the Glasgow Art Gallery and Museums on "Contemporary Art Criticism") took advantage of a variety of public institutions in the city (Newman House, the Provost's House, the College of Surgeons etc.). These were usually attended by the President or the Taoiseach. In emulation of Sir Hugh Lane's Vuillard in his still not permanently secured collection of 39 "modern Continental" pictures, they acquired a further early gouache by the Post-Impressionist painter for the National Gallery, as well as a Daubigny. Further acquisitions included bequests by Lily Yeats of her father's work, a Bassano *Procession to Calvary* for the National Gallery and, on the advice of Evie Hone, a still life by Francisco Bores and a landscape by André Lhote.[31] Once more in 1949 the Council felt the need to reiterate its policy as regards purchasing modern works of art, to which it was not solely bound.

"A visit to almost any modern gallery in any capital city of the world, outside Dublin, is sufficient to demonstrate that the modern idiom in its various manifestations has long been generally accepted. Most modern galleries tend to start where our Municipal Gallery leaves off. In consequence, the few, the very few, pictures that our Municipal collection possesses that are really representative of contemporary painting on an international place, look out of place because they are seen outside their context. On the other hand, to any informed visitor to Dublin, the vast majority of the pictures in Dublin's modern gallery must inevitably appear to be an anachronism. This Society, with its small membership and modest income, has done its best to repair the deficiency. Picasso is represented by a small oil-painting, but by nothing that would give the enquiring visitor any conception of the power and versatility of this painter's work. Bonnard, one of the most honoured names in twentieth century painting, and fast qualifying to become an old master, is well represented by an important early oil painting. Lurcat, Utrillo, Segonzac are each represented by one picture. Rouault, one of the great religious painters of all time, remains unrepresented through no fault of this Society.

Your Council feels that the time has come to call for more co-ordination in the administration of our public galleries, and for some scheme to be devised whereby Charlemont House may be enabled to justify the retention of the word "modern" in its official title. Further, your Council respectfully suggests that the time has come when good photographs and reproductions of all that is outstanding in our various public collections should be made available to our own public and to visitors to our capital city".[32]

The problem was, as always, rising market prices. The tireless secretary R.R. Figgis, enlisted the advice of Basil Ivan Rákóczi, a founder member of the White Stag war-time group of Dublin painters[33] in trying to secure a Matisse through his friend the Abbé Morel, who gave "a brilliant and stimulating paper on "Le Tragique et l'Art de Notre Temps" at the end of the year; but this proved beyond their means.

The setting up of *An Chomhairle Ealaíon*, the Arts Council, in 1951, four of whose founder Board members were also F.N.C.I. Council members, reflected the Society's fundamental role in the nation's cultural concerns ("The visitor to Charlemont House cannot fail to observe that almost everything of significance on the walls of that gallery painted within the last thirty years, has been presented by this Society").[34] When an exhibition of contemporary Swedish art came to Dublin, it was the Friends who organized a reception at Charlemont House. They also achieved a successful settlement of the late Jerome Connor's unfinished and long

Seán Keating
(1889-1977)
An Allegory(1925)
NGI. Cat. No. 1236

overdue Lusitania Memorial for Cobh. 1954 - 5 was an outstanding year: the President supported the Society by agreeing to become its Patron, and far more new members and new acquisitions and bequests were secured than ever before in one year. This was mainly due to James White, newly elected to the Council (on which he is still a valued and now, consummately experienced member) and in charge of an extensive countrywide membership appeal; partly to the most exciting new acquisition, a Henry Moore *Reclining Figure*. This had been exhibited in Kilkenny and at the Living Art Exhibition, but rejected (as the Rouault had been)[35] by the Municipal Gallery's Art Advisory Committee. While Council member Erskine Childers, then Minister for Posts and Telegraphs, wholeheartedly supported the "artistic prescience" and "independence of judgment ... impossible under any system of bureaucratic purchase" shown by the Friends, Council member Lady Dunalley, in her distaste for Moore's sculpture, declared "that she considered modern Art decadent". P.J. Little, Director of the Arts Council, affirmed "that the Society, labouring against a tide of apathy and neglect, had accepted the onerous work of creating a public patronage of art" and must try to persuade any "people of real knowledge and taste scattered throughout the country" to join.[36]

James White's success in recruiting new members was such that he assumed Bobs Figgis's Hon. Secretaryship in 1956, while joining him on the Executive Committee along with Norah McGuinness, Brigid Ganly, C.P. Curran, Terence de Vere White, Sir Alfred Beit, Sir Basil Goulding, Françoise Henry and Thomas MacGreevy (by now Director of the National Gallery). That year the Council was

Thomas Hickey
(1741-1824)
An Indian Girl (1787)
NGI. Cat. No. 1390

expanded to represent all parts of the country (Henry McIlhenny, and later Derek Hill, in Donegal, Sir Chester Beatty in Dublin, Lord Killanin in Galway, Dennis Gwynn in Cork etc.). Erskine Childers and Cearbhall Ó Dálaigh were among those on the existing Council, which was responsible with Bord Fáilte for mounting an exhibition of Japanese prints from the collection of Sir Chester Beatty, a new Vice-President of the Friends; arranging a lecturer from America; a visit to Russborough and a series of exceptional acquisitions. These included important work by Epstein (two works), Chinnery, Maclise, Van Nost, St. Gaudens, James Barry; they were also instrumental in securing Augustus John's portrait of W.B. Yeats for the Abbey Theatre. Other activities included their successful campaign to remove government tax on artists' work entering the country (at the instigation of Seán Keating, P.R.H.A.), a handicap on which the current law has sadly regressed. The 1957/8 year saw the election of Anne Crookshank, then Keeper of Art in Belfast, and John Hunt to the Council, while the executive committee investigated modern French paintings to fulfill Evie Hone's substantial bequest of £500 for such. Over 30 works by her were bequeathed or acquired, as well as a couple by Jack Yeats, a Nano Reid and important paintings by Thomas Hickey, James Barry and Hugh Douglas Hamilton (the latter three for the National Gallery). Visits, a lecture, a festive opening of *Paintings from Irish Collections* (with Bord Fáilte) and a Cork Chapter drew new members.

Speculation over the Lane pictures was revived in 1959 when Sir John Rothenstein gave a lecture on "British Painting since the War". Soon after, an official compromise was reached through the offices of Thomas Bodkin and Lords Moyne and Longford resulting in the pictures' alternating between their two claimants.

By 1960 two problems, which are still major concerns of the Friends, were voiced: that no restrictions exist to prevent works of art streaming out of Ireland, usually for profit abroad; and the steep rise in art prices "and enormous interest in all works of art of value in the international market" were proving preclusive to purchase even at a comparatively early stage in an artist's career. Consequently, "The policy of buying works by promising young artists is the only possible one under the circumstances ... Your committee is not unaware of its responsibilities, no matter how bitterly it regrets the opportunities it has to turn down for lack of funds ... Not one single penny is spent in this country outside this Society to acquire works by living non-Irish artists. The responsibility is totally ours ... and our resources are our members ...".[37] Thus, "two distinguished collectors", Lady Dunsany and Lady Mayer were co-opted on to the Council and gifts did continue to be presented, bringing the total number of accessions to 195. At the end of the year, two new categories of membership were introduced: life (15 guineas) and junior (5/ - per annum) for under 18's and those attending universities or art colleges.

James White's appointment as Curator of the Municipal Gallery in 1960 meant that first Anne King-Harman and then John Turpin shared his duties as Hon. Sec. (since, apart from the extra work of this new commitment, he could not write letters to and from himself as Secretary of the Friends and as Curator of the Gallery). His double position was an enormous boost to both Gallery and Society. In 1962, the Friends' contribution to Anne Crookshank's enlightened purchase of works by Ceri Richards, William Scott, Roger Hilton and Terry Frost for the Belfast Art Gallery and to a collection of Jack Yeats paintings for the Sligo Museum was warmly supported by him. Through Sir Alfred Beit, Kenneth Clark waived his usual fee for an enthusiastically attended lecture on Rembrandt's paintings. In 1963, James White, as Hon. Sec. drew attention to the newly formed Contemporary Irish Art Society, whose aim was to supplement, not compete with the Friends, since the latter had decided not to acquire works by living Irish artists - a welcome and complementary association. That year the Society received Thomas Bodkin's bequest of 38 works of art for distribution and enjoyed a lecture on the Icarus theme by Michael Ayrton. 1964 saw several new members added to Council, some of whom still serve on it, the longest serving member now being James White. He was instrumental in the Friends' next major undertaking: an exhibition in August-September 1964 in the Municipal Gallery, and then the Ulster Museum, of the works acquired by the Society since its foundation. A small but steady flow of acquisitions, particularly through Sir Alec Martin, a long-term supporter, also of the Hungarian artist of Irish blood, Ferenc Martyn, continued along with lectures and visits. Still, "not one single penny had ever been spent by the Corporation on purchasing works whilst the Friends had kept the Gallery alive by putting into it works worth £200,000. Dublin is the only municipality in the world which makes no contribution to purchases of works of art".[38]

The Society also undertook to erect house plaques to Sir Hugh Lane and Walter Osborne. Sadly they did not make any purchases when the first ROSC exhibition was held in Dublin in 1967, partly because their resources had been stretched by the purchase of a Guttuso in 1965. This is an opportunity which has been consistently missed every four or so years during successive ROSC's and would now be financially unlikely. (Proposals to buy Bill Woodrow's superb *Elephant* at the penultimate ROSC at the Guinness Hop Store came to nothing, although the Council bought a fine Albert Irvin for Kilkenny as a direct result of his inclusion in the same show.) 1968 saw the acquisition of an Elizabeth Frink bronze *Cock* and Ivon Hitchens' *Ringed Lily*, further visits, a goodwill address from the now well-subsidized North of Ireland, represented by Capt. Peter Montgomery (urging support for the new galleries in Fermanagh and Derry) and a profit of £800 on the now famous Midsummer Ball at Castletown in collaboration with the Irish Georgian Society, at which Micheál MacLiammóir gave a dramatic performance. By 1969, James White's incipient appointment as Director of the National Gallery, in succession to MacGreevy, led to his handing over the Hon. Secretaryship after nearly twenty years to John Turpin and John Gilmartin, although he still served actively on the Council.

1970 was a historic year in that Dublin Corporation contributed £300 to the sum of £2,700 for a Josef Albers painting, *Aglow*, bought by the Society from David Hendricks - "This was the first occasion on which the Civic Authorities of Dublin contributed towards the purchase of a work of Art for the Municipal Gallery".[39] The Friends also contributed to the purchase of a fine piece of 18th century Dublin silver for the Ulster Museum, bought three contemporary stained glass panels from Evie Hone's collection and turned up in record numbers to a series of visits, including a now legendary one to the Provost's House conducted by Anne Crookshank and Professor Otway-Ruthven. They also voiced deep general concern over the condition and role of the National Museum, leading to the formation of a Museum Committee, and the preparation of a detailed Report.[40] That year, Charles Haughey, T.D., Minister for Finance, proposed the adoption of the Annual Reports. 1971 was marked by a profitable and enjoyable fund-raising Antique Quiz at the King's Inns, chaired by Peter Wilson of Sotheby's, the purchase of a Leopoldo Novoa abstract, *Grand Cris á Cinq Elements*, and visits to the various ROSC exhibits, particularly in Cork. In 1972, when Peter Harbison assumed the duties of Hon. Sec., the total lack of requests for aid made the Friends determined to combat and investigate a general ignorance of their possible aid throughout the country. At the 1973 A.G.M. the eccentric editor of *The Arts in Ireland* magazine, Charles Merrill, called for the appointment of a Minister of Cultural Activities.

The F.N.C.I. celebrated their 50th anniversary in 1974 with exhibitions of selected works presented by the Friends to the Municipal Gallery and others by Sarah Purser, the Society's founder (organized by the Curator, Ethna Waldron and Dr. Elizabeth Fitzpatrick (née Purser), Hon. Treasurer),[41] visits to Emo and Glin and a number of varied but important acquisitions and distributions of bequests. They were rewarded with exemption from income tax (being a charity) and a moderately optimistic response to their proposals on Capital Gains and Wealth Tax, particularly where private individuals were concerned. James White, by now a Vice-President, gave a lecture in 1975, commemorating the centenary of Sir Hugh Lane and welcomed the advent of a new national institution in Dublin, The National Trust Irish Architectural Archive. Dr. Edward McParland addressed the 1976 A.G.M. on the Archive, the same year in which Malahide Castle and some of its contents were secured for the nation, and Lord Norwich lectured in the

National Gallery. In 1977 Ciarán MacGonigal, who had been chairing a sub-committee drawing up a detailed report on the future role of the Friends, took over as Hon. Sec. His outgoing Annual Report of 1979 summed up the position of the Society now that the Irish Museums Trust, Friends of Modern Dublin and the Contemporary Irish Art Society were established, the Hugh Lane Municipal Gallery of Modern Art could avail of Dublin Corporation's annual purchasing fund of £30,000 and taxation problems to the detriment of art works were being addressed. Over the years, many other issues discussed are still as pertinent as ever: e.g. the destruction of historic public monuments and architecture in Dublin; legislation for and classification and preservation of historic monuments and their contents; the documentation, legislation and state aid for the continuing export of works of art of national importance; the vital need to set up a Georgian townhouse as a museum, like those in Charlotte Square in Edinburgh and The Royal Crescent in Bath; the tax on artist's materials and any art work painted less than 100 years ago (now altered but still unsatisfactory).[42] The much discussed extension to the National Gallery was built, and the Royal Hospital Kilmainham has of course been magnificently restored and has become the new Irish Museum of Modern Art.

Since Lord Rosse's death, James White, The Lady Dunsany, Judge Walsh and John Ross have presided over and chaired the proceedings of the Society. Its 60th anniversary was celebrated by the erection of a plaque denoting the original Municipal Gallery in Harcourt Street, the commissioning of a fine drawing of the house by Michael Craig, the stamp designer, for graphic reproduction as a logo, a reprint of the catalogue of the Gallery's original collection in 1908 and the presentation of a major painting, *Ned Kelly by the River* by the Australian-Irish artist, Sydney Nolan, at an A.G.M. addressed by Dr. White at the Royal Irish Academy. The purchase of works of all periods continues to be made or assisted and no-one could be more conscious of the vital need for a wide spectrum of enthusiastic and committed young, actively involved members than the Society's longest-serving but ever youthfully minded Vice-President, James White.

Notes

1. See John O'Grady, *Sarah Henrietta Purser,* Ph.D. thesis, National University of Ireland 1974.

2. Nicola Gordon Bowe, 'Early Twentieth Century Irish Stained Glass in Context', in N. Gordon Bowe, D. Caron and M. Wynne, *A Gazetteer of Irish Stained Glass,* Dublin 1988.

3. 1st Annual Report, the Friends of the National Collections of Ireland, 1924 - 5, rule 2.

4. Ibid.

5. The catalogue was reprinted with a new preface, 'The Municipal Gallery, Sir Hugh Lane and the Friends' (James White) by the F.N.C.I. in 1984 to commemorate their 60th anniversary.

6. See Homan Potterton, *Illustrated Summary Catalogue of Paintings,* National Gallery of Ireland, Dublin 1981, Introduction, pp. xxxiii-iv.

7. Thomas Bodkin, *Hugh Lane and his Pictures,* Dublin 1956, pp. 62 - 3 and for the full story of the protracted affair. See also James White, op.cit.

8. Manifesto of the F.N.C.I., May 1928.

9. See *Irish Women Artists from the 18th Century to the Present Day,* National Gallery of Ireland, Dublin 1987, pp. 107 - 8, p.166; also Hilary Pyle, *Irish Art 1900 - 1950,* Cork 1975, pp. 32 - 3.

10. A copy of this long letter is the first document filed in the records of the F.N.C.I. In her letter, Harrison states they "were to have been married" on his return from America in the summer of 1915, and that one of his principal reasons for tolerating the procrastination of the Corporation was that "Miss Harrison has put so much of her life into the scheme". Bodkin (p. 73) writes, "Lane was never married; the society of women did not seem to give him any special pleasure".

11. For a full list of the pictures in question, see Bodkin, op.cit., pp. 29 - 30. They included four Corots, a Boudin, two Puvis de Chavannes, four Courbets, an Ingres, Daumier, Fromentin, Degas, two Manets, a Monet, Pissarro, Berthe Morisot, Renoir and Vuillard. For the story in detail see Bodkin, op.cit., pp. 28 - 62.

12. Letter from Sarah Purser, March 13th 1927.

13. 2nd Annual Report 1926.

14. Bodkin, op.cit., p. 64.

15. Letter February 1st 1929 from E. Blythe, Department of Finance.

16. Bodkin, op.cit., p. 66.

17. Bodkin, op.cit., p. 67.

18. See *Irish Georgian Society Records,* Dublin 1912, Vol. IV, pp. 23 - 33.

19. Bodkin, op.cit., p. 67.

20. Ibid.

21. 7th Annual Report 1931

22. Letter April 14th 1932 from the Curator of the Municipal Gallery to Sarah Purser.

23. It is worth noting that the Society continued to operate from Dermod O'Brien's house in Fitzwilliam Square while the Chair at the A.G.M. was taken by the Lord Mayor.

24. George 'AE' Russell, that key figure in all progressive cultural ventures in early 20th century Ireland, had been their Vice Preisdent, a foundation member and "generous supporter". Bodkin filled the vacancy caused by his death.

25. 12th Annual Report 1936.

26. 13th Annual Report 1937.

27. Letter dated November 21st 1942.

28. 20th Annual Report 1944.

29. 21st Annual Report 1945.
    25th Annual Report 1949.

30. She and Terence de Vere White both became Council members that year. Norah McGuinness became the dynamic Chairwoman of the I.E.L.A. in 1944. For its origins, see Brian Kennedy, 'Women artists and the Modern Movement, 1943 - 9' and Brian Fallon, 'Irish women artists in the nineteen-fifties', in *Irish Women Artists,* op.cit., pp. 41 - 5 and pp. 46 - 7.

31. Both the latter had featured in the 1950 I.E.L.A.

32. 25th Annual Report 1949.

33. See Kennedy, op.cit., pp. 40 - 1.

34. 28th Annual Report 1951 - 2.

35. Council wrote a carefully judged letter asking the committee to reconsider its decision, but the matter was unresolved for some years.

36. A.G.M. minutes.

37. 36th Annual Report 1959 - 60.

38. Dr. F.H. Boland in Minutes of 1966 A.G.M.

39. Secretary's Report 1970.

40. "The sad position of the National Museum still after 50 years of self-government in the stranglehold of the Department of Education, has to be continually ventilated ... Even if a Minister of Culture is not going to be established, at best the Museum could be restructured ..." (William Dillon, '50 Years of the Friends', *Irish Times,* March 28th 1973).

41. The late Dr. Fitzpatrick was notably active at this time in her countrywide survey of galleries, museums and public organizations.

42. A covenant scheme for would-be purchasers of art works giving adequate tax incentive and provision was first suggested by James White at the 1974 A.G.M.

FROM DUBLIN TO NEW YORK, WITH A DETOUR TO LENINGRAD: AN ART-HISTORICAL ODYSSEY

Marian Burleigh-Motley

For a child visitor to the National Gallery of Ireland in the 1940s, there was something magical in the stories told by the lecturer who, each Sunday, described and interpreted seemingly inexplicable old paintings. But how did the lecturer determine which of the gods was which, and how could he tell the way each layer of paint was applied, and in what order? (And what were scumbles? The word did not appear in my dictionary.) How could the lecturer know what the artist was thinking about as he painted a portrait and how could he be sure that the expression given to the sitter matched his personality? Only one explanation seemed possible. The lecturer must have a direct line to the all-knowing Christian God. But how could someone as sinful as only an Irish Catholic girl could be, ever hope to achieve a similar level of knowledge? For some years I was perfectly happy to listen to and marvel at the man my father introduced as "Paddy" White - more formally known in art circles as James. Later, on James's recommendation, I read Bulfinches's *Mythologies* and 'stories' from the Old Testament (the full text not being considered suitable reading for young Catholic girls; they might, God forbid!, read the Song of Solomon among other suggestive passages), and most climactically, the letters of Van Gogh. It was exciting to discover that even I might learn some of the secrets of the old masters.

But James White had not finished with me. An ardent supporter of all that was new in art - in a society that found the ludicrous sentimentality of the "Bleeding Heart of Christ" perfectly acceptable - James lectured and wrote about Cubism and Abstract art, and I was there to learn a new vocabulary and a new passion. Furthermore, James not only taught us about the great European art movements of the twentieth century, he also almost forcibly interested us in the Irish followers of those movements. For, simultaneously with his lecturing on the old masters, he reviewed the exhibitions of contemporary art which were enlivening the Dublin scene in the 1950s.

My future began to take shape - on the model James White provided. After completing a B. A. at Trinity College I studied art history there, under his direction. I also began to write art criticism, at first for a monthly journal, *The Irish Architect and Contractor* and later as the regular critic for *The Irish Press*. Unfailing in his encouragement, which was badly needed both when I felt inadequate to explain a particularly interesting new artist such as Richard

Kingston and also when the latest exhibition was so bad that I had absolutely nothing to say, he always managed to persuade me to at least try to do justice to the effort of the artist, while never dissuading me from expressing my own opinion.

Working with James on exhibitions and acting as his assistant in the organization of the first Dublin meeting of the International Association of Art Critics in 1953, I learned from his extraordinary organizational skills, although I never mastered his innate qualities of diplomacy. Over many years I never saw him lose his temper or behave inappropriately - even under extreme provocation. Through my work with the Association and their trips abroad, I got to know some of the most distinguished art historians and critics of the day, including Lionello Venturi, James Johnson Sweeney, Herbert Read, and others and began to discriminate between different approaches to art and to art history. During my tenure as Acting Director of the Municipal Gallery of Modern Art in Dublin in 1964-5, I was also able to benefit from James's advice and help as he continued to live over the Gallery after he became Director of the National Gallery of Ireland. But even he was shocked when I arranged the official reception for an exhibition of the works of Francis Bacon on Good Friday. Nonetheless, I was subsequently invited to lecture to seminarians on homosexuality in Bacon's art.

Later, armed with a letter of recommendation from James, I entered the doctoral program at the Institute of Fine Arts, New York University in 1966, and soon after began the New York phase of my career, without abandoning my connections with James. I was fortunate to study modern art under Robert Goldwater, one of the great minds in the field, and Renaissance art under Charles Sterling from the Louvre. I later wrote my dissertation on the Irish artist, George Russell (AE), locating and identifying many 'lost' works, with help from James White, and offering a reading of AE's murals in Ely Place based on Madame Blavatsky's *Secret Doctrine*. One rediscovery from my Dublin days was the presence at the Institute of Gert Schiff, whom I had first met through James at the 1953 Art critics meeting in Dublin. When Robert Goldwater, my second important mentor, died, Gert Schiff kindly took me on as his dissertation student. He remained - despite the potential problems of such a relationship - a good friend until his death in 1990.

During my subsequent years in America I tried to remain associated with museums and their art works even while teaching in the academic world - again following James's example. As Director of the Rutgers University Art Gallery I drew on the skills I had learned from him to organize many exhibitions, including one of the first exhibitions in America of underground Soviet art. So began what was to become my long-term involvement with Russian and Soviet art. In order to familiarize myself with original works of Russian art and architecture I spent the winter of 1975-76 visiting both public and private collections in Leningrad, Moscow, Novgorod, Kharkov and elsewhere. The opportunity to study Russian art from medieval to modern times in both the public displays and storage areas of the major museums was invaluable. I made contact with Soviet art historians and curators many of whom quickly became warm friends, as well as stimulating colleagues. The kindness and hospitality of the professional staff at the Russian Museum in Leningrad, especially, made what might have been a very grim, cold, hard winter, a time to be treasured in memory. The striking similarities between

Leningrad and Dublin in climate, 18th-and 19th-century architecture, slow-moving grey river, ever cloudy skies, and in hospitality, indeed made my three-month stay there more like an extension of my Dublin rather than of my New York life. But Russian nineteenth-century landscape painting proved so similar to American art of that period that I felt I was back in New York in the American wing of the Metropolitan Museum. I was lucky enough to see also George Marian Costakis's famous collection of Russian avant-garde art (of which a portion was seen at the Rosc exhibition some years ago) before its dispersal when he emigrated in 1977. Later, several shorter trips to the Soviet Union to study specific works of art and archival sources enabled me to publish in 1986 a revised and enlarged edition of the basic book in English about the Russian avant-garde - Camilla Gray's, *The Great Experiment* of 1962.[1] Working with members of Camilla Gray's family, including her Russian husband Oleg Prokofiev (son of the composer), I was able to reconstruct a picture of the extraordinary life and death of a young ballet dancer who took on the daunting task of making sense of a turbulent period in Russian art then virtually unknown in the West. During these years I kept James informed of my new-found passion during frequent summer visits to Dublin.

As a member of the faculty of Princeton University in the 1970s and later in the 1980s, I offered some of the first courses in Russian art given at any American university, often working together with colleagues who specialized in Russian literature, history, or music. I was also able to invite James to lecture on the paintings of John Butler Yeats to a Princeton audience which considered that Irish art had come to an end in the 8th century. At Princeton, I continued to be involved with museum work, organizing several teaching exhibitions at the University Art Museum, including an exhibition of fakes which was prepared with five senior students in the Department of Art & Archaeology.[2] James White's training, which was based on actual works of art, not on slides or photographs, provided the necessary connoisseurship skills for this task.

During these years I also translated a book on French Art Nouveau glass, wrote numerous encyclopedia entries on both European and Russian art and catalogued a collection of twentieth-century art for an exhibition in California.[3] In all these undertakings I was encouraged by the example of James White, who ranged widely in his publications and lecturing.

Today, the organisational skills I learned from James have found, I think, a fruitful outlet in my work at the Metropolitan Museum of Art, New York as Head of the Office of Academic Programs. Such an Office could hardly exist in Ireland where museum staffs and budgets are so small. At the Metropolitan, where the staff numbers about 2000 (assisted by 600 volunteers), and the total budget exceeds $77 million, we still face budget deficits and complain about not having enough money, but obviously the opportunities exist for presenting a greater variety of programs. My office acts as a liaison between the Metropolitan and the academic and professional communities of universities and other museums and provides a variety of programs and services in the areas of museum studies and higher education. With a rich endowment specifically designated for fellowships, we are able to give some 30-40 scholars and graduate students each year the opportunity of doing research at the museum, or in some cases of travelling abroad. Other funds are available for summer internships at the museum for both graduate and undergraduate students. For our own staff we offer tuition reimbursement and travel grants to further their professional development.

The Metropolitan Museum's role in higher education goes back to the 1930s when many of the refugee art historians who came to America from Germany found teaching positions at the Institue of Fine Arts - the art history graduate school of New York University. Erwin Panofsky, among others, taught their first classes in the basement of the museum. Even when the Institute moved into its own premises, the connections with the Metropolitan continued. As part of our commitment to the nurturing of future museum professionals and scholars, we offer a joint program whose aim is to train selected doctoral condidates in curatorial skills and responsibilities over a four year period. We also collaborate on a conservation training program. To facilitate the interchange of curators and art historians, several of our curators and conservators (and myself) hold adjunct professorships at the Institute.

In our programming we benefit from our New York location in that over 75% of our visitors have a university degree. While the museum has always offered numerous lectures and gallery talks for the general public it seemed to me when I joined the museum four years ago that we should also address the needs of the more highly educated segment of our audience, including the 15% who hold doctoral degrees and the many members of the museum who are scholars or collectors. Given the intellectual resources of the museum and the generosity of donors I have been able to organize an annual lecture course for that segment of the public. My goal was to extend to the educated public, interested scholars and graduate students, and to our own staff and volunteers an opportunity to increase their understanding of how art history works, and to build a bridge to the public by showing them what academics and museum curators do in the course of their scholarly work. Taught by senior curators and conservators from the museum and by faculty from the Institute of Fine Arts, the first two courses covered a wide variety of art historical methodologies, including the 'new' art history. The most recent series has addressed the question of the original context of works of art in the collections of the Metropolitan Museum. As I prepared this article I realised that, in a way, I am trying through these lectures to anticipate and answer the kinds of questions I had puzzled over as a child in Dublin. For the same audience we also offer scholarly symposia on topics ranging from the Pre-Columbian art of ancient Mexico to the restoration of Renaissance frescoes. The symposia, notwithstanding their scholarly focus, regularly attract audiences of 600 to 700. As a further contribution to higher education the museum publishes a scholarly journal, on whose board I have the honour to serve.[4]

On a more personal note, I might add that I also lecture extensively in our various programs, and try to remain active as a scholar in my chosen field of Russian art by contributing to symposia and exhibition catalogues.[5] In Spring 1991, I offered a graduate seminar on the Russian artist Kazimir Malevich, using a major exhibition of his work at the museum as the focus of the course.

What has all this to do with James White? I could not care so passionately about art history and its methodologies, if I did not care so much for art, and it was James White who first, and forever, showed me the joy and excitement to be found in the experience of works of art. Although interested in the new art history's approach to modernism, as an art historian I remain wedded to the idea so powerfully argued by James, that abstract art has meaning. It was through James's interest in abstract art that I initially came to the study of the Russian avant-garde of the first three decades of this century. So, in many respects my interests and career have been shaped by his teaching and example. Other contributors to this volume have written about James's influence on Irish art and Irish art history so I hope I may be forgiven for choosing to make this a personal tribute rather than a scholarly study. I would like then to offer this short article as an inadequate sign of my personal debt to a much-loved friend and mentor, James White.

Notes

1. Camilla Gray, *The Russian Experiment in Art 1863-1922*, Revised and enlarged edition by Marian Burleigh-Motley, Thames and Hudson, London, 1986; Russian-language edition, 1990.

2. *Problems of Authenticity in Nineteenth- and Twentieth-Century Art*, ex. cat., Princeton University Art Museum, 1973; "Cubism and Post-Cubism", in *Selections from the Norton Simon. Inc.. Museum of Art*, ex. cat., Princeton University Art Museum, 1972; "Art in the Post-war Era", *European and American Art from Princeton Alumni Collections*, ex. cat., Princeton University Art Museum, 1972.

3. Essays on various art topics in *Academic American Encyclopedia*, Arete, 1981; Twenty biographies of Russian artists for *Macmillan Encyclopedia of Art*, forthcoming; *Seven Decades of 20th-Century Art: From the Sidney and Harriet Janis Collections*, ex. cat., La Jolla Museum of Art, 1980.

4. *Metropolitan Museum Journal*. Published annually. Volume 25/1990 includes an index to volumes 1-24.

5. 'Tatlin's *Sailor*: A New Reading' at "Vladimir Tatlin. Leben, Werk, Wirkung: Ein internationales Symposium 1989", Städtische Kunsthalle Düsseldorf, DuMont, 1990; 'Arte russa e sovietica dal 1870 al 1930: lo stato attuale degli studi in Occidente' in *Arte Russa e Sovietica 1870-1930*, ex. cat. Turin, 1989, pp. 60-72.

William John Leech
(1881-1968)
**A Convent Garden,
Brittany (c. 1913)**
NGI. Cat. No. 1245

W. J. LEECH AND THE CONVENT GARDEN

Julian Campbell

In 1913 William John Leech exhibited a painting entitled *Les Soeurs du Saint-Esprit* at the Paris Salon. Two years later, in 1915, the same painting was shown at the Royal Hibernian Academy in Dublin, and then in 1921 at the Royal Academy in London, entitled 'Nun and Lilies'.[1] Most likely this was the painting now entitled *Convent Garden, Brittany*, which was presented to the National Gallery of Ireland by Leech's friend May Botterell in 1952. With its attractive subject-matter, a garden setting, its sunshine and shadow, and its bright colouring and decorative brushwork, it is one of the most deliberately 'impressionistic' of paintings by an Irish artist. Priced at only £28-5-0 when it was first exhibited in Dublin, *Convent Garden, Brittany* remains one of Leech's most popular and best-loved pictures.

Born in Dublin in 1881, Leech had studied at the Metropolitan School of Art, and then at the R.H.A. schools, as a pupil of Walter Osborne. He went to Paris in 1901, and studied at the Académie Julian for a couple of years. He first visited Brittany in about 1903, settling not at Pont-Aven, where Osborne and Roderic O'Conor had painted, but at Concarneau, which also had a thriving artists' colony. Concarneau had a medieval walled town, and great expanses of flat beach at low tide. Leech spent at least part of each year until around 1908 in Brittany, and continued to visit the region until the outbreak of the First World War.[2] In 1908, he painted an important Breton indoor scene with figures, *Interior of a Cafe* (exhibited R.H.A. 1909. Private collection). *Convent Garden, Brittany*, although not dated, shows a considerable change in style from the *Interior*: from a careful, detailed style, somewhat in the manner of Orpen, to looser, more expressive brushwork, and a brighter palette, suitable to its open-air setting. Yet, with its carefully worked-out composition, its experimental technique, and its echoes of other paintings, obviously it was intended as an important exhibition piece. *Convent Garden* brings together a number of important influences, and elements in Leech's own life. The painting repays further study and a certain sense of enigma remains in the picture to this day.

Irish artists had been visiting Brittany since the 1870s and eighties, attracted by its verdant landscape and rolling coastline, its picturesque villages and colourful inhabitants in traditional costumes, which varied from region to region. In particular the women, wore ornate head-dresses and shawls on the occasion of religious festivals. The French artists Gauguin and Bernard, leading figures of the

Henry Jones Thaddeus
(1859-1929)
**Market Day,
Finistère (1882)**
NGI. Cat. No. 4513

Pont-Aven School, were by no means the first artists who were attracted by a sense of the exotic in Brittany and by the pictorial possibilities of the decorative white headwear of Breton women. For example, in 1882 the Cork-born artist, Henry Jones Thaddeus, represented a Breton girl on the beach at Concarneau, in *Jour de Marché Finistère* (N.G.I.). Her cheerful red bonnet, and wide, white ruff with lace trimmings, are beautifully observed. In a painting *Corpus Christi Procession, Brittany* (Allied Irish Banks Collection), probably also dating from the early 1880's, Aloysius O'Kelly shows three girls in simple white costumes in procession on a shadowy road. He uses subdued pale grey and ochre tones, but the face, bonnet and shoulders of the girl in the foreground are dappled with sunlight. With its sensitive treatment of sunlight, and its sketchy brushwork *Corpus Christi Procession* is a surprisingly 'impressionistic' picture by an Irish artist at this early date. Considering it was painted thirty years before *Convent Garden*, it is remarkably 'Leech-ian' in feel.

A tiny panel of a Corpus Christi procession also survives from Edith Somerville's visit to Brittany (private collection). French artist Pascal Dagnan-Bouveret created a humble, but memorable picture of Breton girls in traditional costume, seated on the grass, in *Breton Women at a Pardon*, 1887 (Gulbenkian Foundation, Lisbon).

Although painted in a much more traditional or Realist style than that of

P.A.J. Dagnan-Bouveret (1852-1929)
Breton Women at a Pardon (1887)
Calouste Gulbenkian Foundation Museum, Lisbon

Gauguin, never-the-less the girls' elaborate white headwear merges to form decorative shapes. In a recently-discovered painting *A Song to Spring*, dated about 1897 (private collection), Walter Chetwood Aiken[3] also enjoys, along a horizontal axis, the complex lines and patterns made by the white head-dresses of Breton women.

Aiken charmingly captures a group of girls in the shade of an apple tree in blossom, with a sunny landscape in the background. Nathaniel Hill represents a more sober picture of Breton life in his *Breton Peasants waiting at a Convent Door*, 1884 (private collection). Here, the artist depicts the poverty of the villagers, dressed in threadbare working clothes, and waiting for alms outside the convent. The closed door and bleak walls effectively shut off their lives from the quiet convent courtyard or garden, and there is not a religious figure in sight.

Leech's painting *Convent Garden, Brittany* represents a different world - on the other side of the convent walls: a sunny, secluded garden of lilies and lush grass, bushes and trees. A group of nuns walk and pray, shut off from life outside. In the foreground a young girl, dressed in white, stands among lilies. Her face is uncovered and raised slightly, and she holds a prayer-book in her hands. In the background nuns walk beneath the trees, heads covered by heavy bonnets, figures half-hidden by leaves and shadow. The young girl on the right faces out of the picture, seemingly about to pass out of view, while the other nuns appear almost to 'float' at the top of the picture. This gives a 'frieze-like' effect, adding to the feeling of insubstantiality, as if symbolizing the sisters' withdrawal from the world, and their life of prayer. The decorative costumes of the women and shapes of flowers and leaves, and the unusual a-symmetrical composition, suggest the influence of Gauguin.

Meanwhile, much of the composition is taken up by the garden itself, its lilies and grasses swaying in a pool of sunshine. The tall upright lilies balance the figure of the girls, while the decorative arabesques of flowers and leaves, the swirling blades of grass, seem to have a life of their own. In Chetwood Aiken's painting, the girls in the foreground were shown in shadow, with a sunny landscape behind; in Leech's work, it is the other way around, the trees forming a dark frame at the top of the picture. Leech has used a striking palette: greens and whites, blues and yellows, pinks and delicate mauves.

Sister Mary Benedict Cotter identifies the nuns in the background of *Convent Garden* as 'Les Soeurs Blanche', or 'Les Filles de Saint Esprit' (Daughters of the Holy Ghost), as they are officially known, thus giving the original title to Leech's painting.[4] She recognizes the convent garden at Concarneau, where she herself served for some time. Sister Mary writes that the white habits worn by the nuns in Leech's painting were discarded in 1953. She believes that before the order wore white, the nuns used to wear the dress of the ordinary people; and they do so again today.

A Breton writer, Gweltaz Durand, believes that Leech is the painter: "who best depicted Brittany at that period... better than Gauguin himself, whose theory of simplifying lines and colours tended towards the exclusion of diversity and peculiarity in the depiction of detail, as in the traditional dress; for instance, Gauguin painted the coiffes and skirts of the Breton woman as being plain unadorned fabrics, ignoring the marvellous embroidery and astounding lace, and made the Breton costume similar to any ordinary peasant dress. Leech, on the contrary, in *Convent Garden, Brittany* deals with the young Tregor girl's coiffe and shawl, as carefully as he deals with the plants and foliage in the convent garden. In a very impressionistic way, he exploits the light passing through the lace in the same fashion as the light passing through the foliage".[5]

The girl in the foreground, probably a novice, wears a different costume from the other sisters. Her lace habit and bonnet are light, almost transparent, with decorative floral patterns just visible. The delicate shades of mauve and lilac, as well as white, in which her garment is painted, suggesting the play of sunlight and shadow, are lighter than the heavily painted garden which surrounds her, further adding to the feeling of insubstantiality.

Although entitled *Réligieuse* when exhibited in Brussels in 1938, *Convent Garden* also brings together more worldly concerns: Leech's interest in the human subject, and in the garden. The garden became one of his favourite subjects. The influence of Walter Osborne had remained with him. Osborne's *Cottage Garden with flowers*, 1888 (N.G.I.) had featured a lush bank of lilies, with a man peeping shyly from a doorway behind. In paintings such as *In the Phoenix Park* (N.G.I.) and *Portrait of J.B.S. Mac Ilwaine* (N.G.I.), sunlight is suggested above the trees, but the principal figures are shown in shadow. Osborne's late, 'impressionistic' painting, *In a Rathmines Garden* (private collection) features a group of children

John Singer Sargent
(1856-1925)
Carnation, Lily, Lily, Rose (1885/86)
The Tate Gallery London

in a warm, sunny garden, and a couple of elderly men in shadow at the top of the picture, giving a hint of Leech's efforts in *Convent Garden*.

Perhaps Leech was attempting a grand Garden painting, in the tradition of Monet's *Women in the Garden* 1867 (Musée d'Orsay, Paris). Monet had featured four women in a garden, capturing sunlight and shadow with great mastery. For example, the dresses are pure white in the pool of sunshine, and subtle pale shades of blue, green or grey in the shadow of the trees. Monet's wife and another woman, dressed up in fashionable, flowing dresses, posed for the four figures in the garden. Leech's *Convent Garden* would obviously have appeared 'modern' and 'French' in quality when it was first exhibited in Dublin in 1915. The swaying lilies, and the thick strokes of paint with which the garden is painted certainly show an attempt at Impressionism, and even suggest the influence of Van Gogh. But this is counteracted by the careful drawing and paintwork in the girl's

William Leech
(1881-1968)
**The Sunshade
(c. 1913)**
NGI. Cat. No. 1246

figure, giving a contrast between the stillness of the nun, and the harsh animation of the leaves and grass. Moreover, it is worth asking if a picture painted forty-five years after Monet's *Déjeuner*, and thirty-six years after the first Impressionist exhibition in Paris, can really be referred to as 'Impressionist'?

Leech's painting is much closer in style and spirit to an English painting, *Carnation, Lily, Lily, Rose* 1885-86 (Tate Gallery) by J.S. Sargent, with its representation of figures in white in a garden, its contrasts of whites and greens, the decorative shapes of the lilies, and the enveloping feeling of the garden, without horizon or glimpse of sky. In Sargent's charming painting two children with loose white dresses, or smocks, and bare heads lowered, are absorbed in their activity: suspending fragile, coloured lanterns in a magical garden of flowers and slender grasses. At the top of the picture large, floating lilies form exquisite arabesques. In contrast to the dramatic contrast of sunlight and shadow in *Convent Garden*, the tonality of Sargent's painting is even, but rich, dominated by the resonant blue-green of the garden

William Leech
(1881-1968)
Portrait of a Girl
Private Collection

In Leech's painting the head of the girl is crowned by a slender branch and canopy of leaves. She pauses for a moment, her head raised. In fact, she is more like a young bride than a nun. Her face is painted with sensitivity, her healthy colouring giving the impression of an outdoor life rather than an enclosed life of prayer. The whiteness of her costume, as of the lilies, symbolises purity. But her features in profile: beautifully-drawn eyebrows and large blue-green eyes, slightly upturned nose and full mouth, pointed chin and slender neck, also suggest a worldly beauty. The model is obviously an individual rather than just a type; indeed she is painted with a sense of admiration.

Who is this girl? Did Leech persuade a young nun of the 'Saint Esprit' order to pose for him? Or did he know the girl?

Denise Ferran has established that the model in *Convent Garden* is Leech's wife Elizabeth Saurine.[6] She was a French painter whom he had met in France, and married in London in 1912. She was obviously very beautiful, and Leech's admiration for her is evident. As Ferran confirms, Elizabeth appears in a number of Leech's paintings at the time, notably *The Sunshade* (N.G.I.). This shows a girl with strong arched eyebrows, slightly upturned nose and slender neck, turning to one side. Elizabeth could also be the model in the watercolour *Portrait of a Girl* (private collection). Painted in muted colours, greys, greens and whites, it captures the momentary glance of a girl, both beautiful and ethereal, whose long hair tumbles over her shoulder.

The garden, and especially the painting of plants or flowers in close-up, became a subject to which Leech frequently returned throughout his career. His feeling for nature and his problems encountered in painting in the open air, are expressed in a long letter to the eminent Dr. Helena Wright,[7] who became a close friend of Leech later in his life:

"My dear Helena,

I am writing to you to try to answer questions that you have asked me. The questions you ask are the kind that one cannot answer at the moment because they set one thinking. You said you had come to a place in your work as a painter and stuck. One has to come to several of those sticking places, it's a good sign I think. Now I think you would get over this place if you did as follows. Get a drawing board, good size, *charcoal* (not pencil) and good sized sheets of paper tinted or not, tinted would be less trying to the eyes. Then start to draw landscape instead of painting it. Now I don't mean by drawing what is generally meant by drawing. I am going to take this advice too. I want you to draw not merely to represent what you see but to draw in order to teach yourself to see. This puts me in mind of a definition of a genius - one who sees what others merely look at. I dare say you have come across it too. You must not be in a hurry, and you must not draw or paint everything or anything. You must search till you find some arrangement of lines that speaks to you, then sit and contemplate it for a long time. Till you really begin to understand its construction, it is not a conglomeration of objects, it appears so at first sight, your business is to see them all as one, and draw them as a portion of the earth so that your picture will have body and weight. The more you can feel, the more will come into your work. To give you an example. Last winter I was drawing something that had a lot of perpendiculars and I, the draftsman was standing too. The first day, I did nothing but just look, and the thing gradually began to appear more and more magnificent, and slowly I began to understand why, as I stood there, a perpendicular, I seemed to realize as never before that I was one with the earth and all the surrounding things, that I was not really perpendicular, but only so from my point of view. If you produced all (i.e. the houses, the telegraph poles other people and myself) our so called perpendicular lives would meet in the centre of the earth. Now I was in a fit state to paint or draw something that could not fail to be interesting because I was conscious of so much. My feet were very firmly planted, like the feet of a circus rider on his horse, like him, I felt at an angle, but an angle that was in relation to all the other! so called perpendiculars, and an angle that felt so tremendously right. I was able to draw all the other perpendiculars in consequence at their real angles without any hesitation at all, I simply felt them, each had its own place and there was not other place for it, and like the circus rider I seemed to feel the movement underneath my feet and I was part of it and we all seemed to be swinging round like the spokes of a great wheel, in fact as I drew I was conscious of the revolution of the earth, I seemed to have my back to the direction in which we were going so that all the things I was drawing were following me. Now you see how completely one all the objects I was drawing had become, they had become one with the earth and one with myself, and I could not help suggesting the movement too, and I had become one with my subject since a line drawn through me would meet all the other "perpendicular" lines in my picture. It is amazing to think that someone else would have drawn all those perpendiculars perpendicular to the tiny bit of ground he was standing on and they all would have been parallel to each other and correct from his point of view and the point of view of the academy. Look how dull his drawing would have been. Goodnight Helena."[8]

Notes

1. Ms. Denise Ferran informed me that Leech's *Convent Garden, Brittany* was exhibited at the R.A., London in 1921 under the title of 'Nun and Lilies'. I am very grateful to Ms. Ferran for reading my article, making a few corrections, and offering some valuable suggestions.

2. Those dates were suggested to me by Dr. Helena Wright, a close friend of Leech.

3. I am grateful for Mr. Desmond Fitzgerald for drawing my attention to this little-known artist.

4. Letter written by Sister Mary Benedict Cotter, of the Convent of the Holy Ghost, Luton, to the National Gallery of Ireland, 5 May, 1985.

5. Gweltaz Durand, *Irish Painters in Brittany at the Turn of the Century*, CARN, Winter 1974 - 75 No. 81, p. 6.

6. In the catalogue of *The Irish Impressionists* exhibition (National Gallery of Ireland, 1984), p. 261, I mistakenly suggested that the girl in *Convent Garden* might be Leech's second wife, May Botterell. Denise Ferran has established that the model is Leech's first wife, Elizabeth Saurine, and that she also appears in *The Sunshade*. Ms. Ferran is researching the life and work of Leech for a doctoral degree at Trinity College, Dublin, and for a forthcoming publication on the artist.

7. Dr. Helena Wright, distinguished international expert in Family Planning, met Leech in 1930 and became a life long friend. I am very grateful to the late Dr. Wright for talking to me and corresponding with me about the artist.

8. Letter sent by Leech to Helena Wright. I am grateful to the late Dr. Wright for communicating this letter to me.

LOSING SIGHT OF ART
Ciarán Carty

Let's start with a painter. Too often it's the other way around. The theory comes first (and, not far behind, the critic who propounds it). Art is expected to fit the theory. If it doesn't fit, then tough on the art. It's as if it has become non-art.

Little wonder Mick Mulcahy quit studying at the National College of Art in the early 1970s and headed off for Spain with Mick Cullen, and then alone across to Morocco. He'd no taste for the arid formalism of minimal art. It had: "no body, no soul, no lasting power." As with other expressionist painters who had formed the Independent Artists in the 1960s because galleries wouldn't show their work, he was outside the pale of what then passed for art.

"Always look with the will of Allah!", Arab nomads would tell him as he herded cattle in the Sahara.

"Always look. They'd no preconceptions. They saw everything as it was, not as they expected it to be. They'd look at life with clear brains. Each man, each bird was like the first they had seen. They taught me how to see."

This is back when we first met in 1982. He had a show opening at the Lincoln Gallery (now no more, but responsible for bringing painters like Mulcahy initially into favour). He was painting with the exhilaration of someone who had seen the light: the burning clarity of the desert. His eye-grabbing images assaulted senses with collisions of colour and form. Within a few years, with the New York triumph of the German "wilds", the Irish art taste would catch up on the expressionism it hadn't deemed fit to notice in the 1960s and 1970s. Suddenly this would be the only art to matter. Much to Mulcahy's apprehension. He did not want to be part of any "school" or "movement". "We're all different," he insisted. "we're like a group of fishermen in a town. The only reason we stick together is that we're interested in the same thing, painting or catching fish or whatever."

So what's going on here? Why should labels dictate what is or is not art at any particular time in any particular society? Have art historians and art critics, in cosy collusion with dealers, galleries, the media, art colleges and the market, got too big for themselves? Do they imagine that by defining art they have in some way become its actual creator?

Take a time trip back to Giorgio Vasari. It's surely ironic that the whole process which led in the 20th century to what Hans Belting dubbed "the invasion of art by critics, and, also by the art market", was set in motion by an actual artist. In Vasari's *Lives Of the Artists*, a best-seller when it was published over 400 years ago in the heyday of the Renaissance, this impoverished Florentine painter and architect didn't just list his fellow artists: he attempted to explain their art and put it in context.

Here was the birth of art history as the West knows it, an academicisation of the practice of painting and sculpture which cumulatively over the years has enabled art critics and theorists (quoting Belting again) "to erect a norm of style which in turn seemed to constitute the very meaning of art." Of course this "meaning" would keep changing. By the mid-20th century "isms" proliferated so fast that not even the critics themselves, let alone the bewildered artist trying to catch the eye of dealers and curators, could keep up with the "cult of the briefly new."

This is not to imply that art scholarship is a bad thing. Art needs to be written about. It needs to be put into words. Without documentation it could never have come to be pursued and appreciated to the staggering degree that now prevails. An analogy can be made to religion. It wasn't enough for God to be made man. He needed a Church to propagate His Word. Belief had to be institutionalised. Art too needs a framework of interpretation and study to develop and reach a public. That is its paradox. Through the word, art has flourished and enriched civilisation. But its relationship with the word is in the nature of a Faustian pact. The price too often has been its very soul.

Just as the institution of religion in time has tended to become more important than the truth it was set up to represent, criticism and art history were tempted to amuse their function. Art too often was subsumed into an idea of art. The spirit of discovery gave way to dogma. Instead of interpreting a truth, the interpretation became the truth. "Art, taken purely as art, becomes to a certain extent something superfluous," proclaimed Hegel.

An intimidating infrastructure of self-reinforcing interests grew up around the idea of art: the critics who defined it, the art historians who authenticated it, the dealers who marketed it, the galleries who exhibited it, the colleges who taught it, the patrons who collected it, the investors who hoarded it away in vaults.

New York inevitably became the power broker, the arbiter of taste: Modernism was installed as much as the One True Faith, with a high priesthood to guard its purity. An awed public, impressed by the celebrity of star artists, queued not to look for themselves but to see branch products: a Jackson Pollock, a Frank Stella, a Barnett Newman.

And what of the artists? Tom Wolfe in *The Painted Word* pinpoints their subservience: "Critics issue their absurd fiats and artists hustle to carry them out to the letter."

Not that it was all one way. There were painters like Edward Hopper, Andrew Wyeth and Balthus who paid no attention and kept painting in their own way regardless of fashion. Others like Douglas Huebler and the practitioners of Arte Povera retaliated by creating art that was "beyond direct perceptual experience", so that "awareness of the work depends on a system of documentation." The word in effect became the art. "I'm not really interested any longer in making an object," said Jan Dibbetts.

But this proved something of an aesthetic cul-de-sac. It led to an art shorn of wings, soaring only in the mind.

The more common response has been to reverse roles on the critics. Art criticism and history itself - through pastiche, quotation, playing with signs, self-reference and irony - became the subject of art. But this of course was to fight on the enemies own ground. It could only end in one way, with the emergence of a new movement or ism, neatly packaged by the critics it sought to subvert: post-modernism.

So now it's time for a little sanity. Bring in James White.

James White has always been a joyous exception to this polarisation, a critic and gallery director who at heart is with the artists, who respects scholarship but recognises its limits, who like Mick Mulcahy's Arab herdsman believes more than anything else just in looking and in encouraging everyone around him to look as well.

Here he is in 1979 as director of the National Gallery and chairman of the Arts Council. "People tell me that I'm not a proper art historian. That I haven't the qualifications for the job I've done. I say I couldn't agree more. It's marvellous to be so lucky."

White's first symbolic gesture on coming from the Hugh Lane Municipal Gallery to the National Gallery was to insist on removing the glass from all the paintings. "It was ghastly. You came into the gallery and wherever you looked you saw your own reflection."

Which is what looking at art was in danger of becoming. Just a matter of seeing what you expected to see, a mirror of society's preconceptions of art.

White sought to give the public back its eyes. Because that was how he had come to art himself. Not through scholarship and received opinions but simply by looking. "I had no proper education. I went all over the continent, even to Greece in a cargo boat, going to galleries and museums."

Although White was born in a cottage on Grove Avenue next door to the house where the William Orpen family lived - his mother used to have tea there and she would tell him what wonderful hands Orpen had - Ireland until the 1960s was unfairly deemed to be virtually illiterate in the visual arts. This wasn't because there were no Irish artists but because there was little or no documentation of Irish art.

If this illustrates the need for art to be written about, the 1960s would show that when the word finally caught up on Irish art, the blessings were mixed. Rosc '67 introduced international art to the Irish public. With the Lemass economic boom, an art market developed. Commercial galleries proliferated. Patrons began to build up collections. But the definition of art applied - the art that was considered fashionable, to which the Arts Council gave its imprimatur - had a New York label, against which much of the art being created in Ireland was deemed provincial and outmoded.

This is of course something of a generalisation. The danger in questioning theories is to end up seeming to offer the prospectus for just another theory. Let's keep to specifics. Listen to artists. After all they're at the front line of creativity.

"A painter who loves his art should carefully avoid spending too much time with critics and literary people," warned Georges Rouault. "These individuals, probably unintentionally, deform things by trying to explain everything, taking thought, will, and artistic sensitivities and shearing them just as Delilah sheared Samson."

Dubuffet was just as wary of attempts to explain art. "Ideas are but a faint puff of air," he said. "It is when visions disappear that ideas emerge along with the blind fish of their waters, the intellectual."

What the critic seeks to pin down, the artist - whether painter, sculptor, composer or writer - prefers to keep as a mystery. "In any body of work there's always a pattern to be found," said Graham Greene. "Well, I don't want to see it. When a critic discovers certain keynotes, that's fine and may be of interest, but I don't want to be steeped in his discoveries. I want to remain unaware of them. Otherwise I think my imagination would dry up."

It is precisely this reluctance of artists to rationalise what they are doing that has encouraged critics to do it for them. But the fact that artists, out of their own direct experience of creating art, are convinced that there are certain areas that can be touched only by art - and therefore defy analysis - is surely the point that matters.

In the course of up to 500 interviews conducted by me over the past 15 years with visual artists, writers, dramatists, poets, film directors, composers and performers, both in Ireland and abroad, this is a concern which has found expression perhaps more than any other.

So let us take it as evidence, a form of testimony.

Enter John Behan, sculptor. We're in Hynes pub in Mount Street, sometime in 1977. Behan is a figurative sculptor. But birds, bulls, horses and animals were not at all the done thing when he began exhibiting in the 1960s. He was a founder member of the New Artists Group in 1962 and the Project Arts Centre in 1967. For a while he was a driving force behind the Independent Artists in their attempt to challenge gallery elitism.

"Everyone is born with an ability to see things quite clearly. It is when they get into organised society after their initial childhood that the difficulties begin. Their vision is interfered with. They are told what to see. Ideas of form are planted on them."

"You find it in all societies. Values are imposed. Especially where art has an official tag, as in the Soviet Union or China. The way of seeing becomes completely official. Joy is represented by a sunset going down over a field or ripe corn, and so on."

Which is what happened with much of Western art in the 20th century. Our eyes became isms. Our awareness of beauty was rigged. Too often we were cut of from the staggering potential of our own vision without even realising it.

Picasso had this in mind when he said that "the important thing about me is that my greatest desire is to get back to that state where I would have the vision of a child."

John Behan's images come out of direct experience and observation rather than some theory or the conventions of an ism. "All art is about looking. Like Joyce's epiphanies. Something you see."

A sculptor doesn't explain. The work is its own explanation. "It's just there. You have to understand it or not. All art is a mystery, as life itself is a mystery. But people want it to be a fixed thing. In the same way that they look to religion for the certainty of an after-life, signed, sealed, and delivered."

Even writers, who create with words, profess not to understand how their fiction comes about. "You don't arrive at good prose by reason," says John Fowles, author of *The French Lieutenant's Woman:* we're talking in a study overlooking Bedford Square in London in 1986. Like Graham Greene he sees it as some mysterious power to move people, to make them see a little differently.

"You have to be an adolescent to write a novel. If you were fully mature I don't think you'd ever attempt it. You'd be too much a prisoner of reason." That's the trouble with academics. "Many of them are trained to think rationally and they're upset by things that don't quite fit the pattern they have in their mind. So we're also a bit exiled."

It took incarceration in a mental hospital to recover from several years of heavy drinking for Patrick Graham to liberate his eyes. "Getting rid of the booze was an awful lot more than not drinking," he says. "It was a kind of untying myself from received notions of aesthetics, of life, of politics." It's 1987. His rediscovered zest for painting shows in a series of big expressionist works, some of which are about to go on view in a major exhibition at the Jack Rutberg Gallery in Los Angeles. He now sees painting as the challenge of dealing with the not known. "Getting away from the notion that any dogma or ideology could be law. Because knowing in that way becomes a way of controlling and manipulating truth. Whereas real truth is something ongoing. It is a revealing thing. And if you stop it at all, to put a name on it, you're just into power and hypocrisy."

That's the trouble with style. You know what you're going to see before you see it. The experiencing of the painting becomes merely the consumption of a cultural brand image. "But each picture has to be its own style," insists Brian Maguire. "You don't produce clones."

It's a position that caused his work to be ridiculed when he brought it into Project in the 1970s. By being autobiographical - painting out of his own experience - he was going against the prevailing cult of the purely formal. The fact that in 1982, when we first talked, galleries were finally picking up on expressionism, didn't impress him: "it's only a fashion." Fashion is painting taken over by words. "You rationalise with words. But not with painting. That's the beauty of it."

The older the artist the greater the wariness of words. "You should never come to an artist for any kind of verbal sense," warned George Campbell in 1978, not long before his death. "I see words as classifying rather than interpreting. Suppose somebody tells you that they've bought a red hat. What the hell is red? R-E-D? It's only by painting red that you can know what it means."

A month later, talking with the sculptor Oisín Kelly, the same issue came up. "Too many artists today are trying to be philosophers," he said. "But a philosopher is a man who is in love with wisdom, with abstract ideas. I think philosophy is a full-time trade. These conceptual people are philosophers. They should stick to thought. Whereas an artist is primarily someone who likes things. The woodiness of wood. I am a person who enjoys making things."

His words are echoed six years later by Donald Judd, one of the pioneers of Minimal art. Talking in his studio in Soho in New York, he seeks to distance himself from the Minimal label that has been attached to his art. "The term is a mere concoction." Defining art reduces it to a verbalisation: for him the object matters as much as the concept. "I think about what can be done in the reality of the thing itself. I'm not very much interested in things that are just ideas."

American art is another label he rejects. "I wasn't brought up in Europe so obviously my work isn't European art. But I don't intend to make American art. I'm against the whole nationalistic idea of art which has come back again. Jackson Pollock used to say his art was American only because after all he was American. It was simply American by default."

Judd's fear is exemplified in Ireland by the preoccupation with defining the so-called "Irishness" of Irish art, as in 1990-91 with the five-part Douglas Hyde Gallery "theme" exhibition, "Irish Art in the Eighties." The artists and works that fitted into various categories decided by a number of critics were presented as being representative of art in the 1980s whereas in fact they merely represented the assumptions of the selectors.

The trouble about categorising art under nationalistic labels is that the label gets in the way of the art. Which is why the author John McGahern would consider it an insult to be called an Irish writer. "I know that the colours, the sky, the particular qualities that I inherit are naturally Irish, but I feel that if one doesn't belong to the humankind first, one would be a very poor writer indeed," he says, looking out over Lough Rowen on his farm in Leitrim. It's the summer of 1978. He finds it almost indecent to talk about his writing as such. "The creative act and the love act are in themselves indescribable. Like the sun is indescribable."

Categorising art into decades is almost as limiting as calling it Irish or American. It's a worry of William Rubin, director of painting and sculpture in the New York Museum of Modern Art. To counteract it in 1984 he rehung the MoMA collection so that, as you passed Matisse's cutout "The Swimming Pool", you glimpsed the room with Hans Hoffman and the New York School, and the later Mondrians were within sight of Malevich. "We tend to package art too much time into tidy periods," he says. People forget that Matisse, Leger, Picasso and Miro were painting away and doing great things while Jackson Pollock was painting."

Critics are apt to appropriate art as evidence in support of what they are arguing: colour and form are made to serve as little more than signposts for a theory. "People are always trying to lay a certain trip on a painting," complains Patrick Hall as he prepares his work for an exhibition at the Lincoln Gallery early in 1983. "That's why they often fail to appreciate it. They're trying to detect some message or narrative in it, some nostalgia. Then they can say, oh yes, that reminds me of something."

"What they really want is a confirmation of the known, a sort of imprimatur on their experience, a reassurance of what they are. But you can't relate to a painting that way. You can only relate with a painting in so far as you're prepared to be seduced by it. A good painting should undermine your experience as well as the painter's experience. Being disconcerting is part of what painting is."

It's not just critics who pigeon-hole artists: it's an inherent part of the process of marketing contemporary art. "Dealers don't lay down a law that you must do this or that, but it's implicit somewhere that if you don't, you're cutting your own throat," says Colin Middleton when I visit his study in Bangor, County Down, in 1980. "They build up your reputation on a certain type of painting; that is a Middleton, it couldn't be anything else but a Middleton, so what do you mean by changing your style, people won't recognise it."

Middleton like Picasso defiantly painted in almost as many styles as there have been isms. "The idea of having to stick to one kind of painting all your life to my mind is crazy. What are all the other painters for if they don't open gates for you? I want to wander through when a gate opens. The experience sparks something off in me. You're not imitating when you do that. You're getting in touch with that vein and developing it."

By refusing to keep within the arbitrary perimeters defined for his work by fashionable trends Michael Farrell became something of an outcast in the 1970s, a painter for whom no reassuring label could easily be found.

Acclaimed for his hard edge acrylics in the 1960s and as a leader of the purely abstract wing of contemporary Irish painters ("the one most likely to achieve an international reputation, the only one who has managed to be in the mainstream and Irish at the same time", according to English critic Ronald Alley), Farrell abruptly switched direction, adopting a more personal and human style. Modernism had become too restricting.

"Rothko made his clouds. Someone else did stripes. X did this and Y did that. The powers-that-be found it acceptable. But for me it raised the whole question of identity. Who the hell are you? What's the point of turning out the same thing all the time. I began to feel that I was limiting myself and that I couldn't say what I wanted to say. I limited myself to the extent that I couldn't paint a beautiful woman if I wanted to because it didn't fit in with the kind of artist I thought myself to be."

Not being in a major art centre like New York or Paris can be an advantage for an artist: there is less pressure to toe an aesthetic line. The Danish painter and sculptor Per Kirkeby found this operating from Copenhagen in the 1960s. "It was rather like being Irish," he says before a retrospective of his work at the Douglas Hyde in 1985. "It was outside where the trends were made. There were too few artists to divide into camps, as happened in Germany where painter friends of mine like Baselitz and Lupertz felt obliged to treat minimalists as their enemy."

But the influence of New York gurus like Clement Greenberg, with their dogma that art got better as it became ever more simple and refined, couldn't be altogether ignored. "You felt almost immoral when you didn't develop like that. But why should you try to make your art purer and purer? Why should you pursue what you were doing to the nth point of development until like Reinhardt you ended up with a black canvas or whatever? If you behaved like that you were already born to late. It had all been done. There would be nothing more to do."

As a teacher he likes to repeat to students the advice given to him by his dealer: don't be an intellectual, be an artist. "One of the reasons for doing a painting is that you believe that colour in itself can express something you can't express in language. So it doesn't communicate in an intellectual way. Only stupid ideas are good for making art. Sophisticated ideas are good for making art historians."

Which is why the English abstract colourist Albert Irvin isn't bothered if people say they don't understand his paintings. "Because there isn't anything to understand," he laughs as he supervises the hanging of his paintings for an exhibition at the David Hendriks gallery in 1986. "Painting is for looking at, like the sky. You tell me how much you understand about falling in love and I'll explain my picture to you. Painting is a unique language - just as music is a unique language - in which it is possible to say things that are not available for us to say in any other way."

If he could say what his paintings meant he wouldn't have needed to paint them. "Just as Beethoven wouldn't have needed to put together those three Gs and an E flat and then three Fs and an E."

The Basque sculptor Eduardo Chillida's monumental works at the UNESCO building in Paris, the World Bank in Washington and places in Madrid and San Sebastian are regarded as defining space in a unique way through their stunning balance of form and scale. "But I understand almost nothing about it," he tells me on a visit to Dublin in 1988. "Time is the same. They are brothers. Equally mysterious. It is fascinating to try to understand space even if it is impossible to approach."

Art is a question of reaching for the unknown. "Whatever I know how to do I have surely already done it. Thus I must always do what I don't know how to do."

It's the same for Barrie Cooke; what he paints comes out of the painting. "Paint has the capacity to surprise you if you can be free enough," he says before an exhibition at the Hendriks Gallery in 1981. "The things that you can let the paint do are more than you can think about."

He quotes a remark by Auden about not knowing what you're thinking until you have thought it. "You don't really know what you see until you've painted it. The painting is a process of letting you know what you feel about something. It's not self-revelation for other people but revelation to yourself, it's how you understand the outside world and if someone shares it, that's splendid."

Eithne Jordan, exhibiting at the Project in 1982, puts it similarly. "I'll start out with a vague feeling, but the painting defines it. The nearest I can compare it to is music. You can listen to a piece of music without necessarily understanding it. You just get pleasure from listening to it. It simply appeals directly to the senses rather than to the brain."

Elsworth Kelly, talking at his studio in up-state New York in 1984, suggests this is why he became a painter. "I was very shy as a boy. I spent a lot of time in the woods, bird-watching near the Oradell reservoir. I was very much a loner."

But an art teacher recognised his talent for making pictures of what he saw. "I guess I wanted to communicate and this was a way I could be appreciated. Very often an artist becomes an artist because he can't communicate in any other way."

Kelly has been labelled by some critics as a pioneer of hard edge abstraction and by others as the first of the minimalists. His use of everyday motifs and industrial materials caused some to place him with Andy Warhol in the Pop Art of the 1960s. But to him all such connections are purely co-incidental.

"The art world may have exploded but I'm still carrying on in the old way that really began in Paris with my panel pieces in 1949."

Frank Stella, who revolutionised art as a 22-year-old in the late 1950s with his minimalist black stripe paintings, doesn't think artists should bother too much if critics stick labels on them: it's the function of critics to theorise and artists to make art. "I don't worry about where my art stands," he said in Dublin in 1985. "That's somebody else's problem. My problem is to paint the painting that I have to paint tomorrow."

Which is how it has always been, even when he was being lionised in the 1960s. "If you look at it from my point of view I was just one of many young painters who were becoming known. We were all in the same boat. I didn't feel particularly special. The reverberations were all in other people's minds. We just worried about the next painting."

So too with Willem de Kooning, speaking at his studio in East Hampton in 1984. "I don't know what I am. I can't help what they call me. I don't worry about it. I'm like a house-painter."

Scholarship and critics have their role. The danger is when they fail to recognise the limits of theory. Instead of serving art, of clarifying and documenting art, they presume to know better than the artist. Because they can explain better. "Fiction should undermine the prevailing cognitions," says Nobel author Saul Bellow, "because so many people are being damned by them." We talk over tea at the Westbury Hotel, Dublin in 1985. "Too many writers in modern times show the wretchedness of living through received ideas and those received ideas are still too young to be identified as received ideas.

"First it was Marxism. Then it was psychoanalysis. Then it was existentialism. And then it was structuralism. One thing after another, all fated for obsolescence."

In his novel *Herzog* in 1964 he tried to poke fun at this pre-occupation of modern literature with concepts at the expense of the reality they claim to represent. "The futility of a PhD when an ordinary crisis jumps out at you," he says, wryly. But few critics got the point. "I meant to debunk the life of thought and instead I was identified as a great highbrow, which I wanted least. Lots of people read the book as if they were taking a comprehensive examination in a year's course in Humanities."

As the character Corde complains in a later novel *The Dean's December:* "the language of discourse has shut out experience altogether."

Leon Golub, a New York painter who has been both shunned and lionised by dealers and critics depending on the fashion of the moment, sees this as a fact of life for artists. Instead of whining about it they should seek to exploit it.

"You've got to remember that the art world is just a commodity market," he says on a visit to Dublin in 1988. "Art that is not controversial in the political sense may be easier to sell than art that is. Because people do not necessarily want to have that kind of thing on their walls. That's how America is and we're American artists. We're dealing with that kind of world.

"It takes time for some verification to come through in art. Which is why most artists are poor. Verification means you become a marketable commodity and then you begin to live." Which may mean that the artist is producing what society is prepared to see: the artist has become safe. "That's the irony of it all. But I'm not attacking the commodification of art because that's the world we live in. Unless you have commodification there's no way for the artist to surface."

Artists may look for what they call alternate space. "But it's just as hard to show in alternate space. Believe me I know. They set up their own little territories."

Communist countries are even worse. State bureaucrats merely replace the market in deciding who's in and who's out: a danger that also exists in Ireland where much of art is subsidised through an Arts Council whose taste is almost inevitably the market taste.

The challenge for artists is to operate as far as possible on their own terms within a particular society. Art is by its nature subversive; changing perceptions from within. Golub remarks; "So who's buying whom? That's always the big question. It is the person who buys, so they control you? Or are you infiltrating their space? Well it's probably both at the same time. Nobody wins the whole battle."

For all the confusion of often conflicting styles and isms, critics and art historians have nevertheless served a function in enabling the art of the present century to bring us "an unexpected transcendance beyond our banal, everyday one-dimensionality, surprising extensions of our experience and reality, an immense discovery and penetration of the dimensions and depth of our existence." This is the argument of the radical theologian Hans Kung (banned from teaching by the Pope). At the Goethe Institute in Dublin in 1985 he tells me; "I was much more impressed as a student by my professor of art history than by teachers of theology. He educated us in the spirit of what is beautiful, he educated us to see what is good art."

Much like Mick Mulcahy's nomads in the Sahara. "Always look with the will of Allah."

It's the legacy, too, of James White, with his gesture of taking the glass off the paintings in the National Gallery. Although I interviewed him in 1979, I can hear him as if it's today. "I don't think a painting exists until it can be seen properly and enjoyed," he said.

NOTES ON THE CLEANING AND FRAMING OF PICTURES IN TRINITY COLLEGE, DUBLIN

Anne Crookshank

While working recently on the catalogue of the paintings in Trinity College, I went through the Board minutes and Bursar's accounts fairly thoroughly, and it was through this that I became aware of the endless care and attention paid by the college through the years to its pictures. This did not extend to listing them, though occasionally when a work was commissioned its payment is recorded. Listing was a hit and miss affair. At some periods college officers were more meticulous than at others but some of the most interesting pictures are not recorded at all in the minutes, for instance the Madden bequest of 20 pictures in 1766 is not mentioned on its arrival. But picture cleaning and framing was done by craftsmen, often men employed on other jobs in the College who were accustomed to signing receipts and, perhaps for this reason, some bills have survived. The Board minutes frequently mention the cleaning of pictures because their permission was needed. The artists who painted the pictures may not have been so business-like. Obviously what records survive will not give a complete picture but I feel that it is worth while to publish what facts exist because there is probably no other collection in Ireland better documented where cleaning and framing is concerned.

The first indication that Trinity owned pictures is recorded in a bill. Robert Beale (otherwise unknown to me) paid on 4 Nov 1710 for "cleaning Mending and Varnishing 3 Pictures for ye College £03:00:00:/To a New black Frame for Chanc^{lr} Loftis's picture, and a frame black and gold for Primat Usshers Picture £1:10:06:/ To Glewing and Mending ye Pannol and Frame of Dr Challoners Pict^r. £00:10:06:"[1] Sad to relate none of these pictures certainly survive. There is now no portrait of Luke Challoner in Trinity, the Ussher portraits are both eighteenth century works and though one of the seven portraits of Loftus which the college owns may be the one mentioned here, the frames have all gone.

Irish Carved Frame for
Anacreon Repelling Minerva
Italian School, 17th Century
Madden Bequest, Trinity College, Dublin

The Madden Bequest which contains some of the best pictures owned by Trinity College was not listed till the nineteenth century but on its arrival some of the works were clearly in poor condition and the frames needed repairing, On 17 Oct 1767 James Chapman was paid for work begun in Oct 1766.[2] All the prices were given of course in pounds, shillings and pence.

"To lining, cleaning, and mending the Virgin and Child etc palma 1.14.1(now, after Titian)

to ditto St John in the Wilderness, P Veronese ..13 s (now regarded as a studio work from late in Veronese's career)
To cleaning etc the Marriage of St Catherine .. 11.4
To ditto a Holy Family a round. F:Penni 11.4 (now School of Andrea del Sarto)

To ditto Coriolanus P Lastman 1.2.9
To ditto the Martyrdom of St Stephen L: Carracci .. 6.6 [now 17th century Italian]
To ditto Wisdom admonishing Anacheron And. Sacci m .. 6.6 [now late 17th century Italian]
To Ditto St Caecillia M. Angelo 1.2.9 (now early 17th century Italian)
To Ditto Belshazzar's Feast 1.9.3 (Giulio Carpione)
To Ditto the Death of Agripina. S Ricci 1.2.9
To lining, cleaning and mending a Head of Hesiod. Spagnioleti 1.2.9 (now School of Mola)

James Chapman, who died in 1792, was, according to Strickland,[3] an Englishman, who came to Dublin and having failed as a painter became a picture cleaner, dealer and auctioneer. Pasquin,[4] describes him as a picture faker using artists like John Butts to paint the canvases which he then aged. His cleaning one feels may well have been somewhat carefree, though Strickland mentions an account which I have not found which indicates that his work was considered good by Trinity as he was employed again in 1773 for "mending a bishop and repairing a Queen."

The repair of the frames of the Madden pictures was dealt with by William Wilkinson[5] who received on 19 Sept 1767, £17.14.11 for the following work:

"mends and varnishes frame of St John in the Wilderness ..16.3
Holy Family ..13.6
Mending and Guilding Holy Family over chimney 4.0.0
Gilding the frame of a History picte 4.0.0
For gilding the frame of St Stephen stone'd 1.4..00
For gilding the frame of picture under it 1.3.0
For gilding 2 large frames in Parlour 6.0.0
For ahead Gold frame 1.2.9
For mending and varnishing a large frame in the Parlour ..10.0
Ditto on one side if the Chimnye .. 5.5 "

William Wilkinson's work is unknown to me but he is mentioned by Strickland under the entry for his son John who was a watercolourist. William was a print seller, a publisher and a picture cleaner and presumably he employed craftsmen who dealt with frames. The more important work of making frames was given to the great wood carver Richard Cranfield, 1731-1809, who was employed in the Provost's House when it was being built. On 9 Sept 1767 he was paid "To carving

Irish Carved Frame for
The Expulsion from Paradise
*Attributed to
Leandro Bassano.
Madden Bequest,
Trinity College, Dublin*

and guilding two frames for pictures hung up in the Provost's House £10.0.0"[6] It is just possible that these were for the pair of Leandro Bassanos which formed part of the Madden Bequest. It is interesting that his son John Smith Cranfield, died 1802, was paid on 16 Nov 1790, £3.19.4 for cleaning and varnishing "a whole length picture of his Majesty in the Ballroom at the Provost's House" (presumably the Allan Ramsay given by the first Marquess Townsend when he was Lord Lieutenant of Ireland, 1767-1772). Also included in this account was the Gainsborough of the Duke of Bedford, a portrait of Queen Elizabeth and one of Archbishop Ussher who was described as "one of the fellows of the college in her reign." Except for George III these still all hang in this room, now called the Saloon. All their frames were also cleaned and varnished as were the "4 Statuary Marble Busto's"[7] presumably those of the Duke of Bedford, Richard Rigby and two Roman emperors all of which are still in the room. This bill was countersigned by the architect Graham Myers who was building the Chapel at the time and this may account for the use of John Cranfield on this work as he was a wood carver by profession and later paid for work in the Chapel. One would not think he was suitable as a picture cleaner but he would have been employed because he was on the spot.

Repair work was always needed. Two more frames with gilt mouldings were paid for in Oct 1784 to James Ramsay. As they cost a mere 8 shillings and 8 pence the work must either have been a repair or the gilt was only on the slips. Pictures seem to have been repaired and cleaned quite frequently when they were given to

Francis Bindon (Before 1700-1765)
Provost Richard Baldwin (1745)
(?1668-1758)
Irish Carved Frame, Trinity College, Dublin

or bought by the College. For instance the portrait of Provost Andrews which was bought from a Mrs Norman on 9 Dec 1800 was immediately restored and William Allen was paid on 27 Jan 1801 for "Cleaning, lining and repairing Picture of Provost Andrews £1.0.2 and for reguilding the Frame £3.19.7."[9] The painting was presumably the splendid Anton Maron still in the College.

James Chapman appears yet again when he was paid £6.16.6 on 21 May 1791[10] for cleaning 8 whole lengths and their frames and hanging them. These were the pictures still in the Public Theatre (the Exam Hall) commissioned by the College from Robert Home and finished in 1788. They must have been stored while the building was completed and hence needed a light clean. The frames had been made by Richard Cranfield who was paid £63.4.0 for them. They are portraits of Provost Baldwin, Bishop Berkeley, Archbishop King, William Molyneux. Jonathan Swift, Archbishop Ussher and Queen Elizabeth. They still hang in the position for which they were painted. The eighth, a portrait of Henry Gratton, disappeared sometime about 1800 and there is no record of what happened to it. These pictures are mentioned again on 24 May 1864 when Stephen Catterson Smith the elder who had been appointed Curator of the Pictures on 25 Nov 1863 proposed to "clean, retouch, and revarnish the nine pictures (two more of Edmund Burke and Lord Clare painted by Hoppner and Gilbert Stuart had been added) now in the examination Hall and also to have the Frames of these nine pictures carefully regilt with best gold, all the retouching to be done by himself. The Board agrees to accept Mr Smith's proposal to carry out the above for £150." The Edmund

Burke portrait was in trouble again in 1878 when it is recorded as being "laid down on new canvas" on 23 March and a month later Mr Cranfield (presumably a descendent of Richard) was "employed to clean the picture of Edmund Burke - the cost not to exceed twenty pounds". On 25 April 1908 it had to be repaired again. No restorer is named but at this date J C Nairn of London was cleaning a number of other pictures for the college. Hoppner's picture was defeating the cleaners as by then the bitumen he had used must have made the surface of the picture, seen at close range, look like crocodile skin.

On 9 Oct 1869 Catterson Smith was asked to repair the portrait of the Primate (probably a slip for the late Primate Lord John George Beresford who had died in 1862) for £10.10. This damage, given that the picture hung in the Dining Hall as it still does, is perhaps understandable, though why it should be in trouble again in 1886(2 and 16 Oct) is not recorded, but it is then dealt with by Mr J^{os} Tracy vho was paid £13. Despite the name Joseph this cleaner was almost certainly John Tracy who died in 1911 and cleaned pictures with his brother Edward; both were sons of Joseph Tracy who had died in 1873.

Damage which had occurred in the Provost's House some ten years earlier is less easy to understand. On the 8 Jan 1859 Dr. Lloyd, Dr Todd and Dr Malet were appointed to "enquire into the state of the Pictures in the Provost's House" and reported on 5 Feb 1859 that "of the Pictures in the Provost's House 31 are in such a condition that immediate steps must be taken to preserve them: and that 3 of them, owing to unskilful handling, will require the utmost care to remedy the injuries thay have received. They were the Andrea del Sarto, the Guido (a Virgin and Sleeping Child now just called Italian School c. 1700) and the portrait of George I. Dr Malet estimates that the total cost for repairing and preserving these pictures will be £150." Prices were rising and how one longs to know what they had been up to in the Provost's House to cause such terrible damage. The highest price paid to Chapman had been £1.14.1d while on average each of these cost over £4 each. Maybe the cost of the badly damaged pictures was much higher and caused the average figure to rise abnormally. Catterson Smith was to get £10 for his work on the full length portrait of the Primate in 1869. The pictures in the Provost's House were once more under scrutiny in 1907 when (Nov 2) "Mr Gray and Dr Mahaffy were constituted a sub. Commee "to report on the steps to be taken for "their preservation." On 19 Dec for the first time a J.C. Nairn. the London restorer, was employed and was voted £43.1.0 to pay for work done on the Queen Elizabeth, Archbishop Ussher and Nero and the Dead Agrippina. This last work now and in the 18th century was given to Sebastiano Ricci but in 1907 it was attributed to Domenichino. It was a strange choice to restore at that date because only a few years earlier the College had been considering its sale and sought the advice of Christies whose reply recorded in the minutes of 13 Dec. 1884 stated that it "it would be unsaleable". Three more pictures were given to Mr Nairn for cleaning on 11 March 1908 and he was paid a further 26 gns. The sums paid to Mr. Nairn were not much higher than those given to Stephen Catterson Smith.

Odd small jobs are recorded as the re-varnishing in 1912 (26 Oct) of the portrait of Provost Salmon in the Provost's House but the really big moment came on 12 Dec 1914, shortly after Mahaffy became Provost, when "Sir Hugh Lane attended the Board, and reported at length on the State of the Pictures in the

Thomas Hudson
(1701-79)
**Frederick,
Prince of Wales**
*(1707-44)
Paul Petit Frame (1748)
Trinity College, Dublin*

Provost's House. He stated that they were in a very bad condition, in many cases the paint falling out. He adopted Mr. Nairn's estimate of £234 for the restoration of 48 Pictures, but submitted that 5 more required restoration, which would increase his estimate to £250. 15 should be reframed and the remaining frames washed and cleaned. He also undertook to provide for the effective lighting of the Pictures. The total cost of all this work was not to exceed £300, or, at the very furthest 300 guineas. The cost of carriage to and from London to be borne by the College." These costs were low in comparison to the Victorian and Edwardian figures and may indicate that Nairn charged less because of the size of the commission. But making 15 frames and cleaning the rest for £50 to £60 seems remarkably cheap in view of the fact that Cranfield got £10 for two, admittedly elaborate frames in 1767. They of course were gilded and it is clear gilding was always the really expensive task. At the following meeting, 19 Dec, the Board decided that a contract with Lane would be required and that the pictures should be insured on the journey against loss and damage. Obviously anxious that deterioration should not continue, in the following year on 6 March 1915 the Board accepted the estimate of Daniel Egan to fit plate glass to all the pictures in the Provost House. excepting two, the Bindon of Archbishop Boulter and the George II as Prince of Wales which hung on the stairs and were clearly very difficult to reach. He charged £90 to include "supplying brown slips and strengthening frames where necessary."

Benjamin Wilson
(1721-88)
Archbishop Arthur Price
*(1680-1752)
Irish Carved Frame
Trinity College, Dublin*

The Provost's House was clearly dealt with for the present so the Board turned its attention to other areas of the College, the Common Room where the Portraits were to be cleaned for about £18 and again on 15 Oct 1919 Mr Nairn's estimated 27 guineas for cleaning 5 College Portraits (the situation was not given) and "a supplementary estimate for picture frames amounting to £14.10.0. was approved" on 1 Nov 1919. Lane's plans for lighting the pictures may not have been carried out as on 12 Jan 1921, Jane C. Meldon's estimate of £11.10.0 "for installation for lighting 2 oil paintings in the Provost's House by electric lights and reflectors" was accepted. However they may have been for newly acquired works.

By 1966 the glass on the pictures had been removed and no satisfactory lighting has ever been achieved. Despite the endless use of experts nobody thought of the damaging effect of central heating installed quite early in the century in the Provost's House. As a result the Lastman, painted on panel, virtually split in two. In many cases, in my opinion, cleaning may have meant only revarnishing as the thickness of the deep yellow-brown varnish on many of the pictures was measurable. The removal of old varnishes in recent years has almost always led to a great change in the appearance of the backgrounds of the pictures so that sometimes cleaning may have meant faces only. The relinings have all stood the test of time.

The greatest frame owned by the College is the grand, baroque frame commissioned by the sitter, Frederick, Prince of Wales, for his portrait by Thomas

Hudson, finished in 1748. This was carved by the great French frame maker, Paul Petit. He worked for the English Royal family and the account survives in the Library of Windsor Castle. It is dated 2 June 1748 and says: 'In burnished Gold in the Best manner. Sent to Dublin College £197.7.6'[11] This enormously expensive frame was for a whole length and is carved with complex symbolism. It was quite badly damaged in the fire of 1984 and we can at least pride ourselves that all the restoration, including any necessary carving was carried out by Irish craftsmen under the restorer, Mary McGrath. Two frames certainly carved in Ireland at much the same time and of similar though slightly smaller size, exist around the portraits of Archbishop Price and Provost Baldwin. Unfortunately the bills for these do not exist so we cannot compare the prices. We do however have the price for the elaborately carved but not gilded frame of Bindon's 1739 portrait of Swift in the Deanery of St. Patrick's. This, carved by John Houghton is said by Strickland to have cost £18.13.0 while the painting cost £36.16. If the frame had been gilded it would probably have cost as much as or more than the painting. It was much less than the Petit, however, and one wonders if the Trinity College frame was the only work included in his account.

The pictures are to be found all over the College nowadays: they are no longer confined to the Provost's House, the Dining Hall, the Public Theatre or even the Common Room. Now there is hardly a building without its works of art, mostly in reasonable condition and there are many pieces of sculpture in the grounds so that everyone can enjoy to some degree this little known but important part of Ireland's cultural heritage.

Notes

1. TCD Mun P/4/15/1.
2. TCD Mun P/4/55/11.
3. W.G. Strickland, *A Dictionary of Irish Artists*, Dublin and London 1913, 2 vols. This invaluable book is used throughout the article and will not be footnoted again.
4. Anthony Pasquin, (i.e. John Williams), *Memoirs of the Royal Academicians and an Authentic History of the Artists of Ireland*. London, 1796, reprinted with an introduction by R.W. Lightbown, London, 1970 p.52.
5. TCD Mun P/4/55/51.
6. TCD Mun P/4/55/13.
7. TCD Mun P/4/59/4.
8. TCD Mun P/4/57/25.
9. TCD Mun P/4/ 77/1.
10. TCD Mun P/4/60/5.
11. Duchy of Cornwall Household Accounts of FREDERICK PRINCE OF WALES, vol.XVI, 1748, p.53. This information was kindly supplied to me by Miss Joyce Boundy.

Giovanni di Paolo
(?1403-1483)
The Crucifixion
NGI. Cat. No. 1768

THE CRUCIFIXION

Paul Durcan

Friday afternoon, three p.m.,
Visiting my daughter in the Psychiatric Unit,
Killing time in her cubicle.
I sit. She stands. In the window.
My young hero of loneliness,
Her hands behind her head,
Her plaited dreadlocks,
Her crown of thorns,
A gold sky outside,
Half-astride the sill,
Pretty shrew in the badger's jaws.

You are my father -
Why can't you get me out of here?
Look at my knees -
Are my knees not benign?
Look at my legs - are my legs
Not sheer as nylon stockings in glossy advertisements?
The pain in my head
Has percolated down to my toes.
Father, have you never seen the waterfall at Powerscourt?
Why is it, Father, that all you can say to me is
"Tie up your hair" or
"Be a brave woman and bear it."

Eli, Eli, lama sabachthani?
I am a woman, Father,
In spite of the fact that I've got hairs on my upper lip.
Why will you not accept me for what I am -
A woman with a woman's soul - a roodscreen?
Father, why have you dumped me?

Why can't we go for a walk together in Thomas Street?
I can't imagine anymore what it must be like to be ordinary -
What it must feel like to walk along Thomas Street
And to post a letter in a green pillar box on the corner?

When I tell the doctors that the palms of my hands
Are hurting me,
That I've got a pain in my side,
That my feet are bleeding from being made
To wear shoes that are too small for me,
That personality and nature are not synonyms,
They tell me that I am imagining it all
Or that it's a case merely of childbirth.
Father, have you never seen the waterfall at Powerscourt?

How right they are, Father,
Only they do not know it.
I *am* imagining it all and
I *am* giving birth to the world
In the corner of a carpark.

Father, do you see the new
Carparks they've laid out?
Open the window and take me in your arms.
Call me by that name
You used first call be by, remember?
'My pretty shrew".
Throw out of the window
Your pretty shrew
Down into the carparks.

I want to stretch out
On the gold-paved path
In a dream of velvet loneliness
With carparks all around me
From head to toe,
Under the gleaming hub of your right front wheel.
Father, have you never seen the waterfall at Powerscourt?

IRISH ART AND THE POSTWAR ERA

Brian Fallon

The stereotype of Ireland in the late 1940s and early 1950s has hardened from a plaster cast into something approaching cement, which can scarcely be dented with a hammer. Sixties Revisionism was no doubt an overdue and healthy reaction, but it has dangerously simplified things in turn, often viewing them through the wrong end of the telescope. The present is never as enlightened as we think, nor the past quite as dark.

The conventional picture is that Ireland from some unspecified period - whether it is the late 1920s or the early 1930s - became parochial and inward-looking, cutting off its European links and sinking into an intellectual bog of censorship, chauvinism and religiosity. No doubt there is a vast amount of historical proof for this, but it is one side of the picture; the other side has been deliberately ignored. I use the word "deliberately" quite ... deliberately, since from the early Sixties onwards there has been a great deal of self-interested blackening of the recent past. The reason for this is obvious; by doing so, a dramatic historical chiaroscuro was created by which a new, ambitious generation could stand out in the most dazzling daylight. They seemed to be saying: enlightment, the European dimension, the future, intellectual freedom, are all with us.

Since I am not old enough to identify personally with Ireland in the immediate postwar years - let alone the earlier ones - I hope I can write about them with some detachment. Perhaps the facts can speak for themselves. In the 1940's, Dublin had a number of excellent literary magazines - *The Bell, Irish Writing,* the *Dublin Magazine* (already ageing) and *Envoy.* Myles na Gopaleen was at the peak of his powers in the *Irish Times* and R.M. Smyllie began his patronage of writers - particularly poets - in that paper (Donagh MacDonagh in 1947 edited an anthology of *Irish Times* poems which is now a collectors' item, and for which Smyllie wrote the foreword). On Radio Eireann, Robert Farren and certain others embarked on a policy of getting the best Irish authors to write for radio, and of paying them decently for it. Farren and Austin Clarke - who for many years had his own poetry programme on radio - were the main force behind the Lyric Theatre, which was founded for speaking verse and performing verse plays. It was a time when chauvinism, censorship and obscurantism were repeatedly challenged, particularly by Seán O'Faoláin in *The Bell* and elsewhere. "Revisionism", in fact, had its roots in this period, when it was fresh and relevant and had not yet hardened into quasi-official dogma. To a great extent, the intelligentsia of the Sixties were living on another man's wound; by then, most of the battles had been fought and won, though it may not have seemed like that at the time. For instance, when Myles na Gopaleen pulled Dr. Alfred O'Rahilly to pieces intellectually in the famous controversy over Noel Browne's Mother and Child Scheme, it was really the end of an epoch, and O'Rahilly and his kind receded rapidly into the shadows. Similarly, the Catholic Hierarchy's victory in that particular case seemed to most people then a proof that things had not changed, or very little; yet the prestige of the Church had suffered a suppurating wound. In retrospect, it had misjudged public opinion, behaved with dogmatic stupidity, and alienated not only liberal middle-class opinion but a large section of the underprivileged. It was, of course, one of those chapters of history from which nobody emerges with credit, least of all the senior politicians involved, but what appeared to be a piece of triumphalist meddling was really a clerical defeat. From that date begins the decline of the quasi-clerical Irish state which had reached its apogée with the Eucharistic Congress of 1932, and the growth of secular opinion.

Visual art in Ireland then played very much a second-violin part to literature and socio-political controversy. It was also subordinate to the theatre, which - in Dublin especially - was almost a national obsession, what my painter-friend Tony O'Malley used to call "mummer-worship". Stage actors in the fifteen years or so after the Second World War were household names; to be smiled at in the street by, say, Siobhán McKenna was a guarantee of social success. The literary value of the plays performed mattered less than the quality of the acting, just as the old-style opera-goer cared less about the opera than the quality of the singing. There were connoisseurs of acting who were not necessarily well-read people, but who understood the nuances of stage performance and discussed with finesse the relative merits of, say, Cyril Cusack's Playboy and those of his predecessors.

It was not a golden age in the Irish theatre; the Abbey Theatre was stagnating under Ernest Blythe, and in the Gate the Edwards-MacLiammoir partnership had lost its edge. But it was not all kitchen farce, or Synge and O'Casey revivals, with an occasional imported West End hit. There was, for instance, a great interest in the contemporary French theatre, and plays by Anouilh, Cocteau, Montherlant, and Claudel were frequently performed - Anouilh in particular; Donagh McDonagh even adapted one of his plays under the title "Fading Mansions". French culture was still the one to admire, and there was a keen edge of interest when the philosopher Gabriel Marcel came to Dublin to lecture in 1959.

The two factors which mainly established Modern Art in Dublin were the founding of the Irish Exhibition of Living Art in 1943, and the Waddington Gallery run by Victor Waddington. (An older painter told me recently, without any prompting from me, that he reckoned that the third major factor was the enthusiasm and activity of James White, then an influential art critic but with no position in the official art world). The Living Art is history by now, and though Mainie Jellett and Evie Hone are usually linked with it, at the start at least, they were no more than figureheads. The Living Art in its creative years, which ended in the middle or late 1950s, is synonymous with the generation of Louis le Brocquy, Daniel O'Neill, Norah McGuinness, Patrick Collins, Gerard Dillon, Nano Reid, Oisin Kelly, Colin Middleton, George Campbell, Nevill Johnston. In the background there was the White Stag Group, whose nucleus was a number of Englishmen most of whom - it is an open secret, and can hurt nobody now - were reluctant to face conscription back home, and very naturally preferred to paint in exile.

The atmosphere of the Dublin art world, or rather the advanced circles, was a strange one, at once inbred and outward-looking. Paris was the City of Art , but Paris was cut off by war until 1945, and even then few Irish people could afford to go there very often. "French art" meant Picasso, Braque, Rouault, Dufy, Matisse and a few others; the younger generation of Manessier, Balthus, Dubuffet, Vasarely, etc. was little known in Ireland before the middle 1950s. Abstract art was still considered a special and rather rarified taste, and the New York School was unknown. Some people even had trouble with the late Jack Yeats, who seemed to them to have gone over the top and thrown form out of the window (yet there was such immense admiration for Yeats, and so much faith in him, that he always earned respect even when he mystified his public). Irish painting, on the face of it, was not very advanced and not very international, in spite of its aspirations to be both. Apart from Yeats, it had no genuinely major figure. Why, then, does that generation still appear as something special, something particularly individual and authentic? Perhaps because, for one thing, it emerged out of wartime isolation and deprivation; because it embodied Ireland's first real Modernist generation (Hone and Jellett had brought in an attenuated version of Cubism, but they were too isolated to form a school, even though they had considerable influence).

This school - if it can be called that - grew out of a very particular mixture of "native" feeling and foreign influence. Apart from Yeats, who was *sui generis*, there were no home models for an Irish artist except the Hone-Jellett line. There were Cubist elements in the work of George Campbell, Norah McGuinness and Father Jack Hanlon, but they were little more than a framework; Cubism in the real sense did not take strong root in Ireland. In any case, in the Neo-Romantic Forties, it seemed rather too formalistic and intellectualised, and the same was true of abstract art. Considering that links with Britain had been kept up during the war years (much more so, in fact, than is realised today) it is curious that contemporary British art had so little influence. Most Irish artists and writers of the period knew London well, read British papers and periodicals, and were in fact more anglicised than Frenchified. *Horizon* magazine for instance, edited by Cyril Connolly, gave many people in these islands their first acquaintance with the work of Giacometti, Morandi and Matta. Several Irish artists showed in London galleries shortly after the war, and some even emigrated there, at least for a time. Yet apart from the influence of Ben Nicholson on Colin Middleton, British artists made little impact here. In the early 1950s, it is true, there was a tremendous row about the proposed purchase for Dublin of a Henry Moore "Reclining Figure", a brief flare-up of public hysteria set off by a titled eccentric called the Dowager Lady Beatrice Dunalley. The fact remains that Moore had little influence on Irish sculptors.

The old tradition - largely an Anglo-Irish one - of Irish emigré artists living and working in France was virtually dead. The almost inevitable conclusion is that Paris Modernism was known here mainly at second hand, through reproductions and magazine articles and the like - there were, after all, few modern pictures in Irish hands, for people to see. The late Oisín Kelly told me once that his favourite sculptor was Ernest Barlach, yet he had hardly seen him in the original; he knew his work from a 1930s book of black-and-white photographs. Picasso came largely at second hand, filtered through the work of immigrant Jewish painters such as

Jankel Adler, who had a considerable influence in Britain and here. Even the Tate Gallery had as yet relatively few Modernist works in its collection. The type of large modern art book, with excellent colour reproductions and a scholarly text, was decades in the future. Modern art, after all, was still a minority enthusiasm, and it was only in the 1960s that it finally replaced the old "academic" tradition and became an official style.

Irish Modernists, then, were a small sect with little power and little financial support, apart from the buyers which Waddington could find for them. They made up for this by idealism and total commitment of a kind which is hard to understand today, now that the art world has become so thoroughly commercialised. At once avant-garde and isolated, they made up for this by an emotional immersion in the Irish landscape - Collins and Reid, for example - a kind of intimate, personal, moody Romanticism or Neo-Romanticism (Campbell and O'Neill) or refloating a "Celtic" style in a modern Idiom, as in Oisín Kelly's sculpture. Gerard Dillon and a few others found a new vitality in the life of the West of Ireland, a tradition popularised by Paul Henry a generation earlier, or in the back-streets of Belfast. Others, like Norah McGuinness, continued the "tasteful", upper-middle-class Anglo-Irish tradition in a mildly Cubist manner and with a transparent use of colour learned mostly from Frenchmen such as Dufy. The Fifties was not a happy decade for Europe; the illusion of peace in 1945 had frozen in the permafrost of the Cold War, and rationing, Welfare State austerity, and postwar disillusionment were the norm in most countries. The temporary eclipse of the older European traditions had also opened the door to the most blatant Americanisation, even if the new art of the American avant-garde remained very little known. In Ireland, it was an uneasy period of transition; de Valera and the power of the Church seemed to have been there for ever, and until the 1960s saw the development of Lemassian pragmatism, there was a dismal feeling that the old ideologues remained at the helm. Attempts at coalition governments were not very encouraging, and in any case the Opposition parties were even more hidebound than Fianna Fáil; neither the Left nor the Right had much to offer, and so politics stagnated in the Centre, as they had done for years. Wartime neutrality had kept Ireland safe, but cliques of discontented intellectuals felt that they had been deprived of participation in the great political dramas and confrontations of the mid-century. The early moves towards a Common Market, born essentially out of the experience of defeat and occupation shared by France, Germany, Belgium, Holland (though not England), saw Ireland left firmly on the outside.

So when Sixties affluence and exuberance finally arrived - and in Ireland they came late, and never to the extent that they did in Britain and the US - the preceding decade was made by contrast to look a depressed and discouraged one, uncreative and provincial. In fact, it had been the reverse; in spite of impoverishment and official neglect or disapproval - the Irish Government relinquished very slowly and reluctantly its support for the type of Free State "official" art popularised by Seán Keating - the Forties and Fifties laid the foundations for most of what came after them. They were years of impassioned debate and intellectual ferment, which produced new and challenging thinking, good writing and brilliant journalism, a new generation of artists, relentless self-criticism (too much, in fact), the birth of the Arts Council and the foundation-stone for a national symphony orchestra. Superficially an age of defeat, the Fifties had in fact been one in which the massive walls of conservatism and reaction had gradually been mined from underground, so that in the end they collapsed with a suddenness which surprised most people. In the Sixties, at last, censorship was quietly phased out; the National Gallery was given new funds, and the Dublin Municipal Gallery was revitalised - again, James White had a considerable role in both. But what seemed like a revolution was in fact the culmination of years of fighting the good fight.

It is ironic, then, that one of the victims of progress should have been the Living Art itself. As Modernism slowly became the accepted, everyday style, and galleries such as the David Hendriks (originally Ritchie Hendriks) Gallery and Dawson Gallery took it up, it became superfluous. Its standards declined, in spite of the emergence of new talents such as Camille Souter and Patrick Scott; by the late Sixties it had become little more than a shallow, provincialised reflection of international art fashions, popularised in this country by agile eclectics and opportunists with both eyes levelled like javelins on the main chance. Attempts to rejuvenate it in the Seventies proved abortive; the Oireachtas Art Exhibition, a despised affair for years, took on a new lease of life, and the Independent Artists produced a new generation of Wild Ones and angry young men (and women).

In the Eighties, efforts to resuscitate it again have proved one thing - that it is a corpse. Art movements have their span, and there seems little point in filling old wine bottles with Coca Cola. In any case, the international ambitions of most young Irish painters and sculptors have made the idea of a "native" group exhibition largely irrelevant. If you aim at the Sao Paolo Biennale or the Cologne Art Fair, why bother with the conquest of your own backyard? Yet the present burgeoning of visual art in Ireland (not just in Dublin) and the new-found confidence of Irish artists, could not have existed without the energy and idealism of a few small cliques of people in the darkest years of the Second World War.

THE CURIOUS CRAFT OF ART CRITICISM: WITH DR JAMES WHITE IN PARIS AND OXFORD

Tony Gray

When I heard that James White - or Paddy White as I knew him - had been appointed Director of the National Gallery of Ireland, I couldn't believe it. I couldn't believe that the sane and sober authorities who decide these things, would ever in their wildest dreams appoint a fellow-journalist to such a responsible position.

This statement probably calls for some qualification. The only thing that Paddy and I had in common - and I have to call him Paddy because that was how I knew him, just as he then called me Tony, as everybody now does, though in those days I was called George, after my father, and wrote under my given initials, G (George) H (Hugh) Gray or GHG - was that we both, at the same period, did what is known as "art criticism", Paddy for the *Irish Press*, and I for the *Irish Times*.

One would be entitled to ask - and indeed I often felt, when I had savagely panned some earnest young painter who took life far more seriously than I dld at that period, that we should have been asked - on what basis did we feel ourselves qualified to pronounce on the diligent output of fellow-Irishmen who had elected to go in for painting instead of writing for the newspapers ?

But again, there is no easy answer to this one. Do you have to be a Cordon Bleu chef before you can wave away a steak as inferior ? Do you have to know how to blend Pinot Noir and Pinot de Charentes before you can say that in your opinion Roederer Kristal is a better champagne than Veuve Clicquot ? Do you have to know how to play, much less compose, a single bar of music to be able to say with total conviction that Mozart is a far more interesting composer than Eric Coates? Because that's really what it comes down to in the end.

Paddy White and I approached the road to art criticism by very different routes. In the last term before I left school, I vaguely toyed with the idea of becoming an artist, but much more in the hope I believe, of persuading my parents to let me spend a few months in Paris, which was what I wanted most passionately to do, than from any deep and abiding interest in art as an end in itself. In the evenings I attended Life Classes at the National College of Art - where my tutors were Seán Keating and Maurice MacGonigal - and in my spare time I painted a lot of terribly bad and highly pretentious pictures, which, quite rightly, were instantly rejected by the Royal Hibernian Academy. When the war broke out and any hope of getting to Paris was shattered, I quite happily went into journalism, because at that period the Palace Bar seemed to be about as close as I was going to be able to get to the cafés of Montmartre or the Boulevard St Michel until after the war.

Paddy, who worked in what my editor, Smyllie, always called "the world of commerce" - for one of the tobacco companies - never had any notions of becoming a painter, but was intensely interested in the whole subject of painting and had made himself an expert on various specialised aspects of art, and more particularly, art history.

I became an art critic by accident, as a result of plaguing Smyllie for more money. When I first joined the newspaper in 1940, straight from school, I was paid 38 shillings a week as a junior leader-writer, but was able to augment that meagre salary by flogging the books we had decided not to review to Greene's in Clare street, because one of the perks of the job of junior leader-writer in the *Irish Times* at this stage was the disposal of books for review. When I left Smyllie's editorial department because at the age of nineteen I couldn't stand working from 9.30 p.m. every evening until 4 a.m. the next morning, hours that allowed little opportunity for socialising, I sadly missed the revenue all those neglected review books had brought in. And when James Lawler died or Arthur Power resigned, I forget which, Smyllie thought he would get me off his back by letting me review the art exhibitions, at a guinea a go. I remained - and still do - very interested in art, but no more than I am interested in music or books.

Paddy White may have worked for Players for a living, but he lived for art, and I think he only fully came alive when, shortly after the war, the International Art Critics Association was launched. Ireland was invited to become a founder member, and an Irish branch was formed of which he immediately became in effect the director, though he had a much more humble title, Hon Sec, or something of the kind.

This extraordinary institution was an offshoot of UNESCO - the letters stand for the United Nations Educational, Scientific and Cultural Organisation, if I remember rightly - and our titular head in Ireland was Tommy MacGreevy, though he rarely graced any of our meetings, which were usually held in Paddy White's house. Dr Thomas MacGreevy was at that time Director of the National Gallery. I went to the meetings, because Paddy had invited me, and during this period got to know him quite well.

I had always read his reviews with interest. He was far kinder than I was, always judging the work of young artists against the background of what it was they were trying to achieve - whatever "ism" or other they were into. I didn't know enough about the development of modern art to be able even to hazard a guess what it was they were trying to do, so I simply judged them by the effect that their work had upon me. I have always regarded painting as a form of communication, and if a picture did not say anything to me, or excite my imagination in any way, as Yeats's canvases invariably used to do, or stimulate me into looking again at some aspect of the visual world as Francis Bacon's tortured images always did, I would dismiss the whole exhibition in what I hoped was as amusing a manner as possible, because I also regarded it as one of the functions of the critic to entertain his readers. Paddy White would probably have agreed with me on this, but not to the extent ever of being unfair to the painters.

Not long after the Irish Art Critics Association had been formed, plans began to be made for the first International Art Critics Association get-together, at UNESCO headquarters in the Avenue Kleber in Paris, in the summer of 1949. Paddy White was extremely enthusiastic about the whole idea and intended to go, at his own expense if necessary, if the *Irish Press* proved unwilling to pay his expenses. Tom MacGreevy was also going - indeed so far as I remember he contributed a paper, in impeccable French, naturally - and I said that I would try it on Smyllie, though I wasn't very optimistic as it didn't seem to me that anything that I could possibly write about a meeting of international art critics in Paris could be of any possible interest to the readers of the *Irish Times*. On the other hand, by this time I had succeeded Brian Inglis - who himself had succeeded the Hon Patrick Campbell - as Quidnunc of the Irishman's Diary, and it was just possible that he would agree on the basis that it wasn't a bad thing to get the Irishman's Diary out of Ireland and across to the continent for a week or two.

Smyllie agreed, but for quite a different reason. I had never been to Paris, and he felt that this was a defect in me which should be remedied as soon as possible and so he agreed to let me have two weeks' expenses in France - a week to cover the conference, and a week to see something else of France, plus the fare of course.

Paddy White and I travelled together, without our wives, because no matter who was paying our expenses, times were hard, and neither of us had money to spare. We travelled via the mail boat from Dun Laoghaire to Holyhead, the Irish Mail to Euston (sitting up all night naturally; no such luxuries as sleepers in those days); breakfast in one of the Lyons corner shops in London, then by tube to Victoria, by rail to Newhaven, across to Dunklrk on board an SNCF steamer, and then from Dunkirk to Paris, St Lazare by French Railways. From the moment we left Dunkirk I was craning at the train window for my first sight of the Eiffel Tower. Paddy, who had been in Paris before, was quietly smiling, I think, at my wild excitement, but as we walked out of the dark cavern of the Gare St Lazare and into the bright golden sunshine of an August evening in Paris, he became every bit as excited as I was. And I still hadn't caught a glimpse of the Eiffel Tower.

I would like to think that we walked down the Rue de Rome and the Rue Auber to the Opera, but I don't think we did; I think we went down into the Metro and took a train to the Palais Royale, where Paddy had booked us both into a hotel he'd stayed in before, the Hotel Montpensier, in the Rue de Richelieu, just a few hundred yards away from the Comédie Francaise and backing on to the gardens of the Palais Royale. And very good it was, too; it's still there, by the way, I checked on it last year.

When we'd unpacked, and emerged from the hotel into the evening sunshine, I did at last see the Comédie Francaise, and the Louvre, and Rue de Rivoli and the Place Vendôme and the Place de la Concorde and eventually, poking its rusting head out of the heat haze, the Eiffel Tower, and my first staggering glimpse of the Champs Elysées sweeping away and up to meet the sky at the Etoile, where the Arc de Triomphe still dominated the skyline. We were walking across Paris to join some friends of Paddy's for dinner. They lived in a second floor apartment, not far off the Champs Elysées and we had dinner with the windows open and all the smells and sounds of Paris hanging in the hot air. I don't remember what we ate,

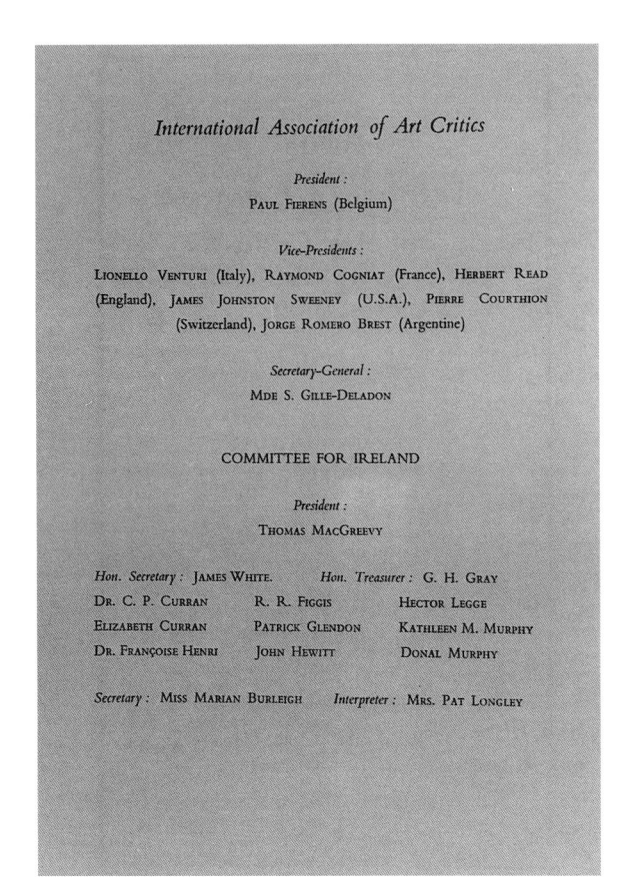

A.I.C.A. 4th Congress, Dublin, 1953
Congress Programme

International Association of Art Critics

President:
Paul Fierens (Belgium)

Vice-Presidents:
Lionello Venturi (Italy), Raymond Cogniat (France), Herbert Read (England), James Johnston Sweeney (U.S.A.), Pierre Courthion (Switzerland), Jorge Romero Brest (Argentine)

Secretary-General:
Mde S. Gille-Deladon

COMMITTEE FOR IRELAND

President:
Thomas MacGreevy

Hon. Secretary: James White.   Hon. Treasurer: G. H. Gray
Dr. C. P. Curran   R. R. Figgis   Hector Legge
Elizabeth Curran   Patrick Glendon   Kathleen M. Murphy
Dr. Françoise Henri John Hewitt   Donal Murphy

Secretary: Miss Marian Burleigh   Interpreter: Mrs. Pat Longley

---

but it was all delicious, with wine, lots of wine, white and red and sparkling, coming up all the time. I don't remember who was there, either, but it seemed to me that the conversation was sparkling too, and that Paddy White seemed to be as completely at home in this sophisticated, international setting as I felt alien; I was bursting with admiration at his shyly adequate French, not fluent enough to argue passionately, obviously, but *suffisament* to parry adroitly any awkward questions and politely to deflect the attention of the company in somebody else's direction.

As we walked back to our hotel in the warm, magical Parisian dusk, stopping at a sidewalk cafe for a brandy, I knew that my first instinct had been right; that whatever I did later, I should have started out here, in Paris. But it was too late now. I had a job, and a wife, and a very young son.

But that night was the start of a week I have never forgotten, have never been able to forget. I don't remember much about the conference, except that the dignitaries who sat at the top table were always in trouble with the delegates in the main body of the hall because, in typical French style, they took three hours over luncheon, and the afternoon sessions always had to be curtailed. I think they included people like Sir Herbert Read, from England, J Johnston Sweeney, an American critic, Raymond Cogniat of France, Pierre Courthion of Switzerland, Pierre Francastel, Lionello Venturi, and a lot of others I ought to have been familiar with, if I had been doing my homework.

What I remember were the two-hour long lunches every-day, with pitchers of delicious red wine as a standard accompaniment, tours of the fabulous galleries out of hours, with no hordes of muddled masses to get in the way, visits to working artists' studios, like that of Georges Braque - and he was there during our visit, an amiable and self-effacing 58. He told Patrick Heron, who was with us, that in Cubism "L'objet, c'est tout" - visits to the theatre to see Roland Petit dancing In the Marigny in the Champs Elysées, and Serge Lifar dancing Petroushka in the Paris Opéra, and hours and hours just spent walking around Paris, learning about it, learning to love it, though I do remember that Paddy White did take a trip to the Loire to enjoy what he told me was the most unforgettable banquet he had ever attended at one of the chateaux, I think it was Chenonceaux, complete with huntsmen and horns with a fanfare for each of the innumerable courses.

The next Art Critics' Conference was held in Dublin in 1953 - due very largely I think, to Paddy White's enthusiasm and efficiency, and partly perhaps to the Irish Government's anxiety to establish itself on the post-war map of cultural Europe as rapidly as possible, if need be by subsidising such unlikely international follies as an art critics' conference - and the working sessions were held in Newman House. In between times, we were given a reception by the Provost of Trinity College, and another by the Minister of Education at the Department of External Affairs in Iveagh House, St. Stephen's Green, and that was only the first day. On the second day there was an exhibition of contemporary Irish painting at Victor Waddington's Galleries in South Anne Street, and a reception at Newtown Park given by Senator E A McGuire, proprietor of Messrs Brown Thomas of Grafton Street. On the Wednesday, as well as an exhibition in the Dublin Painters' Gallery, there was a reception given by Seán T O'Kelly, the President, at Aras an Uachtaráin in the afternoon, followed by another at Patrick Sarsfield's old house in Lucan that evening; it was then and still is the residence of the Italian Ambassador. And so it went on, for fully a week. According to the programme, James White was still Hon Sec, though my recollection is that he did all the work. The President, Tommy MacGreevy, rarely felt the need to do any more than be there and be charming, in French and English, to anybody of any importance. I notice, from the same programme that I was Hon. Treasurer at this period but we can't have had any funds for me to treasure, or I would have been sussed out and sacked instantly. I have never been able to manage my own financial affairs, let alone anybody else's. No, the fact that there was an International Art Critics Conference in Dublin in 1953, and that it did, to some extent at least, establish Ireland on the cultural map of Europe and introduce a number of influential art critics to some extremely good Irish artists, who were then scarcely known abroad, was entirely due to James White's single-handed and single-minded efforts.

By the time the next International Art Critics' Conference came around, in 1955, things had changed. The world had more or less returned to normal after the war, and international conferences were no longer such a novelty. Also, we were all a lot better heeled; both Paddy White and I brought our wives to this one, which was held in Oxford and London. In Oxford we stayed at Wadham College, in rooms belonging to students who were "down" for the long vacation; ours belonged to a Chinese student with a name like Wu or Lu and he must have been as impressed as we were by the deep score-marks in the stone steps, gouged out by the passage of fifteen or more generations of students' feet. Needless to say,

A.I.C.A. 4th CONGRESS, DUBLIN, 1953

RECEPTION BY H.E. THE PRESIDENT OF IRELAND

Delegates at the A.I.C.A. 4th Congress, Dublin 1953 (Tony Gray is in the front row, five from the right, and James White is in the top row, second from the left)

Wadham was an instant success with the foreign delegates, particularly the Americans; they loved the students' quarters, and the old dining room, where we ate public school food and drank very good claret at refectory tables under a vast hammerbeam roof. At lunch, on the final day, we were allowed to taste Oxford's famous Audit Ale, a very strong brew, originally developed to confuse the minds of the accountants who went to the university every year to do the annual audit.

But at Oxford, for the first time since its inception, the International Art Critics' Association seriously got down to the task of considering what it was really there to do and the result was a lot of very serious talking.

What transpired, or so it seems from my notes, was that the first function of such an organisation was to hold a conference every year or two in a different country to allow the international art critics an opportunity of seeing as many original works of art as possible, so that they would not any longer be obliged, as they had been during the war, to base their opinions on reproductions, however good. The second function seemed to be the inauguration of a system of archives of contemporary art in each country. The point of this was that as art seems to escalate in value everywhere, unlike almost anything else except perhaps vintage motor cars, detailed archives of every exhibition of contemporary art should be kept by the Art Critics' Association in each country so that in the years to come, if a painting is put on offer at Sotheby's, it will be possible to check the date and place where it was first offered for sale, and, indeed, even the price, not that that matters a great deal.

But it would be a mistake to give the impression that the Oxford conference was all work and no play. We paid a visit to Windsor Castle which included a tour of the private apartments, and several of the more distinguished art critics were far more interested, I noticed, in the curious markings on the floor of one of the galleries than in the Canalettos which hung on the wall. They were, I discovered by the simple process of asking an attendant, marks to enable the Duke of Edinburgh to play badminton in the evenings. We also visited Henry Moore in his extraordinary house in Much Hadham, in Essex, extraordinary because it was really a very ordinary country cottage, with a big garden full of reclining and crouching and squatting and prostrate figures, fashioned by Henry Moore himself, and some of us had afternoon tea with cream and cakes with Mr and Mrs Henry Moore, and others of us repaired to the village inn and drank pints of bitter.

After three or four days in Oxford, we spent another three or four in London, where the formal meetings of the Conference were held, as far as I remember at the Arts Council, and where we also were given a very jolly reception. There was an even jollier champagne reception at the Tate Gallery one evening; it was extremely pleasant to wander around among all those sculptures with a glass of Moet in your hand.

But at the ordinary sessions, the talk went on. The next thing was the question of settling on a permanent and internationally-accepted system of art critic terminology, to me a truly dreadful thought. Up until then, art critics had used words in exactly the same way as the caterpillar in *Alice in Wonderland* used them, to mean exactly what they intended them to mean. As I wrote at the time: One critic uses 'realism' where another would use 'naturalism'; one uses 'Impressionist' in the strict sense, meaning a painting in the idiom of the French Impressionists at the turn of the century, where another uses the term 'Impressionist' to indicate that the painter about whom he is talking is more concerned with capturing an impression of the subject before him, than producing an accurate description of it. Added to that, there are a great many art critics who regularly use obscure jargon, often to disguise the fact that they are not quite sure whether a certain picture is any good or not, and they don't want to commit themselves prematurely. And this is only in one language; the Art Critics' Association even at that time had 310 full members representing 25 nations from all over the world, including a few Iron Curtain countries like Yugo-Slavia and Poland.

I think it was this discussion that separated the boys from the men, so to speak. I know that after it, I decided to withdraw, gradually but firmly from the Art Critics' Association but I know also that James White kept right in there arguing, and he was right. I think the big difference between James White and the rest of us - and in this category I would include Tommy MacGreevy, who was moderately serious about being Director of the National Gallery, but never very serious, I believe, on the subject of art criticism - was that James (or Paddy) genuinely believed in art criticism as a useful element in what was his real, basic interest, the history of art, and the best method of presenting it to the public.

In that aim, he has been far more successful than any of the rest of us.

Matthew James Lawless
(1837-64)
The Sick Call (1863)
NGI. Cat. No. 864

THE BIRETTA
Seamus Heaney

Like Gaul, the biretta was divided
Into three parts: triple-finned black serge,
A shipshape pillbox, its every slope and edge
Trimly articulated and decided.

Its insides were crimped satin; it was heavy too
But sported a light glossy tassel
That the backs of my fingers remember well,
And it left a dark red line on the priest's brow.

I received it into my hand from the hand
Of whoever was celebrant, one thin
Fastidious movement up and out and in
In the name of the Father and of the Son AND

Of the Holy Ghost ... I placed it on the steps
Where it seemed to batten down, even half-resist
All of the brisk proceedings of the Mass
The chalice drunk off and the patted lips.

Sanctuaries. Marble. Kneeling boards. Vocation.
Some it made look squashed, some clean and tall.
It was antique as armour in a hall
And put the wind up me and my generation.

Now I turn it upside down and it is a boat -
A paper boat, or the one that wafts into
The first lines of the *Purgatorio*
As poetry lifts its eyes and clears its throat.

Or maybe that small boat out of the bronze age
Where the oars are needles and the worked gold frail
As the intact half of a hatched-out shell,
Refined beyond the dross into sheer image.

But in the end it's as likely to be the one
In Matthew J. Lawless's *The Sick Call*
Where the scene is out on a river and it's all
Solid, pathetic and Irish Victorian.

In this case, however, his reverence wears a hat.
Clerical yet domestic, loved in crises,
He sits listening as each long oar dips and rises,
Sad for his worthy life and fit for it.

Jacques Yverni
(*fl. 1410-38*)
The Annunciation
NGI. Cat. No. 1780

THE AVIGNON ANNUNCIATION
Eileen Kane

The Annunciation with Saint Stephen and Donors is one of the most attractive paintings in the National Gallery of Ireland. It was acquired in 1965, during the Directorship of Dr. James White from the firm of Wildenstein and measures 1.51 m in height by 1.93 m in width without the frame. It was painted in tempera on wood prepared with linen and gesso and is in good condition despite having been transferred to a new support.

The moment in the Gospel story of the Annunciation which the artist has chosen to represent is one full of suspense. The Angel Gabriel has spoken to Mary conveying to her the divine invitation to become the Mother of God. He kneels, waiting for her response. Mary had been reading, before the angel came. Now she turns towards him rising as she does so from the cushion on which she had been kneeling before an altar, her left hand marking the page of an open book upon which are written the words *Magnificat anima mea dominum*, "My soul magnifies the Lord". Rapt in thought, she inclines her head and with her right hand, draws together the edges of her cloak at her throat. She has not yet spoken, but already her acceptance is known to the Father. He opens his hands, and, in the rays which emanate from them are seen the dove of the Holy Spirit and a tiny Infant. This moment of confident suspense is marvellously wrought. As we look, we watch, our eyes moving constantly between Mary and the angel. Behind the angel, to the left of the picture Saint Stephen and the two donors also watch, waiting, as we do, to hear Mary's reply.

This is a very beautiful picture. In composition, it is finely calculated. There is a lovely sense of interval between the figures of St. Stephen, the angel and Mary, the head of the kneeling angel dipping in relation to the heads of the other two figures, so that the three heads are not on a straight line. Above the angel's head appears God the Father, and again that sense of interval can be seen in the spacing between Him, the Infant he dispatches, the dove of the Holy Spirit and the inclined head of Mary. Mary stands within an aedicule, a little five-arched building like a *ciborium* placed over the altar at which she has been kneeling. The aedicule is elegantly designed, its slender columns and gently rounded arches framing and drawing attention to the graceful figure of the Virgin Mary and the altar at which she stands. Over on the left of the picture, the two kneeling donors are on a smaller scale than the rest of the figures. That is in accordance with a

Jacques Yverni
(fl. 1410-38)
Annunciation (Detail)
NGI. Cat. No. 1780

long tradition in medieval art. Here they fit well into the composition, tucked in between St. Stephen and the angel Gabriel, providing relief from the monumentality of the major figures in the drama.

In his handling of colour, the painter of the Annunciation shows the same sensitivity and sureness of touch evident in the composition. There is a predominance of pinks and red. These are distributed over the picture with, once again, an unerring sense of interval, the pink of the angel's robe responding to the pink of the Virgin's dress, seen on her body and in the folds of drapery which spill out beneath her cloak. The red of Saint Stephen's dalmatic and of the altar-cloth close in the picture at either side, finding a response in the shading of the angel's wing and in the diminutive figure of God the Father, surrounded by a blue wavy cloud in the upper part of the composition.

As we look at this painting, however, certain questions arise in our minds. We wonder who the donors might be. The man is evidently a canon. We can tell that by his costume - a white pleated surplice worn over a soutane, with an almuce or fur cape thrown over his left shoulder. His head is tonsured. Who is he? There is no escutcheon to indicate his identity. And who is the lady beside him? She appears to be dressed in black, though some traces of lighter colour on her cloak would suggest that it may originally have been green. Her hair-style is unusual, as is the very high collar, with pointed wings rising straight up behind her ears. Are we looking at a brother and sister? There is not sufficient difference in the ages for them to be mother and son. We also wonder at the strange, and surely extremely rare repetition of the pattern of St. Stephen's vestment in the covering on the altar. Indeed, it is not just the pattern, but the colour too, as if both vestment and altar-cloth had been cut from the same length of material. Finally, the picture is puzzling in that it is not easy to place, merely by looking at it, in the history of European painting. Its style is International Gothic, with a strongly Italian emphasis. But it is not completely Italian. So where did it originate? Who could have painted it? And to what date can it be assigned?[1]

The previous history of the painting provides partial answers to some of our questions. In 1853, when it was first brought to public notice, it was in a private collection in Lyons.[2] It was reported at that time - and there is no reason to doubt the report - that the painting came from a church in Avignon. Unfortunately, no details were given as to which church. Nor do we know whether the church in question still exists or whether it was one of the many religious foundations, churches, chapels, convents, monasteries and friaries which were suppressed during the Revolution of 1789 and in the years which followed. A thorough search of the lists, drawn up at the time, of pictures and other works of art confiscated from the religious houses of Avignon during the Revolutionary period, has produced no clear reference to this *Annunciation*, though a number of paintings on the same theme are mentioned in them. However, the mention of Avignon provides a starting-point in the attempt to place the picture in its historic context.

The most notable single fact about the history of Avignon in the late Middle Ages is that for about seventy years in the fourteenth century, the city was the residence of the popes. From Clement V (1305 - 1314) to Gregory XI (1370 - 1378), seven popes lived there. These men, particularly popes Benedict XII (1334 - 1342) and Clement VI (1342 - 1352) built and decorated an immense and splendid papal palace, which still stands, towering over the city and the river Rhône. To decorate the palace, they brought together teams of artists from many different countries of Europe, and, in those teams, the Italian element predominated. Under Pope Clement VI and his successors, Innocent VI (1352 - 1362) and Urban V (1362 - 1370), the official position of Pope's Painter, or *pictor pape*, was held by Matteo Giovannetti, from Viterbo. It is to Matteo Giovannetti that the paintings in the chapels of St. Martialis and St. John in one of the towers of the palace, may be attributed, as well as what remains of the frescoes in the hall known as the *Grande Audience*. These frescoes reveal Matteo as an artist of great narrative skill, an artist with a strong and inventive interest in the depiction of pictorial space, which he accomplishes through the use of architectural elements. The language of his architectural details is Italian Gothic, and he employs fictive mosaic - "Cosmatesque" - decoration of the kind one might expect to find in Rome at that time. In his interest in space and in his figures he also reveals the influence of the great Florentine painter, Giotto.

One of the most important events in the history of the arts in Avignon had already occurred before the arrival of Matteo Giovannetti. That was the presence there for the last few years of his life of the greatest Sienese painter of his generation, Simone Martini.[3] Simone may not have painted in the papal palace: there is certainly no trace of such activity, either in what remains of the paintings in the palace itself, or in the archival documents which have so far been examined. He did, however, leave some very important and beautiful frescoes in the porch of the cathedral of Avignon, Notre-Dame-des-Doms. These frescoes

Jacques Yverni
(fl. 1410-38)
Madonna and Saints Triptych
Archivio Fotografico della Soprintendenza per i Beni Artistici e Storici, Torino, Galleria Sabauda

consisted of a Christ figure in the pediment and a Virgin and Child with the donor Cardinal Stefaneschi, in the lunette beneath it. The paintings were in such a damaged state that in the 1960's they were detached and are now exhibited in the palace.[4] When they were detached, the under-drawings, or *sinopie* were revealed. These are drawings of extraordinary finesse in which the delicacy of line combines with a strength and sureness of touch which are typical of the work of Simone, qualities which would mark the work of the followers of Simone working in Avignon later in the century, as may be seen in some frescoes by an anonymous painter in the church of Saint-Didier. The Saint-Didier frescoes include some angels which are evidently closely inspired by the example of the great Sienese master.

Simone Martini was a friend, during his Avignonese days, of the renowned Italian poet Petrarch, who also lived at Avignon. For Petrarch, Simone painted the frontispiece of a volume containing the poems of the Latin poet Virgil, one of the most lovely examples of manuscript-painting to come down to us from the fourteenth century. There was also a tradition, long current in Avignon, that Simone painted portraits of the poet and of Laura, the woman he had first seen at a distance in one of the churches of Avignon and for whom, in his poetry, he expressed such an idealized love. In the porch of Notre-Dame-des-Doms, up to the year 1828, when it was wantonly erased, there existed a fresco representing Saint George fighting with the dragon. In this picture, so it was said, the portrait of Petrarch could be seen in the features of St. George and that of Laura in those

Jacques Yverni
(fl. 1410-38)
Madonna and Saints Triptych (Detail)
Archivio Fotografico della Soprintendenza per i Beni Artistici e Storici, Torino, Galleria Sabauda

of the princess liberated by the valiant saint.[5] The loss of this fresco was greatly lamented in Avignon. Perhaps it is only understandable that when the Annunciation now in Dublin came to light, the two donors should have been identified as Petrarch and Laura. However, it is now virtually certain that such an identification can be ruled out.[6]

There is, in the Galleria Sabauda in Turin, a most interesting painting, in which are evident the qualities of elegance, and gracefulness of line characteristic of the tradition of Simone Martini. This is a triptych of the Virgin and Child with, in the side panels, Saint Stephen and Saint Lucy. The triptych is signed: *Jacobus Yverni d. .vinione pxcit* ("Jacques Yverni from Avignon painted this").

It is rewarding to compare the triptych in Turin with the Dublin Annunciation. In both there is that same atmosphere of quiet restraint, a certain elegance, even a hint of languor. The proportion of gold background to floor-space and the positioning of the figures in relation to this is similar in the two paintings. Between the facial features of the Virgin and the Saint Lucy in Turin and the Virgin of the Annunciation, there is a strong resemblance. The hands, in the way they are painted in the two pictures, are very alike. The handling of the drapery folds is very similar, particularly in the case of the figures of the Dublin Virgin and the Saint Lucy in Turin. On stylistic grounds, then, an attribution of the Dublin Annunciation to Jacques Yverni, painter of the Turin triptych, seems very reasonable.

In 1853, when it was brought to public notice by Monsieur Albin Chalandon, the Annunciation was attributed to Simone Martini. No doubt that attribution was based upon the fact that the elegance and the graceful subtlety of line characteristic of Simone are reflected in the Annunciation, but even at that time, the attribution was not accepted by the critics.[7] Beyond the suggestion that the painting was by an Avignonese artist,[8] however, no other name was mentioned in connection with it until 1956, when Jacques Dupont referred to it, almost casually, as being by Jacques Yverni. In Dupont's eyes, the Saint Stephen in the Annunciation was a direct copy of the Saint Stephen in the Turin triptych.[9] Since 1956, the Annunciation has received a number of notices in the critical literature and its attribution to Yverni has not been put in question.[10]

Jacques Yverni is one of the most fascinating artists of the School of Avignon. References to him are found in the archival documents at Avignon between the years 1410 and 1438. By the latter date he was dead, the most likely date of his death being sometime in 1437. In the course of the centuries, according as their works disappeared, replaced in the churches and religious houses of Avignon by others more in keeping with constantly changing fashion and taste, the artists of the Middle Ages fell into oblivion. In the 17th and 18th centuries, Avignon clothed itself in a new mantle of buildings, and the medieval artists, their names, even their existence, were forgotten. At the time of the Revolution, terrible destruction was wrought. Then, all works of art which could be found, of whatever period, were confiscated, some to be preserved, others to be sold, but what little was left of the once marvellous wealth of medieval material was despised as exemplifying the "bad taste" of the past and was dispersed or destroyed.

Towards the middle of the 19th century, in that general renewal of interest in everything which had to do with medieval civilisation, the archives of Avignon began to be searched for the names of the artists of the past. Paul Achard, Archivist of the Department of Vaucluse, of which Avignon is the principal city, was the first to undertake this work. In 1856, he published a first list of names of artists to whom he had found references in the archival documents.[11] Among them was that of Jacques Yverni. The information Achard had found concerning Yverni recorded a payment to the artist in 1427 for four banners painted for the city of Avignon. Two of these were small, intended for the city's brigantine plying on the river Rhône, and two were large, for the general procession held in the city that year. It was not until 1889 that two more pieces of information on the artist were published. These had been found by Canon Requin, a researcher of great diligence, who spent many years examining the documents dating from medieval times which were still held by the notaries practising in Avignon.[12] The first of Requin's documents showed that in 1434, Yverni took on an apprentice named Guillaume Barthélemy; the second was a description of a painting which once hung in the church of Saint-Agricol, in Avignon, in which François de Nyons, Abbot of the Abbey of Saint Genevieve in Paris, was shown kneeling at the feet of Saint Genevieve. The Abbot was accompanied by his coat of arms and an inscription which concluded with the signature: *Jacobus Yverni me pinxit* - "Jacques Yverni painted me".[13] A third researcher who found references to Yverni in the archives of Avignon was Gustave Bayle.[14] In 1898, Bayle published two further documents concerning the artist. The first of these recorded another payment for a banner. This banner was commissioned in the year 1412 by the Avignonese Council of War, and it was intended to be carried to Arles "for the honour of this city" by the Avignonese troops whose task it was to prevent the forces of the antipope Benedict XIII (Peter of Luna) from succeeding in their attempt to reach Avignon by way of the river Rhône. Bayle's second document also came from the Council of War. It is dated 4th December 1426, and in it we find Jacques Yverni acting as a witness to a decision by the Council to gather an army in order to declare war on Geoffrey le Meingre, called Boucicaut, and to besiege him in the fortress of Livron. To all this information, some further details were added by Pierre Pansier, who found the name of Yverni among those to whom payment was made by the syndics of Avignon for their activity on behalf of the city during the long siege of the papal palace in 1410 and 1411 when it was occupied by the partisans of Peter of Luna.[15] Once again, Yverni had provided banners, this time for a general assault on the palace on 10th March 1411. The banners were decorated with the city's arms, consisting of three keys. Other documents published by Pansier referred to property owned by Yverni in Avignon itself and on its outskirts.[16] Thus, over the years, information on Jacques Yverni had gradually accumulated. Given the thoroughness and the dedication of those who had been searching the archives, particularly of Canon Requin and Pierre Pansier, it might have seemed futile to hope for any further finds among the same or parallel material. That has not been the case. Returning to the archives of Avignon has produced a harvest of gleanings which has been well worth while. The personality of Jacques Yverni has come into sharper focus and his place in the artistic context of Avignon has been more clearly defined.[17]

The first reference to Jacques Yverni in the archives at Avignon occurs in the year 1410 when he is mentioned as paying his contribution to the war-loan raised by the city in order to besiege Roderic of Luna, brother of the anti-pope Benedict XIII, and his Catalan followers in the papal palace of Avignon which they had occupied.[18] In the next two years, Yverni continued to play his part in various ways on behalf of the city. We have seen that he provided banners for the Avignonese troops but not all of his ways were peaceful or confined to artistic activity. There is an intriguing document which records the end of a story of which one would dearly love to know the details. The document is a payment made on behalf of the Avignonese authorities to an armourer to cover the cost of replacing a breastplate which Jacques Yverni and two other men allegedly stole, "during the war", from a servant of the Lord of Châteauneuf Calcernier.[19]

The documents provide information on three works of art by Yverni which are now lost. The first of these was for Avignon itself, the second for Aix-en-Provence and the third for the town of Cavaillon. The painting for Avignon has already been mentioned. It was the picture of Saint Genevieve which once hung in the church of Saint-Agricol. It is in fact a work of considerable interest for the career of Yverni because the donor of the picture, François de Nyons was a very prominent personality in the Avignon of his day. Even though he was Abbot of a Parisian Abbey, he continued to be active in the affairs of his native city of Avignon. He had been a canon of the cathedral of Notre-Dame-des-Doms and *Primicerius* or Rector of the University of Avignon before his appointment to Paris in 1406, and he played a prominent role on behalf of the city in the "War of the Catalans" in 1410 - 1411.[20] He died in Avignon in 1413. Clearly, the choice of Jacques Yverni to paint the Saint Genevieve picture must have brought considerable prestige to the artist.

The painting commissioned from Yverni for Aix-en-Provence is also one which not only must have brought considerable prestige to the artist in his own day, but indicates to us now that he must have enjoyed a high reputation in Avignon. The donor was the Seneschal of Provence, Pierre d'Acigné, who, as the representative of the King of France, was the highest-ranking official in the area. It was into his hands that Roderic of Luna surrendered the papal palace at the end of the Catalan war, in November 1411. There are no traces left of the altarpiece which Pierre d'Acigné asked Yverni to paint. All that is known about it is derived from the one document which has been found in local archives.[21] From this we learn that it was commissioned to hang in the cathedral of Saint Sauveur at Aix-en-Provence on an altar recently constructed by the Seneschal "beside the altar and the tabernacle of Corpus Christi". Judging by the price paid for it, 112 gold florins, it must have been a large work. Beyond the title given to it of the "Altarpiece of Our Lord Jesus Christ" we do not know what it represented, but we may surmise from its intended position in relation to the tabernacle of the Blessed Sacrament that it may have represented scenes from the Passion of Christ, or, less likely, the Last Supper. The date of the document which refers to this altarpiece is November 11th 1413.

The third documented work of Jacques Yverni was commissioned from him in January 1422. It consisted of four stained-glass windows for the cathedral of Cavaillon.[22] Two of the windows were to be round and two were to be of normal shape. In the contract, the subjects to be represented in the windows are not specified. It is stated simply that they will be indicated to him, but that the figures are to be in colour and the rest of the glass to be white. The donor of these windows was a *barbitonsor*, or barber, called Philippot Borée, and the price to be paid was not to exceed one hundred florins. Like the other two documented works of Yverni, these windows have disappeared without trace. They may very well have been destroyed as early as 1562 when much damage was done to the cathedral of Cavaillon by the Baron des Adrets, during the religious wars.

There is no reference in the documents which have so far been explored, to the triptych in Turin. There is peripheral documentation, in the sense that there are several references in the archives both at Avignon and at Aix-en-Provence to members of the Piedmontese family of Ceva, whose escutcheon appears on the Turin picture. For instance, there was a 'noble Nicholas, Marquess of Ceva' in the service of Avignon as captain of a detachment of soldiers and crossbowmen during the siege of the palace in 1410 and 1411. It is quite possible, therefore, that the commission for this triptych originated in the time immediately following the war.[23]

Besides these references to specific works of art, other documents have come to light which provide details about Yverni's personal life. We know, for instance, where in Avignon he lived. His house was in the parish of Saint Agricol, in the district known as the Bishop's Gate and was situated between the old walls of the city and the "new" wall constructed by Pope Innocent VI in the latter half of the fourteenth century. The house had a yard and a garden and was surrounded by other people's gardens, except on the eastern side, where it faced the public road. His neighbours included a dyer, whose garden was next-door, a butcher and a merchant. In addition to this house, and some other property in the city, Yverni also owned some land outside the walls of Avignon. This consisted of a vineyard, a meadow and some arable land in the district known as the Clos Vieux.

Finally, from all the documentation concerning Yverni, we know that he was present in Avignon on various dates between the years 1410 and 1435. There is no reference to him, at present known, for the years 1414 to 1416, or between 1418 and 1420. He was already dead by March 1438, when his widow Margaret was disposing of her property prior to marrying her late husband's former apprentice, Guillaume Barthélemy.

The dates between which Jacques Yverni's activity in Avignon is documented, mark the period during which the International Gothic style reached its full maturity. This style flourished in the context of the princely and ducal courts throughout Europe, but particularly in certain centres of high artistic activity. The survival of the Turin triptych and of the Annunciation indicates that Avignon, after the departure of the popes, had kept abreast, stylistically, with developments in what had by then become more favoured centres. Furthermore, there is archival evidence for the activity of other artists in the city, besides Yverni. The two most important of these were Bertrand de la Barre, sculptor and painter, and Guillaume Dombet, painter and artist in stained glass. From the work of these men, no paintings survive, but Bertrand de la Barre is quite probably the author of some carved figures of apostles which come from the tomb of Martin of Selva, Cardinal of Pamplona,[24] which he was making in 1407,[25] and to Guillaume Dombet may be attributed some fragments of stained glass in the cathedral of Saint-Sauveur at Aix-en-Provence. The period of the International Gothic style was a time of decline in Avignon, after the brilliant and expansive years of papal residence. It was marked by wars and hardship, yet, from the documentary evidence, it is clear that artistic activity in the city never ceased completely, even in the darkest moments. Did not Jacques Yverni, as well as Bertrand de la Barre and Guillaume Dombet all make a livelihood from their art in this period? In the 1430s and especially in the 1440s, there was a considerable renewal of artistic life not just in Avignon itself, but also in the surrounding area as well. This is evident from the documentation, especially concerning Guillaume Dombet, who worked in Aix and Marseilles, as well as in Avignon and Tarascon and for a variety of patrons.

Clearly, the Avignonese Annunciation is a work which the National Gallery of Ireland is fortunate to possess. In itself, it is a fine and beautiful picture, but in what it represents historically, it is a rare and valuable work. In the context of the School of Avignon, it is one of the very few survivals from the period of the International Gothic. For Jacques Yverni, it is, with the Turin triptych, one of only two works which not only attest to his style, but bring him to special attention and distinguish him from his contemporaries, as an artist who is remembered both as a name in the archival documents and as the author of still extant paintings. *The Annunciation* is a painting to cherish.

Notes

1. Tentative answers to some of these questions were proffered in: E. Kane 'A Fifteenth Century Avignonese Annunciation in Dublin', in *Gazette des Beaux - Arts,* 6ème période, t. LXXXIII, no. 1263, April 1974, pp.193-204.

2. *Bulletin du Comité de la Langue, de l'Histoire et des Arts de la France*, 3ème Section - Archéologie, t.1, 1852 - 1853, p. 112.

3. Simone Martini died at Avignon in 1344.

4. On the Simone frescoes see: F. Enaud, 'Simone Martini à Avignon.' in *Les Monuments historiques de la France*, no. 3, Paris 1963.

5. Cf. M. Laclotte et D. Thiébaut, *L'Ecole d'Avignon,* Paris 1983, p. 140.

6. For a discussion of the various putative portraits of Petrarch see P. de Nolhac, *Excursus on "L'Iconographie de Pétrarque"*, in his *Pétrarque et l'Humanisme*, nouvelle édition, Paris 1965, Vol. ii. pp. 245 - 257.

7. Cf. G. Bayle 'Contribution à l'Ecole avignonaise de peinture (XVe siècle), in *Mémoires de l'Académie de Nîmes*, Nîmes 1897, p.71.

8. Bayle, loc. cit.; L. - H. Labande, *Les Primitifs français de la Provence occidentale*, 2 vols. Marseille 1932, p. 244 No. 273; G. Ring, *A Century of French Painting* 1400 - 1500, London 1949, p. 234.

9. J. Dupont, 'Quelques exemples des Rapports entre la France et l'Italie au XIVe et au XVe siecles' in *Cahiers de l'Association Internationale des Etudes Françaises*, 1956, p. 37. In this article, Jacques Dupont was also accepting the attribution to Jacques Yverni of some frescoes in the castle of La Manta in Piedmont. These frescoes are no longer considered to be by Yverni, but are attributed to the Turinese painter Giacomo Jaquerio, or to his circle. On Jaquerio see A. Griseri, *Jaquerio e il Realismo Gotico in Piemonte*, Turin, n.d.

10. Cf. especially the following: M. Laclotte, *L'Ecole d'Avignon,* Paris 1960, p.68; A. Châtelet and J. Thuillier, *French Painting from Fouquet to Poussin*, Geneva 1963 p. 29; M. Roques, *Les Apports néerlandais dans la Peinture du Sud-Est de la France*, Bordeaux 1963, p. 148, note 21; E. Castelnuovo, *Il Gotico internazionale in Franciae nei Paesi Bassi*, pt.2, Milan 1966; J. White, 'National Gallery of Ireland: Recent Acquisitions', in *Apollo,* vol. LXXXV, no. 60 (n.s.), February 1967; J. White, *National Gallery of Ireland*, London 1968. p.64 and pl.XI; C. L. Ragghianti, 'Pertinenze Francesi nel Cinquecento, Codicillo', in *Critica d'Arte*, n.s.122, March - April 1972, p.87; E. Kane, op. cit. 1974; M. Laclotte et D. Thiébaut, *L'Ecole d'Avignon,* Paris 1983, pp. 62, 64 & 215.

11. P. Achard, 'Notes sur quelques anciens artistes d'Avignon', in *Archives de l'art français*, t.4, Paris 1855 - 1856, pp. 177 - 92. See also : Idem, 'Notes historiques sur les peintres et les sculpteurs du département de Vaucluse', in *Annuaire du Département de Vaucluse*, Avignon 1865, pp. 145 -90.

12. H. Requin, *Documents inédits sur les peintres, peintres-verriers et enlumineurs d'Avignon au 15ème siècle*, Paris 1889.

13. This information was taken from a book of inscriptions to be seen in the churches of Avignon, written in manuscript in the middle of the 18th century by the Canon de Véras. See: J.R. de Véras, 'Recueil des épitaphes et inscriptions qui sont dans les églises d'Avignon ... 1750', Bibliothéque Municipale d'Avignon Ms. 1738 fol. 51r. On the picture of Saint Genevieve and François de Nyons see also E. Kane, 'A Propos de Jacques Yverni et d'un abbé avignonnais de Sainte-Geneviève de Paris', in *Mémoires de l'Académie de Vaucluse*, 1981, pp. 113 - 123.

14. G. Bayle, 'Contribution à l'histoire de l'école avignonaise de peinture (XVe siècle)' in *Mémoires de l'Académie de Nîmes 1897*, Nîmes 1898, p. 20.

15. P. Pansier, 'Les Sièges du Palais d'Avignon sous le Pontificat de Benoît XIII', in *Annales d'Avignon et du Comtat Venaissin*, 9e année, 1923, p. 62 note 6.

16. All the items of information concerning Jacques Yverni which had been found in the archives of Avignon up to about the year 1930 were published in two important studies, the first by L. - H. Labande, *Les Primitifs français. Peintres et peintres-verriers de la Provence occidentale*, 2 vols., Marseille 1932 and the other by P. Pansier, *Les Peintres d'Avignon aux XIVème et XVème siècles*, Avignon 1934.

17. All the archive material relating to Jacques Yverni, both newly discovered and already known is to be found in: E. Kane, 'Jacques Yverni of Avignon', in *The Burlington Magazine*, vol. CXXIX no. 1013, August 1987, pp. 491 - 498.

18. Archives de Vaucluse (hereafter A. de V.) EE 741, Siège du Palais. Comptes de la Ville 1410 - 1412 fol. 70v.

19. A. de V. Siége du Palais. Pièces.

20. On this picture and on François de Nyons see: E. Kane, 'A Propos de Jacques Yverni et d'un abbé avignonnais de Sainte-Geneviéve de Paris' in *Mémoires de l'Académie de Vaucluse,* 7e série, T. II 1981 pp.113 - 123. It had been argued that the Saint Genevieve picture was an indication that Yverni came from Paris and had kept up contacts there. In view of the information now available, there are no longer any grounds for this opinion.

21. Archives des Bouches du Rhône, Dépôt d'Aix en Provence, Notaires: Muraire 308E/85 fol. 5lr.

22. A. de V. Notaires d'Avignon, Martin 295 (no pagination).

23. If this is accurate, then the date of the Turin work might be about 1412 - 1415, although stylistically it looks more like a work executed in the middle of the 1420's.

24. The figures are preserved in the Musée du Petit Palais at Avignon.

25. A. de V. Notaires d'Avignon Martin 197 (no pagination).

PIERRE THOMAS LE CLERC'S ILLUSTRATIONS FOR DESMARAIS' POEM JÉRÉMIE

Raymond Keaveney

Apart from its rich collection of Oriental material, the Chester Beatty Library in Dublin also contains among its treasures some fine examples of Western art, including illustrated manuscripts, a superb collection of prints and a small holding of drawings. Among the latter is a set of six small pen and wash compositions by the little known French artist Pierre Thomas Le Clerc, best known for his activity as a supplier of designs for engravings. The six designs relate to Le Clerc's commission to supply illustrations for François Desmarais' poem *Jérémie avec sa prière et sa lettre aux captifs prêt à partir pour Babylone*, published in Paris in 1771. The drawings are important as, heretofore, our only knowledge of Le Clerc's style has been obtained through the study of the engravings made from his fashion designs. Few drawings by him have so far been published.

What knowledge we possess of Le Clerc's career and oeuvre is relatively scant. No extensive survey of his life has ever been written and what little has appeared has been minimal and for the most part repetitive. A number of 18th and 19th century authors included him in their compilations, Heineken (1790), Charles Le Blanc (1856); J. Renouvier (1863); Roger Portalis (1877); D. Guilmard (1880); and Emile Bellier de la Chavignerie (1882), all of whom concentrate on his activity as an engraver and provide a listing, either brief or reasonably substantial, of his output. More recent, yet just as modest, have been the contributions in Thieme-Becker and Bénézit. Illustrations of engravings after his designs have appeared in a number of publications devoted to French fashion of the 18th century, a genre in which Le Clerc was particularly active, most notably Roger-Armand Weigart's *Galérie des Modes et Costumes Français* (1956).

The most substantial modern account of Le Clerc's career is that included in Yves Sjoberg's volume in the series surveying the holdings of French 18th-century engravings at the Bibliothèque Nationale (Paris 1974, Vol. XIII). According to Sjoberg the artist was born in Paris about 1740 and received his training under L.J.F. Lagrenée l'aîné at the Académie Royale. Active almost exclusively as a supplier of designs for engravings, he produced compositions in a number of genres: allegory, portraiture, arabesques and fashion plates. He exhibited some paintings and drawings at the salon in 1796. Le Clerc most likely resided in Paris throughout his lifetime as he signed himself "Leclerc Parisinus pictor historicus". The address given when he exhibited at the salon in 1796 was 33 Rue des Noyers. We possess no record of his date of death, though we know he was still active in

1799 when he produced two compositions for *Le Manuel Republican* (15 May 1799). Apart from providing brief accounts of his career, few writers have paid any critical attention to Le Clerc's work, only Jules Renouvier, in his survey of art during the Revolution, has commented on his style. He saw in Le Clerc's compositions symptoms of the decline in French drawing under the influence of the Academy - prior to its being regenerated through the study of the antique.

Le Clerc supplied seven designs for François Desmarais' poem *Jérémie*, six of which are presented here along with their engraved versions[1]; the seventh, a design for the decorative frontispiece has been lost. François Desmarais (nicknamed Torchon), a minor figure in the French Enlightenment, was born in Paris on 8th January 1736. He was reputed to have been the natural son of Louis XV and a lady in the entourage of the Queen, though this is unlikely. Educated at the *Collège des Mathurines or Trinitaires* he made his vows in that order in 1756. He was soon appointed confessor to the King in keeping with the tradition that the order supplied the royal chaplain. Active at court and in the literary world of Paris until 1776, he then retired to Regniowez in the Ardennes taking up religious duties there. Though resident in the provinces for the remainder of his life, Desmarais continued to be occupied with State affairs, publishing pamphlets on cultural and legislative topics, an activity which brought him into conflict with the authorities on more than one occasion. In 1775 he was imprisoned when his church and priory were sacked. Besides his involvement with national issues, Desmarais also took considerable interest in improving the life of the people in his local community at Regniowez, providing educational facilities for them, founding a college there in 1786, encouraging the local textile industry, organizing charitable institutions and endowing the town and religious institutions with works of art. He died in 1808.

The poem *Jérémie* was written early in Desmarais's career, while he was still resident in Paris and at a time when his ambitions were primarily literary rather than socio-political. He had acquired a taste for ancient languages during his student days and had written some verses in Latin early in his career. *Jérémie* is essentially a recounting of the writings of the Old Testament prophet Jeremiah and is based on the Biblical texts. It is dedicated to 'Madame' (Marie Antoinette). Published in Paris in 1771, *chez G. Desprez*, in Rue Jacques, the project was prepared in 1770, the date appearing on three of the six drawings. Desmarais was obviously very happy with the choice of artist as a short notice commenting on his designs was included in the publishers introduction: "M. Le Clerc est le compositeur des desseins, d'après le plan et les idées de l'Auteur. On voit briller dans son ouvrage une hardiesse sage, une touche délicate, et un imagination qui frappent et qui enchantent. Nous osons assurer que le nom de ce jeune Artiste deviendra célèbre un jour."

That Le Clerc's career did not quite live up to the expectations quoted by the publisher is perhaps due to the fact that he never again received the support and direction given him by Desmarais and Desprez. Certainly his designs for *Jérémie* display much promise and ability. A feature of the publication is that every plate (all printed in reverse direction to the drawings) is accompanied by a commentary provided by the author, each explaining the content of the relevant illustration. It is conceivable, though we have no way of proving the supposition, that these commentaries were first supplied to Le Clerc, who, following Desmarais'

Mission de Jérémie.
(Jeremiah's Mission)
Drawing and Engraving

instructions, based his designs on their content. This would appear to be the procedure indicated in the publisher's foreword. The lack of complete correlation between commentary and drawing, particularly as evidenced by the discrepancies between Desmarais' description of the city of Taphnis in the fifth vignette and Le Clerc's disregard for suggesting the beauty of that city, indicates that the commentaries, rather than describing what is actually contained in the engravings, were initially conceived as a guide for the artist as to how to represent each scene.

Leaving aside the decorative frontispiece, for which we have no drawing, the first illustration to the text shows the young prophet Jeremiah announcing to King Sedecias the destruction of his empire, (Jeremiah ch. 20, v. 4 and f.). The *Explication de la Première vignette* reads as follows[2]:

Jeremiah's Mission

The Prophet, aged fifteen, announces to King Sedecias the ruin of his empire. He shows him the temple, the destruction of which is imminent if he does not return to the way of the Lord. The King appears frightened by his threats: around his house are assembled, on the one side, the Princes of the people, and on the other, the Priests and false Prophets. The former, by their mocking aspect and their insulting behaviour, show their distain for Jeremiah and his predictions: the others, through the intensity of their gaze and the grinding of their teeth, show their consuming hatred for the man.

The High Priest Strikes Jeremiah

The second plate illustrates the persecution of Jeremiah, showing him struck by the High Priest Phassur (Jeremiah ch. 20, v. 2). The *Explication* is as follows:

The High Priest Phassur, long annoyed with the Prophet and driven to despair by the predictions which he had been making to the people in the Temple, has him whipped and beaten ignominiously. He pursues his vengence. On his orders, soldiers seize Jeremiah and take him to prison. We see him represented close to the Temple where the event occurred, close to the great gate of Benjamin: women, the elderly and the young, all appear touched by the sight of this sad spectacle.

The following plate continues the theme of Jeremiah's persecution and represents the imprisonment of the prophet (Jeremiah ch. 38, v. 6). The *Explication* to the third vignette reads:

Jeremiah Thrown Into A Pit

The King of Jerusalem, solicited by the High Priests and the Princes of the People, grants them permission to have Jeremiah thrown into a filthy pit. His tormentors lower him down, suspended from ropes. Jeremiah looks on them with eyes that display tenderness and in an attitude which shows him interceding to Heaven on their behalf. He looks to further exhort the People to penitence: one sees the profile of the High Priest Phassur; his eyes, his attitude, his gestures, all demonstrate the joy in his heart. To his right is an Equerry; he has just executed the orders of the Prince.

The next illustration, the fourth in the series, depicts the prophet seated among the ruins of the Temple with the city of Jerusalem in flames all about. The *Explication* to the vignette reads:

Jeremiah Seated Among Ruins of the Temple

The Prophet is seated among the ruins of the Temple, in a most touching attitude. He views with dismay the ruins of Jerusalem, still burning. His hands are raised to Heaven and the grief is painted on his features: one glimpses the remains of the beautiful colonnade of the Temple, the urn where the Jews purified themselves, and some fragments which proclaim the magnificence of the house of the Lord. Under Jeremiah's feet are loose blocks of marble, overturned columns, broken capitals, fragmented reliefs, and signs of destruction everywhere. In the backround, one can see the flames, still rising from the ruins of the City which is virtually reduced to ashes.

The fifth plate shows the martyrdom of Jeremiah at the hands of his compatriots in the town of Taphnis in Egypt. (This event is not recorded in the Bible. A number of extra-biblical sources indicate that the prophet was stoned to death in Tahpanhes in Egypt though St. Jerome refers to another tradition which maintains that Jeremiah died a natural death. See Pseudo-Epiphanius: *De Vitis Prophetarium*, in *Patroligia Graeca*, vol. 43, col. 400, and also Isidorus Hispalensis: *De Ortu et Orbitu Patrorum*, ch. 38 in *Patrologia Latina*, vol. 83, col. 142). The *Explication* to the vignette reads:

The Martyrdom of Jeremiah

One sees a view of Taphnis, one of the most beautiful Cities in all of Eygpt. The Jews, who for a long time have been angry with Jeremiah, who has been denouncing them with dreadful reproaches for their failure to heed the way of the Lord, have him brought to the

Le Grand-Prêtre frappe Jérémie.
(The High Priest Strikes Jeremiah)
Drawing and Engraving

Jérémie jette dans un fosse.
(Jeremiah Thrown into a Pit)
Drawing and Engraving

Jérémie assis sur les ruines du Temple.
(Jeremiah Seated Among Ruins of the Temple)
Drawing and Engraving

Martyre de Jérémie.
(The Martyrdom of Jeremiah)
Drawing and Engraving

Lecture de la lettre de Jérémie.
(The Reading of Jeremiah's Letter)
Drawing and Engraving

public square; there they throw him to the ground and set upon him, some with sticks and others with stones. The Holy Prophet is seen in a most touching state: he raises his hands to Heaven, and while expiring, prays for his executioners. An Angel appears in the distance, on a bright cloud, with a palm in one hand, and bears him the crown of martyrdom.

In the sixth and final vignette an elderly man in chains is depicted reading the letter which Jeremiah had written to the captive jews in Babylon (Jeremiah 29, v.1 and ff.). The accompanying *Explication* reads:

The Reading of Jeremiah's Letter

One sees the Jews in chains, and on the point of their departure to their place of exile. The elderly, the women, the young girls, and the infants still being nurtured, are all depicted in a most striking manner. One of the Elders, holds in hid hand the letter from Jeremiah: he reads it publicly, covering it with his tears. The people listen with dismayed attention: some turning their eyes to Heaven, some to the earth; the women covering their faces with their hands, with the young women appearing wrapt in a more bitter sorrow.

Returning briefly to Jules Renouvier's comments on Le Clerc's art, the nineteenth-century writer criticised his paintings and costume prints in particular, as he considered they displayed neither originality nor distinction. He was not, however, completely blind to Le Clerc's limited talents and acknowledged that in his drawings the artist showed ability, a sentiment which echoes the appreciative comments, quoted earlier, printed in the publisher's foreword to *Jérémie*. The six drawings illustrated here are in many respects awkward and lacking in finesse; but they are free from those anaemic qualities which characterized so much of late eighteenth century French art. Le Clerc's compositions are rendered with a sense of vitality and in his compliance with the author's directions he has shown himself an able storyteller and a competent designer. The stylistic roots of his art are evidently grounded in his study of the masters of the seventeenth century rather than the antique and his development was consequently limited as he lacked the vision to exert a modern synthesis of the traditional and the antique, a faculty which was fundamental to the formation of the neo-classical idiom which revolutionised eighteenth century European art.[3]

Notes

1. The author wishes to thank the Trustees of the Chester Beatty Library, Dublin, for permission to reproduce the drawings, and the Bibliothèque Nationale, Paris, for permission to reproduce the engravings. All the drawings are in pen and ink with grey wash. They each measure 13.5 x 9cm. Four of the drawings are signed by the artist, with two carrying the date 1770: *Mission de Jérémie; Le Grande-Prêtre Frappe Jérémie* (dated); *Jérémie Assis Sur Les Ruines Du Temple* (dated); *Marytre De Jérémie*. The drawings carry no inventory number.

2. The original French translations of the *explications* are as follows:

   Mission de Jérémie.

   Le Prophete, âgé de quinze ans, annonce au roi Sedecias la ruine de son empire. Il lui montre le Temple dont il prédit la destruction prochaine, s'il ne retourne pas au Seigneur. La Roi paroît effrayé de ses menaces: auprès de son trône sont, d'une côte, les Prince du Peuple, et de l'autre, les Prêtres et les fauz Prophètes. Les première témoignent, par un ris moqueur et par des gestes insultants leur mépris pour Jérémie et ses predictions. Les autres experiment, par le feu de leur regards et des grincements de dents, toute la rage dont ils sont animes contre lui.

   Le Grand-Prêtre frappe Jérémie.

   Le Grand-Prêtre Phassur, irrité depuis long-temps contre le Prophète, et désespéré des prédictions qu'il faisôit au Peuple dans le Temple, l'en chasse en le frappant ignominieusement. Il pousse plus loin sa vengeance. Des soldats, par son ordre, se faisissent de sa personne, et le traînent en prison. On la voit représentée à côté du Temple, parce qu'elle y etoit vraiment pratiquée proche la haute porte de Benjamin: des femmes, des vieillards, des jeunes gens, paroîssent attendris à la vue de ce triste spectacle.

   Jérémie jette dans un fosse.

   Le Roi de Jérusalem, sollicité par le Grand-Prêtre et les Princes du Peuple, leur accords la permission de faire jetter le Prophète dans une fosse pleine de boue. Ses borreaux l'y descendent, suspendu par des cordes. Jérémie les regarde avec des yeux où la tendresse est peinte, et semble interesser le ciel en leur faveur. Il paroît vouloir encore exhorter le Peuple à la pénitence: on voit de profil le Grand-Prêtre Phassur; ses yeux, son air, ses gestes, annonce la joie de son coeur. A sa droite est un écuyer; il vient faire executer les ordres du Prince.

   Jérémie assis sur les ruines du Temple.

   Le Prophète est assis sur les ruines du Temple, dans l'attitude la plus attendrissante. Il jette un regard consterne sur les débris de Jérusalem qui fument encore. Ses mains sont élevées vers le ciel, et la frayeur est peinte sur son visage: un appercôit un reste de la belle colonnade du Temple, - 'urne où se purisioient les juifs, et quelques vestiges qui annoncent la beauté et la magnificence de la maison du Seigneur. Sous les pieds de Jérémie sont des marbres détachés des colonnes renversees, des chapiteaux brisés, des basreliefs rompus, et toutes sorte, de débris épars. Dans le frond, la flamme se fait appercevoir sortant encore des décombres de la Ville qui est presque toute en cendres.

Martyre de Jérémie.

L'on voit Taphnis, l'une des plus belles villes de toute l'Egypte. Les juifs, irrités depuis long-temps contre Jérémie, qui leur faisoît de sanglants reproches de s'y être retirés contre l'ordre de Dieu, le traînent cruellement au milieu de la place publique: ils le jettent par terre, et l'assomment, les uns à coups de batons, les autres à coups de pierres. Le S. Prophete a la physionomie la plus touchante: il éleve les mains au Ciel, et prie, en expirant, pour ses borreaux. Un Ange paroît au loin, sur un nuage éclatant, une palme à la main, et lui apporte la couronne de martyre.

Lecture de la lettre de Jérémie.

On appercôit les Juifs enchâinés, et fut sur le point de partir pour le lieu de leur exil. Les vieillards, les femmes, les filles, et les enfants encore à la mamelle, y sont représentés d'une manière frappante. Un des Anciens respectable par son age, tient dans ses mains le Lettre de Jérémie: Il en fait publiquement la lecture, en l'inondant de ses larmes. La Peuple l'écoute avec une attention consternée: les une levent les yeux au Ciel; les autres les ont fixés sur la terre; les femmes se couvrent le visage de leur mains, et les filles semblent être absorbées dans la plus amere douleur.

3. Bibliographic Sources

Carl Heinrich von Heineken: *Dictionnaire des artistes dont nous avons des estampes, avec une notice détailée de leurs ouvrages gravés,* Leipzig, J.G.I. Breitkopf, 1778-1790; Charles le Blanc: *Manuel de l'amateur d'estampes..,* Paris, 1854-1890, 4 vols; J. Renouvier: *Histoire de l'art pendant la Révolution, considéré principalment dans les estampes, ouvrage posthume de Jules Renouvier: suivi d'une étude du même sur J.B. Greuze,* Paris, 1863; Roger Portalis: *Les Dessinateurs d'illustration au dix-huitième Siècle,* Paris, 1877, 2 vols.; D. Guilmard: *Les Maïtre Ornemantistes, dessinateurs, peintres, architects, sculpteurs et graveurs. École Française, Italienne, Allemande et des Pays-Bas...Publication enrichie de 180 planches...et précédée d'une introduction par M. le Baron Davillier,* Paris, 1880, 2 vols.; Bellier de la Chavignerie: *Dictionnaire général des artistes de l'é française depuis l'origine des arts du dessin, jusqu'á nos jours,* Paris, 1882-1885, 5 vols.

Sir Alfred Chester Beatty
(1875-1968)

THE COLLECTING TECHNIQUE OF SIR ALFRED CHESTER BEATTY

Brian P. Kennedy

The difference between the true art collector and the dabbler has been explained as follows:

> Collecting is a form of self-indulgence, but by and large it is a beneficial one. Probably the simplest differentiation between the dabbler and the genuine collector is that the latter has stilled once and for all any inhibition against spending money on the inanimate objects of his choice. Once this resolute state of mind has been reached and some money is available, progress is assured.[1]

Alfred Chester Beatty (1875-1968) was, without doubt, a genuine collector and his self-indulgence proved to be to Ireland's inestimable benefit. His bequest to the Irish Nation of his magnificent library of oriental, near eastern and western art places him in the front rank of distinguished Irish cultural benefactors. Ireland now possesses splendid treasures including jade books, dragon robes, rhinoceros horn cups, Batak bark books, Persian miniatures, Korans, woodblock prints, snuff bottles and some of the earliest known copies of the Greek New Testament on papyrus.

The Chester Beatty Library, situated at 20 Shrewsbury Road in Dublin, has been frequented by scholars, foreign visitors and the interested public since it was first opened on 11 August 1954 by the Taoiseach, Eamon de Valera. Its founder was born in New York in 1875 and his paternal grandparents were Irish, Robert Beatty from Armagh and Catherine Louisa Armstrong from Mountrath, County Laois. Alfred Chester Beatty studied for a year at Princeton University and then moved to Columbia University to study mine engineering. He graduated in 1898 after receiving 91% in his final examinations. Living in America until 1911 and then based in Great Britain until 1950, Beatty became a wealthy and influential business man. His mining company, Selection Trust, pioneered the adaptation of new technology to open-pit mining. Most of Beatty's success came from his company's copper mines in Northern Rhodesia (now Zambia).[2]

It was his childhood interest in mineral samples which led Beatty into the field of art collecting.[3] By 1914 he owned over 1,600 Chinese snuff bottles made mostly from semi-precious stones. A visit to Egypt in the winter of 1914 fuelled his interest in art by exposing him to the world of Arabic manuscripts. He purchased

Japanese Inro
Yoyusai (1772-1845)
Two Swallows Flying Past Willow Fronds
Courtesy of the Trustees of the Chester Beatty Library, Dublin

a residence near Cairo and spent most winters there for the next twenty-five years. In 1917 Beatty visited Japan and China. While there, he bought manuscripts, scrolls, albums and decorative objects. These items formed the nucleus of an art collection which expanded at a phenomenal rate throughout the 1920s and 1930s. During the same period, Selection Trust surged forward to become a group of companies with mining interests in many countries. Beatty's knowledge of mining was of considerable assistance to the Allied war effort throughout the Second World War. He served on a number of British Government committees and was Vice-Chairman of the United Kingdom Commercial Corporation established to further wartime trade.

Beatty had paid his first visit to Dublin in 1937 and had enjoyed browsing in the antique shops along the quays.[4] After the war, he began to spend weekends at an estate in County Kildare which had been purchased by his son, Alfred Chester Beatty Junior. In 1950, aged seventy-five, he decided to retire from the busy world of mining and to move to Dublin where he purchased a residence in Ailesbury Road, Ballsbridge, and a site for his library at nearby Shrewsbury Road. 'Ireland', he declared, 'is the best country in the world in which to retire. The country has atmosphere. The people have so much charm. Life goes on as it did elsewhere until 1939'.[5]

Although Beatty only stayed in Dublin from May until September each year, preferring to winter in the warmth of the south of France, he gained a pre-eminent role as a patron of the arts in Ireland. He presented paintings to the National

Binding of Persian Manuscript, painted and lacquered
(Iran 17th Century)
Courtesy of the Trustees of the Chester Beatty Library, Dublin

Gallery of Ireland[6] and oriental weapons to the Military Museum at the Army's Curragh Camp. His greatest gift, however, was that of his world-renowned library.

Ireland was not slow to honour Beatty. In 1951 he was appointed as a member of the first Arts Council and was awarded honorary doctorates by both Trinity College, Dublin, and the National University of Ireland. He was made a Freeman of the City of Dublin in 1956 and the following year became the first Honorary Irish Citizen. In 1954 Winston Churchill proposed that the 'World Copper King' should receive a knighthood which was duly conferred by Queen Elizabeth II. Sir Chester Beatty became a favourite guest of Irish politicians and was the subject of many feature articles by journalists eager to recount stories of a man whose conversation included references to wild west gunfights, copper discoveries in Africa, priceless manuscripts and a long list of kings, presidents and prime ministers whom he counted among his friends. He was good-humoured, gentlemanly and, above all, generous. While living in England, his charitable interests included cancer research and in Ireland he supported the Wireless for the Blind Fund. In a final tribute to Beatty, the Irish Government honoured him with a State funeral, the first foreign-born citizen to receive this distinction. In 1975, a condition of the Chester Beatty bequest was fulfilled admirably by the Irish Government when a new exhibition gallery was opened to the public.

Art collecting is a peculiar addiction and it affects its victims in different ways. A few examples will suffice - Calouste Gulbenkian was enormously secretive, Randolph Hearst was a voracious magpie collector, John Ringling bought huge paintings (the more square yards of canvas the better), John Pierpont Morgan was a cheque book collector (money was no obstacle), Sir Denis Mahon is a scholar collector.[7] Alfred Chester Beatty is typical of the *grand amateur*. This is not to suggest that he lacked knowledge. He could not read any oriental languages but he acquired an extensive knowledge of oriental manuscripts. He relied on the basic requirement of all good collectors, a discerning eye, the same quality required to be able to evaluate mineral samples. Beatty insisted on seeing every object which entered his collection. He relied on dealers and scholars but held a firm grip on the collecting policy and on the purse strings. He knew how to delegate and made able use of his full-time librarian - Mr. F.M. Kelly (to 1927), Mrs. Joan Kingsford Wood (1927-46), James Wilkinson (1946-57) and Dr. R.J. Hayes (Honorary Librarian 1957-67, Librarian and Director 1968-76).

There are many criteria on which the acquisition of an art object can be based, quality, rarity, age, value, aesthetic or artistic merit. But the fundamental criterion underlying Beatty's approach was: 'Quality, quality, always the quality'.[8] He argued: 'It is not worth buying books that are not first-class, as it ruins the average of the collection and ties up a lot of money and gets one nowhere'.[9] Quality is in fact the hallmark of the Chester Beatty Library's collections. Beatty had extreme self-confidence and trusted his own judgement implicitly. He was a trend setter, not a follower. His pursuit of Armenian manuscripts, for example, saw him ahead of other collectors. He told Wilkinson: 'I should not be surprised if they come into fashion'.[10] He did not pursue big names only: 'I am satisfied, and the policy I want to pursue... is to back our joint judgement on quality and forget about the artist. In the next 25 or 30 years they will know more about the artists'.[11]

Of course the collector always had to be prepared to take a risk. Beatty explained: 'I have found in mining that if the thing is possible, and the price is moderate, the only sound way to find things is to take a chance. The number of people who warned me about losing money in Rhodesia, and never finding copper there, would surprise you, particularly if I gave you some of the names'.[12] Luck has a role to play: 'It is like jades. Everyone condemned eighteenth century jades. Where do you get such jade books as we have? - there are no such books in the world that I know of. That famous one which we have, which is one of the most famous in the world - I would be ashamed to tell you what it cost, and it was bought from one of the regular dealers who had just received it in a shipment from China'.[13]

Beatty had a very sensible attitude to the age of art objects: 'The idea of concentrating on and only buying these very early things is absolutely foolish to my mind... You might as well condemn paintings by Van Gogh or Degas or Cezanne as they are not painted in the 16th century'.[14] He was also sensitive to price, a trait he felt was lacking in 'museum people': 'It is curious how nearly all the Museum people, when they write recommending or speaking highly of a thing, never seem to put the price in. The price is rather an important factor, it seems to me'.[15] But Beatty was never mean regarding price. He had a clear idea about what each particular object was worth and he was not afraid to pay a high price. He told Wilkinson: 'If I pay a big price it will only be for some superb Artistic MSS'.[16] Dealers knew that if they offered Beatty a manuscript before they placed it on the open market, and if it was of sufficient quality, he would pay as much or more than the market rate to acquire it. Wilkinson advised his friend, Bill Archer, who worked in the Indian Section of the Victoria and Albert Museum: 'Sir

Chester is anything but ungenerous over purchases of things of real value to the collection. You also know that he is not much interested in anything that is in poor condition'.[17]

Knowledge of the special interests of his rivals was always of special concern to Chester Beatty. He often discovered that the dealer supplying him with manuscripts was also supplying another leading collector. It was important to win exclusivity from a dealer and therefore clever tactics were required. He advised Wilkinson about how to handle a new dealer in Japan: 'I think we should return the things we do not want, unless we have to return so many that it is going to kill that as a future market. We certainly should not buy all the poor things he sends, but we might take a few in the first shipment if it is going to help us as to future purchases... if the condition is too bad we should, of course, turn them down'.[18] Dealers and scholars often announced their discoveries as 'unique and sensational'. In the face of such exciting declarations, the collector requires a calm and level-headed outlook in order to evaluate the real nature of any discovery. Beatty was aware, nonetheless, that each letter announcing a discovery was worth pursuing. For example, in response to an American scholar who had just returned form Persia announcing a great find, Beatty offered sage advice: 'It sounds to me a good deal like a gold mine you hear of with ore running at 5 ozs to the ton, and then you make a long trip across the desert, in tremendous discomfort and find it is only a pipedream. But, still, the collection at Shrewsbury Road was built up a good deal from chasing pipedreams, and it is very, very interesting and well-worth following up'.[19]

Chester Beatty used a special system which he had devised early in his collecting career in order to categorise his art collections. He employed the system extensively after he settled in England and used it when visiting dealers's shops, museums and libraries. The system was based on a code - 'A' for excellent, 'B' for good and 'C' for not of adequate standard. 'B' items were rarely retained. The 'A' items were classed form 1A to 25A. Beatty did not want anything dirty and would reject material on the grounds that it was 'unhealthy' or 'grubby'.[20] He told one correspondent who had sent him a manuscript on approval: '... unfortunately it is a rather dirty copy, and not quite fine enough for my library. I much regret being unable to accept it as it is a very attractive book'.[21]

Regular visits to the British Museum and to the Bibliothèque Nationale in Paris allowed Beatty to acquire an extensive knowledge of oriental manuscripts. During the 1920s and 1930s, he visited all of the great museums and libraries of Europe except the Vatican Library which he did not see until 1964 when he was received in private audience by Pope Paul VI. On each of his visits to the great oriental collections in London or Paris or Constantinople (Topkapi Palace), Beatty would bring a little notebook which he filled assiduously with handwritten notes about the manuscripts he studied. He classed the manuscripts he was viewing in accordance with his ABC system and added the letters DCFI (Don't Care For It) or NFFI (Not Fit For Collection) or FFI (Fit For Collection). The use of such handwritten records and codes is a characteristic of many dedicated collectors. From 1911 until 1957 Sir William Burrell kept detailed records of all his expenditure on art works by writing entries into a total of twenty-eight school exercise books.[22] Henry Yates Thompson recorded the prices he paid for manuscripts by using a code based on the word BRYANSTONE where B is 1, R is 2, Y is 3 etc.[23] Beatty had codes agreed with some of those scholars who scouted

Chinese Jade Book:
The Diamond Sutra
*Frontispiece showing Buddha Enthroned
Dated A.D. 1732
Courtesy of the Trustees of the Chester Beatty Library*

for manuscripts on his behalf. Eric Millar of the British Museum's Department of Manuscripts worked for Beatty discreetly during the early 1930s. On one occasion, Millar sent Beatty a telegram from Egypt in coded language based on mining terminology. The message read: 'Silver mine very rich has three shafts (stop) Gold mine rich four shafts (stop) should buy them without fail especially silver mine'.[24] Rich meant old, shaft meant century, silver mine meant manuscript one (a third century text of Daniel) and gold mine meant manuscript two (a fourth century text of Genesis).

The only way Chester Beatty could attempt to execute his plan to create a library of the best quality examples of Western, Islamic and Oriental manuscripts and *objets d'art* was to become a master of delegation. Following his decision to site his library permanently in Ireland, he told Wilkinson: 'The thing is getting so complicated and there are so many different lines. The thing is to organise the different departments and supervise the people who are doing the work and make sure that they are doing it properly. When it is once started on the right lines it will need very little attention. That is the system I used when organising Selection Trust. It would have been impossible for me to carry out all those details in connection with all the various mines in different parts of the world'.[25] In effect, the technique which Beatty used to organise his art collections was exactly the same technique he had used to build up his mining company. He employed experts to vet potential purchases, offered a fair price, accepted only the highest quality, and took the final decisions himself. Beatty did not make the mistake of depending exclusively on either scholars or dealers. He employed both and recognised that the dealers were businessmen like himself who were experts in their trade. The scholars offered academic confirmation of the quality of his purchases and also, on occasion, gave him insider information about owners of fine manuscripts who might be open to a generous purchase offer.

The good will of the staff of the British Museum and the Victoria and Albert Museum was guaranteed by Beatty's willingness to involve himself in joint purchases. He recognised that the museums had limited purchasing power but expert knowledge, so he offered to assist the purchase of items which both he and the museums wanted. He showed excellent business sense in the way he went about these purchases. He told Wilkinson: 'I think the fairest way to make these divisions is for the party who buys them to divide them into two lots and give the other party the choice, and when we have selected our lots, if there is any particular miniature that the other person prefers we can make a trade afterwards. That is what was done by old Kruger in dividing up an estate between two brothers... one divided it and gave the choice to the other'.[26]

Beatty's relationship with his dealers was excellent because he treated them in a professional manner and they responded likewise. One example will suffice to demonstrate the point. Beatty wrote to Wilkinson in 1961: 'I received a most charming letter from [Clifford] Maggs. It seems we got both the Ethiopic lots - 111 and 112. I put in a bid for £45 each and he bought them for about £55 each. He offered to forego his commission as he exceeded my estimate, and if necessary pay something towards the cost. I wrote that of course I would not consider that, but I appreciated his generosity, and I am delighted with them'.[27] Beatty established a network of dealers who knew his requirements and were paid well to fulfil them. Maggs was one of the London dealers frequented by Beatty, others included Probsthain, Colnaghi, Sparks, Kegan Paul, Quaritch, Craddock & Barnard, Luzac, Zaehnsdorf, Bluett and Spink. He purchased regularly at Christies but, for some reason, he always sent anything he had to sell to Sotheby's where it was usually sold anonymously as 'Property of a Gentleman'. In Cairo his main sources for Islamic manuscripts were Messrs. A. Sarkissian and A.S. Yahuda. He also bought Islamic manuscripts in Barcelona from Senor S. Babra, and in Paris from Demotte & Co., from Monsieur J. Acheroff and from Monsieur A. Caracotch. Beatty also established a formidable network of scholars who, acting in their private capacities, purchased material on his behalf. There was an unwritten agreement in the major museums that staff could purchase material for private collectors because it might come back to the museum eventually by gift or bequest.

University scholars and museum experts were essential to Beatty's publications programme. Although he could be secretive about how he came to acquire items in his collection, most notably the biblical papyri, he was anxious to have the material published in scholarly editions and available to the public. The cost of producing Beatty's catalogues was staggering. The Persian miniatures catalogue alone cost £6,000 in 1936.[28] It was published in six volumes, four volumes of plates and two volumes of text. Beatty was proud of his reputation for producing fine catalogues and he sent each one, on its publication, to a distinguished list of people including other collectors like Sir Ernest Oppenheimer, Charles Dyson Perrins, George Eumorfopoulos and Lord Rothschild, all of whom, like Beatty himself, were members of the Roxburghe Club in London. This exclusive club, dedicated to the printing of rare texts and manuscripts, was named after John, Duke of Roxburghe, a celebrated collector of ancient literature, who died in 1812.

Indian painting:
Maharao Ram Singh of Kotah on a White Charger Attacking a Water Buffalo
*1855 A.D.
Courtesy of the Trustees of the Chester Beatty Library, Dublin*

The emphasis which Beatty placed on financing publications by eminent scholars reveals the depth of his respect for the contents of his collections. He was aware of the importance of the material which he collected even though his library was a personal one containing books which he liked to read, handle, study and examine. His ignorance of oriental languages led him to request books from his librarian in a rather naive fashion. He would ask Wilkinson to show him 'the manuscript with the horse'. He had many manuscripts with illustrations of horses but his clued-in librarian would know which one he meant and would offer him the appropriate Persian manuscript. A similar instance is recorded in a letter to Wilkinson: 'When you consider some of the pictures we have got they have great charm. Take, for example, that picture of the blackbirds and the hawthorn trees. Even if it was painted in the 19th century it is a very beautiful painting'.[29] Beatty viewed his library as primarily an exhibition library rather than a scholarly one. Certain scholars would come but what made the library most relevant to the Irish people was its potential to introduce them visually to many of the cultures of the world. Beatty stressed the importance of illustrations by having many of his manuscripts broken up, though not the most important ones. While this is regarded as reprehensible by many museologists today, it meant that many illustrations could be viewed by the public instead of just one illustration being exhibited at a time.

During the 1920s, Beatty set himself the target of matching the British Museum collection in each area in which he wished to specialise: 'I want to compare our collection with the British Museum collection of the same class of material'.[30] He made a list of the major oriental collections of the world in terms of quality and quantity. He regarded the British Museum as the greatest museum in the world. Berlin was second, Paris third, Cairo fourth, Leyden and the Bodleian at Oxford joint fifth. Beatty constantly looked to the British Museum with envy and it was a real thrill for him to find that his own collection equalled or surpassed it. He wrote to Wilkinson in 1951: 'I have a remarkable collection of those Cambodian MSS; in fact, quite unique. I do not think the British Museum have anything like it, and now we have those other rare Chinese MSS equal to the British Museum. I would like to know how the British Museum are off for Batik MSS'.[31] In another letter, Beatty wrote: 'Apparently there are no makimonos in the Fitzwilliam Museum or any of the Cambridge Libraries, as far as I understand, and none at Oxford, either in the Museum or the Bodleian, so it looks to me as if the only collection of importance is in the British Museum'.[32] Beatty wished to rival not only public collections but private ones also. He had a particular wish to surpass Robert Garrett, his 'old classmate' of the 'Class of '97', who had bought Islamic manuscripts from Beatty's dealer, A.S. Yahuda, and had presented them to Princeton University.[33]

By 1952 Beatty felt that his collection was almost complete. He wrote contentedly that it was 'very satisfactory that we have taken the cream of the rare texts from the East'.[34] He established a policy of filling in the gaps in the collection and instructed Wilkinson to buy Jesuit Relations (rare books written by Jesuit missionaries to the East), Japanese prints, Icons, woodcut and copper engravings by Albrecht Durer, Siamese and Nepalese manuscripts, Tibetan bindings, Burmese manuscripts (only those with miniatures because he already had a good many Sutras), and Batak bark books from Sumatra. He also wished to build up an excellent reference library of books about all aspects of oriental art. The Jesuit Relations were purchased because they were 'decidedly cheap', about £25 each in 1955,[35] and because they were 'very important in a Catholic country like Ireland'.[36] In another sign of deference to his host country, Beatty purchased fine Irish bindings because the Irish visitors to his library would be interested in them.[37]

Prior to launching his policy of 'filling the gaps', Beatty asked Wilkinson to commission a series of assessments of the world's great oriental collections to find out where precisely the Chester Beatty Library ranked among them. He had been pleased with an assessment in a Victoria and Albert Museum catalogue of 1952 which described the Chester Beatty collection as 'the largest and most important private collection in the world'.[38] Wilkinson set to his task quickly and by April 1953 had completed it.[39] The detailed reports written by distinguished experts provided Beatty with the ideal basis on which to conduct his final assault on the art market. In addition, he had the support of loyal friends because, when he moved to Dublin, his librarian was not the only person to move with him. His publisher Wilfred Merton, his book binder Miss Ida Dyson, and his banker James Hosking also settled in the Irish capital.

Throughout the 1950s, Beatty brought many experts to Dublin at his own expense to study his collections and to write books about them.[40] He offered his guests paid transport to Ireland for all their family, one week's hotel accommodation in Dublin, at the Shelbourne Hotel or the Royal Marine Hotel, Dunlaoghaire, and another week's expenses to travel around Ireland on holidays. In return Beatty received the best advice available from an enthusiastic and

Two Bullfinches on the Branch of a Cherry Tree (1805). From a Japanese Woodblock Printed Book **Shashin Kacho Zue** Illustrated by Kitao Shigemasa *Courtesy of the Trustees of the Chester Beatty Library, Dublin*

grateful group of scholars. He depended on his experts to give him evaluations about how his subsidiary collections were progressing. For example, Dr. P. Voorhoeve of Leiden University established Beatty's batak bark book collection. Dr. Voorhoeve was enthused by the speed at which he was able to build the collection. By 1958, it comprised of forty bark manuscripts, one paper scroll and four bamboos.[41] Dr. Voorhoeve advised: 'I think we are running neck and neck with the British Museum, we have passed the John Rylands (in Manchester) and apparently we have passed all the collections in America. Of course, we can never equal the Dutch collections, but one would not expect that'.[42]

Stuart Simmonds of the School of Oriental and African Studies in London came to Dublin each year from 1960 to 1962 while preparing a catalogue of Pali manuscripts (Pali was an old Indian dialect of the Buddhists which had been spoken by the Buddha himself). In July 1963, Simmonds reported the progress he had made in purchasing Pali manuscripts for Beatty: 'I have now established pretty certainly that Sir Chester's collection of these mss. is far and away the largest outside Bangkok'.[43]

The most spectacular addition to the Chester Beatty Library during the 1950s was the creation of the Japanese print collection and especially of a superb selection of the presentation prints known as *surimono*. Beatty already possessed a large number of quality Japanese books and scrolls but he required prints to complete his Japanese collection. The first step in his acquisition strategy was to contract an expert to purchase the material. Beatty showed great prudence when he chose Jack Hillier in 1954, the same year this renowned Japanese print expert joined the staff of Sotheby's. The next decision which Beatty made was to buy one big print collection on which he could found his own collection. Early in 1954, Wilfred Merton alerted Beatty that the famous Cooper collection had come on the London market. Wilkinson advised that the collection had an entrancing effect and Hillier also recommended it as of high quality. In May 1954, Beatty bought the Cooper collection from Messrs. Kegan Paul for £4,250. It offered a total of 450 prints and these were sifted gradually into the categories 'A', 'B' and 'C'. All the 'C' items were sold (there were not many), only a few 'B's were retained and the 'A's were divided into 'A+', 'A' and 'A-'.[44]

In 1955 Beatty was asked if he would allow his Japanese prints to be exhibited during the annual cultural festival called *An Tóstal*. Beatty was delighted and offered the collection on loan to an exhibition held at the Regent House, Trinity College, Dublin. The exhibition was opened by President Seán T. O'Kelly on 10 May 1955. There were 132 prints by 26 artists and Beatty paid all the exhibition expenses. The catalogue was prepared by Wilkinson and it included an introduction by James White.[45] The attendance numbered about 2,500 visitors for the three weeks of the exhibition and Beatty was pleased that, for many Dubliners, he had offered them their first chance to view fine Japanese prints of all types - black and white, coloured, tall pillar prints and *surimono*.

Between June 1954 and February 1956, Beatty added over eighty prints to his collection. But he would not allow Hillier to spend more than £125 on any single print. In both Hillier and Wilkinson's opinion, this price limit prevented Beatty from making a great instead of a very good collection. But Beatty simply had a mental block about the idea of paying more than £125 for a Japanese print. He felt that the Americans were pushing up the prices beyond reason and he could not bring himself to give chase. Wilkinson tried to persuade him by suggesting that 'one real prize is worth twenty good ones'[46] but it was to no avail. Most of Beatty's prints were acquired from two Parisian dealers, Madame Hugette Beres and Mademoiselle Densmore. By 1960, Beatty reckoned he had spent £3,600 on his Japanese print collection and Hillier told him that it was already worth between £15,000 and £20,000.[47] Beatty was especially pleased with his *surimono* and this part of the collection is now regarded as the best in Europe.

The collections brought together by Sir Alfred Chester Beatty are the result of an extraordinary collecting career of over seventy years. His collecting technique required a high level of organisation, considerable wealth, formidable enthusiasm and total dedication. On his ninetieth birthday, 7 February 1965, Beatty announced that he had ceased collecting. He had won an assurance from the Taoiseach, Seán Lemass, that the Irish Government would secure the future of his library which he had pledged to offer to the Irish State in his last will and testament. After Sir Chester Beatty's death in 1968, the management of the Chester Beatty Library became the onerous responsibility of its Director and a Board of Trustees. The contents of the Library are a national asset of huge importance and they deserve the generous support of the Irish Government. It is rare that a country is offered a gift as magnificent as the Chester Beatty Library and there is a national obligation to make the best possible use of it. It is a sincere hope that the Library will live and grow as the legacy of a great friend and patron of Ireland.

Notes

The author wishes to thank the Board of Trustees of the Chester Beatty Library (C.B.L.) for permission to quote from the correspondence of Sir Alfred Chester Beatty.

1. Frank Herrmann, *The English as Collectors*, London, 1972, p. 22.

2. Arthur J. Wilson, *The Life and Times of Sir Alfred Chester Beatty*, London, 1985, offers an entertaining popular biography of Beatty's career as a mining magnate.

3. C.B.L., Beatty's unpublished memoirs, p.1.

4. For a detailed account of Beatty's years in Ireland, see Brian P. Kennedy, *Alfred Chester Beatty and Ireland 1950-68: A Study in Cultural Politics*, Dublin, 1988.

5. *Irish Tatler and Sketch*, May 1956.

6. See Brian P. Kennedy, 'Alfred Chester Beatty and the National Gallery of Ireland', *Irish Arts Review*, Vol. 4, No. 1, Spring 1987, pp.41-54

7. The following are useful books on art collecting and collectors: S.N. Behrman, *Duveen*, London, 1952; Pierre Cabanne, *The Great Collectors*, London, 1964; W.G. Constable, *Art Collecting in the U.S.A.: An Outline of History*, London, 1964; Douglas Cooper (Ed.) *Great Private Collections*, London, 1964; Frank Herrmann, *Sotheby's: Portrait of an Auction House*, London, 1980; Ralph Hewins, *Mr. Five Per Cent: The Biography of Calouste Gulbenkian*, London, 1957; H.P. Kraus, *A Rare Book Saga*, London, 1979; Richard Marks, *Burrell: Portrait of a Collector*, Glasgow, 1983; Aline Saarinen, *The Proud Possessors*, New York, 1958; Francis Henry Taylor, *Pierpont Morgan*, New York, 1957; Alan G. Thomas, *Great Books and Book Collectors*, London, 1975.

8. C.B.L., Beatty to Wilkinson, 26 Mar. 1955.

9. Ibid., 22 Oct. 1953.

10. Ibid., 21 Apr. 1947.

11. Ibid., 20 Nov. 1953.

12. Ibid., 10 Nov. 1953.

13. Ibid., (see also William Watson, *Chinese Jade Books in the Chester Beatty Library*, Dublin, 1963).

14. Ibid.

15. C.B.L., Beatty to E. McGilligan, 10 Jan. 1958.

16. C.B.L., 25. Feb. 1948.

17. C.B.L., 8 Feb. 1955

18. C.B.L., 5 May 1956.

19. C.B.L., Beatty to Wilkinson, 22 Oct. 1953.

20. Author's interview with Jack Hiller, 25 May 1984

21. C.B.L., Beatty to Robert Steedman, 16 Apr. 1942.

22. See Richard Marks, *Burrell: Portrait of a Collector*, Glasgow, 1983.

23. Frank Herrmann, *Sotheby's: Portrait of an Auction House*, London, 1980, p. 190.

24. C.B.L., 10 Feb. 1930.

25. C.B.L., 9 Dec. 1953.

26. C.B.L., 5 Dec. 1952. Details of Beatty's joint purchases are recorded in the archives of the British Museum (Standing Committee Minute Books, 1923-63, and Board of Trustee Minute Books, 1963-8) and of the Victoria and Albert Museum (Chester Beatty files, 1923-58).

27. C.B.L., 16 Dec. 1961.

28. C.B.L., Beatty to Wilfred Merton, 21 Apr. 1936

29. C.B.L, 10 Nov. 1953.

30. Ibid.

31. C.B.L., 2 Nov. 1951.

32. C.B.L., Beatty to Wilkinson, 14 Jan. 1954.

33. Ibid., 15 May, 1951.

34. Ibid., 5 Mar. 1952.

35. C.B.L., Joan O'Neill to Mme. Costantina dalla Fusine, 16 Dec. 1955.

36. C.B.L., Beatty to Merton, 20 Nov. 1953.

37. C.B.L., Beatty to Wilkinson, 18 Feb. 1955.

38. Ibid., 10 Jan. 1952.

39. The scholars who assisted Beatty and Wilkinson in preparing the survey of the world's great oriental collections were: Basil Gray, Jacob Leveen, Sirarpie der Nersessian, David S. Rice and Basil Robinson.

40. Among the scholars who came to Dublin at Beatty's invitation were: Arthur Arberry, Bill Archer, J.D.A. Barnicott, Signor Cerulli, I.E.S. Edwards, Richard Ettinghausen, Basil Gray, Jack Hillier, Dom Louis Leloir, H.C. Lowe, Henry McAleavy, Sirarpie der Nersessian, Berthe van Regemorter, David S. Rice, David Talbot Rice, Basil Robinson, A.F. Shore, Stuart Simmonds, T.C. Skeat, Robert Skelton, R. Soame Jenyns, P. Voorhoeve, William Watson and S. Cary Welch.

41. C.B.L., C. Cruess Callaghan to Beatty, 7 Nov. 1958.

42. C.B.L., P. Voorhoeve to C. Cruess Callaghan, 25 Nov. 1958.

43. C.B.L., S. Simmonds to R. J. Hayes, 10 July 1963.

44. The major sales of Beatty's surplus Japanese prints took place on 18 Feb. 1957 (Sotheby's, 'Property of a Gentleman') and on 12 Feb. 1963 (Sotheby's, discarded prints from the Cooper collection).

45. J.V.S. Wilkinson, *Japanese Prints from the collection of Sir Alfred Chester Beatty*, Dublin, 1955. James White has been a Trustee of the Chester Beatty Library since 1980.

46. C.B.L., 29 Mar. 1956.

47. C.B.L., Beatty to E. McGilligan, 16 Apr. 1960. The reason that the figure of £3,600 cited by Beatty is less than the £4,250 paid originally for the Cooper collection is because allowance has been made for the considerable prices achieved from the sales of duplicate and other unwanted prints.

Seán O'Sullivan
(1906-1964)
**Fr. Senan Moynihan
O.F.M. Cap.**
Private Collection

FATHER SENAN O.F.M., CAP.: THE CORPULENT CAPUCHIN OF CAPEL STREET

Benedict Kiely

Whether we mean it in joy or in sorrow, in peace or in wrath, in kindliness or in utter viciousness, a lot of us have a habit of saying now and again, out aloud so as to be heard or to our own secret souls: Sgriobhfaidh mé leabhar orra: I'll write a book about them.

Now: as a man who was a staff journalist for twenty five years of suffering and a freelance for as long again, I have a way of saying to myself; Editors I have known, I'll write a book about them.

It could be a long book for I have known a lot of them. But it would by no means be a nasty book for although editors may have their little human weaknesses, they are not, by no means, among the worst of mankind.

To begin with: I cherish with affection the memory of the editor who sent me off on many a pleasant journey. The first of those journeys was made as far back as 1940; just a little before my twenty-first birthday. I had been absent from my home-place for three years and the second half of those three had been spent in an orthopaedic hospital, Cappagh, close to Finglas, which was then a village on what were then the northern outskirts of Dublin city. On my way back home through Dublin I called into this editor's office. I had already written something for him. He had paid me well and written me kindly letters. I was anxious to meet him. I was also naturally hoping that he would ask me to write something else for him: and to my great delight and over a cup of tea, he said; "what would you like to write now".

Like a child in catechism class I had the answer all ready to reel off, whether I knew what it meant or not. So I said, with all the charming modesty of the young: "oh, something like Hilaire Belloc's, *The Four Men.* You know: that book he wrote about Sussex. The sort of book that any man would like to write about the County he came from. The sort of book that you would like to write about the Kingdom of Kerry".

That last sentence was, for me, a clever touch. For that particular editor was a corpulent Kerryman with a beard.

"Done", he said. "Write me, not a book now, but five thousand words about your native Tyrone. Set about it how you please. And God go with you. And

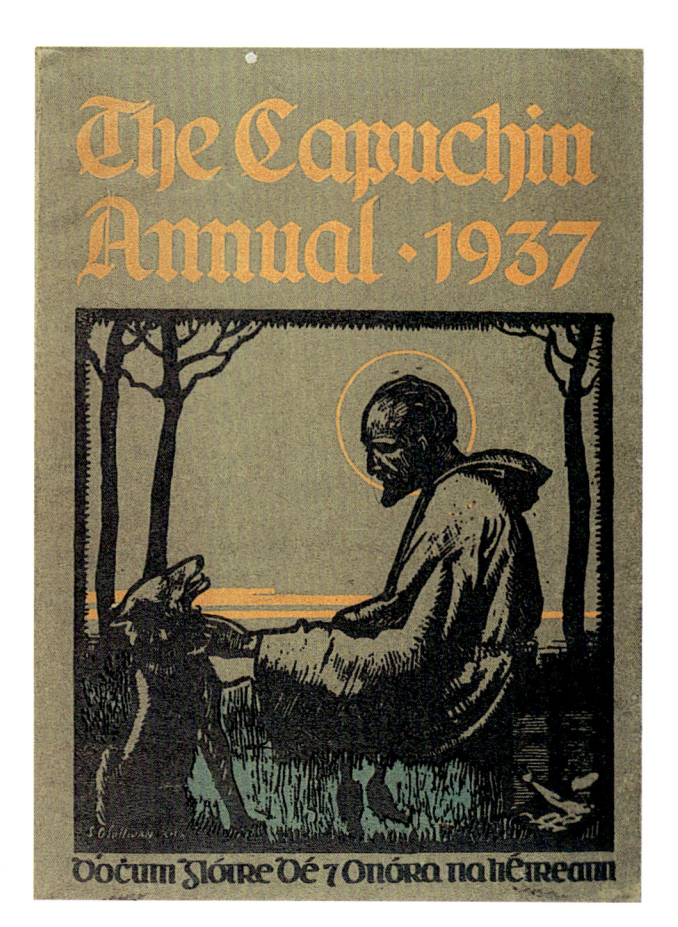

**The Capuchin Annual
1937**
*Cover Designed by Seán
O Sullivan R.H.A.*

mind your health. And if you fall into enemy hands up there, give them nothing but your name, rank and serial number".

This was the way I set about writing that article. It was to cycle, and I was again back in cycling form, from Maghery where the Ulster Blackwater, sleek, deep and full, flows into Lough Neagh, from Maghery, I repeat, all the way across O'Neill's Tyrone to my native town of Omagh. No main road did I follow: but zigzagged this way and that, and called in on old friends, and drank tea and ate soda-bread in meadows where people were making the hay. No hurry in the world was I in and I had all the time in the world, and the time of my life.

John Hewitt, the poet, whose friendship I was later privileged to have, wrote about his own part of County Armagh, on the southern shore of Lough Neagh, in that same fatal year of 1940: "Once walking in the country of my kindred, up the steep hill to where the towertopped mound still hides their bones, that showery August day, I walked right out of Europe into peace..."

Well, I cycled mostly and walked a bit and sat around a lot, and it was a lovely way to come home, and I owe the joy of that journey, and the memory that still stays with me, to a stout bearded Kerryman who wore the habit of a Capuchin friar.

Other journeys were to follow. Around Sligo and Leitrim. Once and all the way and around the rim of the Nine Counties of Ulster. Then to Killarney and the mountains of Sliabh Luachra to write a long study of Aodhaghan O Rahille, the poet. And to Derrynane House to honour the Liberator and see the place transformed into a museum. And to the ruins of Dunboy on Bantry Bay. And all along the route that the great Donal Cam O Suilleabháin followed on his fearful wintry march, in the Elizabethan wars, to O'Rourke's place in Leitrim.

In memory I covered all that ground again when, faraway in Pregow, I heard of his death and he faraway in Australia. He had written to me not long before the end. He had made a long journey from Kerry to find his last resting place.

So I wrote: Father Senan Moynihan died in Australia and when a legend dies so faraway from its origin and growth, there is a danger that it may be oer-readily forgotten. In the case of Senan, that would be a great pity. It was odd, I remember, to notice how few of the people who should have been there were at the funeral of the poet, Padraic Colum. The weather of that day, I will admit was one of the worst that ever blew or poured on the side of the Hill of Howth, where the poet was buried. But Padraic had lived to such a fine old age that a lot of people thought he was already dead: and he had lived most of his years elsewhere than in Ireland. The legend was lost.

Senan was a corpulent humorous man and, like the most corpulent of all humorous men, or the most humorous of all corpulent men, he was not only humorous in himself but the cause of humour in others. So it is only fitting that my memorial to him should begin with a funny story about him. Seán O'Sullivan, the painter, used to refer to him, and to his face and in the most pleasant manner, as Friar Tuck. His very name and something of his warm affability are immortalised in Maurice Walsh's novel, "Blackcock's Feather". But it was Seán O'Sullivan who twisted a nursery rhyme in his honour. For one of Senan's undeniable gifts was that of making distinguished and influential friends, among them, Eleanor Lady Yarrow. And once, when Senan was ill, she brought to visit him, Lord Dawson of Penn, physician to the King of England:

> "All the King's doctors,
> And Dawson of Penn,
> Came over to put Senan
> Together again".

As I think I have said: my own first meeting with Senan was in late 1939. *The Capuchin Annual*, which he edited and created, I had first encountered at the end of 1936 when it was in its eighth year of publication. That would be the issue dated for 1937, a book of about 330 pages and not the mammoth of five hundred pages that the *Annual* was later to become, and selling in 1937 for a modest thirty old pence. Today it seems simply unbelievable that so much should have been given away for so little, for next to nothing. I was seventeen years of age at the time and I feel I had only the vaguest idea about the remarkable nature of the publication, from several points of view. Now I look at it with something like awe.

It had retained, and was always to do so, some of the marks of the religious and missionary magazine. After all, it did go out to the world under the banner of a religious and missionary order. So: a Capuchin, Father Fintan, had an article eight pages long, including illustrations, on missionary life; eight pages out of three hundred and thirty. Thereafter the publication took off in a way in which few periodical publications produced by a religious order had ever done before, in Ireland or, insofar as I know, any where else.

It is interesting to remember that in 1936-37 you could purchase, among other things, and for half-a-crown, or thirty old pence, nineteen reproductions, eight of them in colour and all of them frameable, of works by Seán O'Sullivan. They are all here in this *Annual*. The frontispiece, indeed, was the painter's imagination of Matt Talbot, the saintly working man of Dublin on his bended knees. But the long essay that went with it, "One Man's Years", by the novelist Francis MacManus, was a most unusual piece of hagiography cum social and literary history.

Roibeard O Farachain's first collection of his poetry had, I was later to find out, made its first, (partial, I think), appearance in the issue of the previous year. That 1937 *Annual* carried his poem on the death of G.K. Chesterton: facing that striking photograph of Chesterton reading a book on a bench on the Brighton seafront. And O'Faracháin also contributed a Thomistic essay, "God and Man and Making", on which various people from Eric Gill to Leonard Feeney, SJ. commented. Some gathering! Thomism was the done thing at the time. Yet that essay in aesthetics, like many another feature in the *Annual* might very well stand up to reprinting.

Then D.L. Kelleher who wrote whimisical glamour books about Ireland and Irish tourism, had a set of seventeen simple poems. Michael McLaverty was chief among the contributors of short stories. Gabriel Fallon wrote about the Abbey Theatre. Who knew it better? Seamus MacManus wrote about that golden and eternal old road to Frosses and to the grave of the poetess, Ethna Carbery.

Then there was a photograph of John McCormack in the full regimentals of a Papal Count, and a gratulatory letter about the *Annual* to Senan from the singer at Moore Abbey on the banks of the Barrow. The *Annual* for 1946-47 was to carry a copious feature, text and photos, on McCormack: one of the features that I specifically mean when I speak of reprinting separately as books.

That photo of and letter from the great singer were only details in that 1937 Annual. But I mention them because they remind me that when I came to live permanently in Dublin, and got into the habit of calling into see Senan, I went in one day to that office in Capel Street to find him with Maud Gonne MacBride, John McCormack, Jack Butler Yeats, Thomas MacGreevy and Michael O'Higgins. Who all seemed to have dropped in casually at about the same time. A scene well-set and goodly company. Molly Baxter, Senan's secretary made the tea: a pleasant stout, quiet, slow-moving lady who was possibly, one of the great secretaries of all time, not excluding Machiavelli.

That room in that office at Number Two, Capel Street, on the banks of the Liffey, was an extraordinary place. The office of Capuchin Periodicals then filled the four-storey house except for the ground floor which was occupied by a draper's shop under the reputable name of Lemass. The room where Senan and his socius or right-hand-man, Father Gerald, (frail and saintly and good humoured, and a McGann from Belfast), sat, was up at the top, a combination of office and art gallery, with Jack Yeats and Seán Keating and others on the walls. Those most valuable paintings were, after the passing of Senan, to find other homes.

The office was also, off and on, known as the Pope's Boudoir. Because the famous Eoin, Pope O'Mahony, rushing hither and yon on one of his many missions of mercy would sometimes rest for the night in that room on a splendid oaken settle, watched over, as by attendent angels, by the best of contemporary Irish art. The caretaker of the office was a lovely old lady called Annie. For a lot of her life she had worked for a certain Dublin firm that dealt in stationery, mostly envelopes, and she had been paid a lavish ten bob a week. One morning, after something like thirty years faithful service, she was late for work and was fined six pence. When Senan heard that story he offered her the post of Chatelaine in Capel Street. Then on one occasion Eoin O'Mahony, who was down there in Cork from where, like many another of the name, he originated, had to journey in a hurry to Dubin and needed accommodation for a night, and sent this telegram:

> "Annie, c/o The Capuchin Fathers, 2 Capel Street: Arriving tonight, stop, leave bedroom door open, stop, Pope".

Senan had that telegram framed and hung on the wall.

From the comings and goings in that wonderful office it seems logical to proceed to talk of Senan's luncheons and, now and then, dinners, almost invariably in the Clarence or the Gresham hotels. Some long-nosed, longfaced Malvolios, who were never invited to be there, used to cast eyes up and groan a bit that a member of a Mendicant Religious Order should have an account in class hotels. But apart from the spreading of bonhomie, which should surely be a Franciscan activity, Senan's occasions almost always had, to my memory, some pretty shrewd business purpose connected with the welfare and progress of Capuchin Periodicals: the *Annual*, the quarterly *Bonaventura*, and the monthly, the *Father Matthew Record*.

The guests covered what you might call a wide field: from Paddy the Cope to Frank Sheed, from Peter F. Anson to Seamus MacManus, from Delia Murphy and her songs to Father Terence Connolly, a Jesuit, of Boston, who did a lot of good work on Francis Thompson but who misfortunately, got up once in the Abbey Theatre to put some theological posers about Mr. Yeats', "Purgatory". A lot of people assumed that he was a clerical obscurantist and trouble-maker when he was only an earnest, and typical, American student. In his honour and for his benefit I once heard Thomas MacGreevy sing the entire opus of, "The Star-Spangled Banner", and in prime voice, too.

But all this was peripheral to Senan as an encourager of the arts, which indeed he was. He had his weaknesses and his prejudices. To begin with, he was a Kerryman, and Kerrymen have their impulsive and dictatorial twitches. He was very close to Jack B. Yeats and second to none in admiration of his work. But he had a blind spot where The Brother was concerned. As he had also for that most notable of all the editors I have known: R.M.Smyllie. And Senan seemed to regard the Irish Academy of Letters, founded by W.B. Yeats and Bernard Shaw and now as good as or as bad as, extinct, as a sort of subversive organisation which, as a former president, I can assure anybody, it never was. Senan's political vision allowed for only one sun and there were jokes about the number of times that Eamon de Valera's picture appeared in the *Annual*. But Senan did encourage painters, sculptors, musicians and writers with, I think, his judgement, at its best when he was looking at pictures.

He paid well. Omnibus paribus, as they seldom are, he had generous ideas on advances and retainers. Often, looking at him or just meditating on the unusual sort of man he was, I wondered how, (although I knew the externals of the story), he had ever found his way into a religious order. For it seemed to me that he would have belonged better as features editor on some big New York magazine. But time and place mark all men. Another joke about him was that if he had not become a Capuchin he might, like his Kerry compatriot and friend, Denis Guiney, have ended up managing Clery's vast department store.

His periodicals included for a while, *The Irish Bookman*, under the editorship of J.J. Campbell. It had a short life but a good one. Since the editor was a Belfastman, and a notable one, it was the Dublin periodical that gave the best display to Ulster writers, the only one, perhaps, that at that time tried to balance the two cities not against but with each other. It was beginning to create between Belfast and Dublin the sort of intellectual community that could have been valuable. But like many a good idea, including civilisation, it didn't last long enough.

Then there was, or was to have been, *The Irish Music-Lover*, with Michael O'Higgins, the great singer, to vet the matter on music and myself, the dogsbody, standing by to do the journalism. It never got off the ground nor into the heavenly and harmonious air, because, by that time, the end was near, and rising costs were beginning to batter at the market of the upper-class magazine. And not only in Ireland.

His days, and the company he gathered around him, I remember with great affection. Father Gerald who did those marvellous black-and-white drawings of Franciscan life, or the humorous aspects thereof. Richard King, the artist in stained glass. Sam Mulloy and his camera. Mairín Allen and James White and Thomas MacGreevy who were so well worth listening to when they talked about pictures. Larry Egan, the circulation manager, Seamus (J.J.) Campbell, David Kennedy, Seán Feehan, Joe Tomelty, Francis MacManus, Robert Farren, Jimmy Montgomery, Joe O'Connor of Fossa. And a dozen or more, others. There were quarrels off and on. He was human. So were they.

But always my memory goes back to that moment and that meeting at that time of life (for me) when a young man has nowhere in particular to go and thinks his experience is unique. There I was, in a state as near to gloom as I have ever allowed myself to be: and muttering about Hilaire Belloc walking in the Valley of the Arun and about how fine it would be to write in that way about well-known, well-loved places. And that stout Franciscan said: "Take this as an advance. To help you on the road. And go home, and throw a bag over your bike, and cycle across Tyrone, and bring me back what you get."

Which, as I said, I did. And wrote something called "Long After O'Neill". Copying a title from Michael J. Murphy who had written in, *The Bell*, a fine piece called, "Long After Carleton".

That was a happy journey. And God and Senan, who sits now at his right hand, know when again it may be possible to make such a journey. Even if a hero by the name of Colm Toibín did surpass Cuchullain by marching all along The Baleful Border, and writing a whole book about his journey.

JAMES WHITE

Louis le Brocquy

I am one of those people who can remember the cool rather foggy climate in which the visual arts were immersed in Dublin fifty years ago. In those dark days contemporary art, the art of our time, was scarcely recognised much less understood. Victor Waddington did his remarkable best, as did a number of others, but progress was slow, visibility poor.

Peering through our provincial mist, it was difficult at that time to see what if any vital art lay hidden behind and beyond the settled hulk of academic values. Mainie Jellett and Evie Hone, dual beacons on the same headland, could not be wholly ignored. In a clearing in the general fog a minimal interest was shown in Jack Yeats, whose great nostalgic works were at least *widely* misunderstood. Here and there a modernist torch was raised - and a few blowlamps - but generally our prospects were as obscure as those of the art we professed.

For the people of Ireland forty or fifty years ago art held no great interest. The story was still told of Michael Collins on the run, a literary gathering (*AE At Home*) and George Russell's offer of a night's shelter. Collins' grateful refusal, but could Mr. Russell perhaps suggest somewhere equally safe? "Well, there's always the National Gallery".

That was the climate, the indifferent state of affairs into which, with considerable courage and personal initiative, James White emerged as art critic among us. Certainly there were other enlightened critics at the time; Arthur Power, Edward Sheehy, David Sears, Stephen Rynne, but no one as I remember brought us quite the same indefinable combination of open-minded insight and human concern as did James White.

Although his extraordinary qualities shone from the first, I believe it was from the moment when James, with his marvellous and lovely Aggie, moved into the top flat in Charlemont House in 1960 that his dual devotion to painting and people became truly operative in effecting a gentle revolution, a tenacious assault on public and political indifference towards creative art and our cultural institutions. Almost at once the Municipal Gallery was transformed by its new Curator from the empty mausoleum I remembered into a comparative hive of human activity. The story is well known. Lectures, assemblies, discussions and exhibitions were regularly organised and for the first time Dubliners generally became involved in art, familiar with their own remaining collection.

Edward McGuire
(1932-86)
James White (1981)
NGI. Cat. No. 4348

The story moves on to Merrion Square and with it a perceptive and generously public-minded Director. I believe many would agree that it was during the years 1964-80 that the National Gallery, in step with our time, entered the life of the Nation. It is certain that the Nation entered the National Gallery, brimming over its reconstructed galleries, filling its sympathetic restaurant and bringing at last to this great collection the intellectual and social habit of its varied life. An irrevocable change had occurred. Michael Collins' hypothetic hide-out was no more.

Today, nearing the end of the century, all is indeed changed. Art is widely regarded, desired, valued, supported commercially, equated with football or tennis in its new power to attract popular interest and good will. Public galleries are crowded and will be more so as vigorous new museum directors devise further social and pedagogic links with their public. But let us not forget in our new climate of popularity the still bleak scene of merely thirty years ago nor, through his rare enthusiasm and sustained effort, the transformation effected by James White - effected with a tact and sensibility that regarded an opponent as a friend to be persuaded.

And so it is on a bloodless victory, epitomised you could say by this one man, that museum art in Ireland can today look to a public response undreamed of in the past. What will remain largely unknown to that public, however, is the personal concern and unfailing help which we artists over the long years have learned to count upon from my old friend.

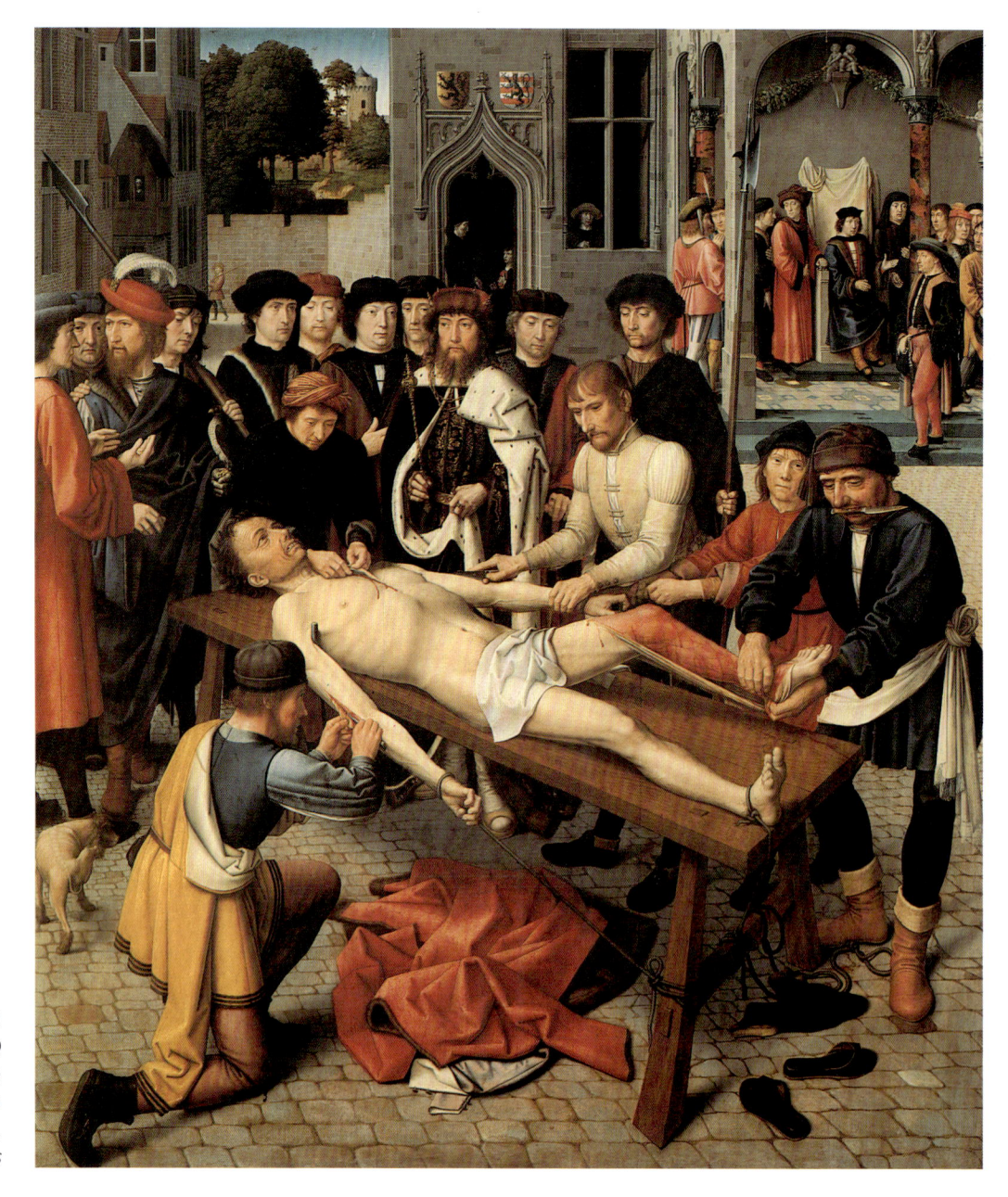

Gerard David
(c. 1450-1523)
Le Jugement de Cambyses
Groeningemuseum, Bruges

COMING EVENTS
John Montague

In the Stadsmuzeum at Bruges, there is a picture by Gerard David of a man being flayed. Four craftsmen are concerned with the figure on the table: one is opening the leftarm, another lifting away the right nipple, a third incising the right arm while the last (his knife caught between his teeth) is unwinding the results of his labour so as to display the rich network of veins under the skin of the left leg. The only expression in the faces of those looking on is a mild admiration: the Burgmeister has caught up the white folds of his ermine gown and is gazing into the middle distance. It is difficult even to say that there is any expression on the face of the victim, although his teeth are gritted and the cords attaching his wrists to the legs of the table are stretched tight. The whole scene may be intended as an allegory of human suffering but what the line of perspective leads us to admire is the brown calfskin of the principal executioner's boots.

John Butler Yeats
(1839-1922)
John Quinn (1908)
*(1870-1924)
The National Portrait
Gallery, Smithsonian
Institution, Washington
D.C.*

NATHANIEL HONE AND JOHN QUINN : A CORRESPONDENCE

Homan Potterton

At the time I worked in the National Gallery of Ireland between 1971 and 1973, one of the myriad activities which the Director, James White, was engaged in was the preparation of the John Butler Yeats exhibition which was held at the Gallery in 1972. James wrote the catalogue[1] and the Exhibition - held fifty years after the painter's death - was the first 'one-man show' of the artist's work. Since Yeats is arguably the greatest portrait painter Ireland has ever produced, the tribute was long overdue. It was neither the first nor the last time that James White would devote his energies to a neglected aspect of Irish art.

It was through James's Catalogue that I first heard of the American lawyer and art collector who was John Butler Yeats's principal patron and benefactor, John Quinn. Now some twenty years later and living, by coincidence, just a stone's throw from where Quinn once lived on Central Park West at 70th Street in Manhattan, it seemed an idea for me to rummage through Quinn's voluminous correspondence (housed in New York Public Library) and search for a topic which would interest James in his retirement.[2] Like John Quinn, James White has always been kind and encouraging to unknowns - just as he was to me all those years ago - and this record of Quinn's patronage of the Irish landscape painter Nathaniel Hone (whom Quinn regarded as unknown) is dedicated to James with the warmest affection and gratitude.

John Quinn (1870 - 1924),[3] who has been credited with having assembled 'the most important modern art collection in the United States before the Depression'[4] was a remarkable figure. The son of Irish immigrants - his father had a bakery in Ohio where John was born - he obtained a law degree by attending night classes at Washington's Georgetown University. After completing graduate studies in international law at Harvard, he moved to New York at the age of 25 where he soon established a reputation as a brilliant financial lawyer and set up his own law firm in 1906.

Quinn had inherited a deep love of Ireland from his parents and even before his first visit 'home' in 1902, he had engrossed himself in Irish nationalism and literature. He formed an Irish Literary Society in New York in 1902 and arranged an American lecture tour for Douglas Hyde in 1905. He sponsored the Abbey Theatre's American tour in 1911 - 12 and when the authorities in Boston and Philadelphia attempted to close down their production of 'The Playboy', he

Walter Osborne
(1859-1903)
Nathaniel Hone (1896)
(1831-1917)
NGI. Cat. No. 987

defended them in court and waived his fee. He brought John Butler Yeats to America as his guest in 1907, and when Yeats remained in New York for the rest of his life, that was also mainly as Quinn's guest.[5]

Quinn remained loyal to the cause of Irish culture throughout his life although after his initial enthusiasm he subsequently tired of the many demands made upon him by the Irish. In 1909 he wrote: 'I am sick of the Irish. They are suspicious, vindictive, uncertain in temper, ungrateful, lying ... The best Irishmen are in this country. Those in Ireland are so convinced of their own superiority that they are not aware that they border on the verge of professional mendicancy ...'.[6]

Quinn's earliest collecting activities were as a bibliophile with a particular focus on manuscripts and first edition works of W.B. Yeats, Synge, Lady Gregory, Douglas Hyde and other writers of the Irish literary revival. In 1909, however, he decided that his book collection was complete and that he would concentrate on art. He wrote: 'I am going to stop putting hundreds and in fact some thousands a year into books. In fact I have got my collections about complete and I am not going into new lines of book collecting. I am going in for some good art, however. After all a picture is a more living thing than a book. It represents life, or a moment of life and the older we get the more interest we ought to show in life and the less in a printed transcript of it'.[7]

The first pictures which Quinn bought were Irish. Beginning in 1902 he bought works by Yeats, father and son, and by AE. Then came his interest in Nathaniel Hone whom he described as 'the greatest landscape painter Ireland has ever had, and one of the great landscape painters of the world'.[8] But in time Quinn moved on from Irish art: he took up Augustus John (who painted his portrait), Gwen John and, beginning in about 1910, modern French art. Between that time and his death just thirteen years later, he amassed 'an unparalleled collection of modern art'.[9] This consisted of over two thousand objects including more than fifty works by Picasso and as many by Matisse, Derain and Rouault as well as important paintings by Cézanne, Van Gogh, Gauguin and Seurat. In 1913 he was the prime force behind the celebrated 'Armory Show' in New York - the art exhibition which introduced 'Modern Art' into the United States.[10]

After his death Quinn intended that his Collection would be sold. He gave instructions to his executors to that effect[11] and, to the dismay of many people, after a Memorial Exhibition[12] of some of the works in New York in 1926, the Collection was disposed of by means of auctions in New York[13] and Paris[14] as well as through some private sales.

Quinn probably first heard of the painter Nathaniel Hone[15] in the same way that he first heard of John Butler Yeats. He read a review by T. W. Rolleston from 'The Dublin Express' of the Yeats-Hone exhibition which Sarah Purser organised in Dublin in October 1901 and wrote to 'J. B. Yeats' to enquire about the pictures in the exhibition.[16] When a reply came from Jack Yeats informing him that that there was not merely one J.B. Yeats, but two, there began an association, which in the words of John B.'s biographer, was to 'profoundly alter both men's lives, as well as Willie's and, to a lesser extent, Jack's'.[17] The following summer (1902) Quinn paid his first visit to Ireland where he met the Yeats family, Lady Gregory, Edward Martyn, George Moore, Douglas Hyde and others. On this occasion he also first made the acquaintance of George Russell (AE), 'spent some pleasant hours'[18] with him, and bought several of his paintings. Their friendship was to continue until Quinn's death: the two men corresponded regularly from 1903 until 1923[19] and Quinn's collection included more than sixty paintings and drawings by AE.

Quinn did not meet Hone on this first visit and, although he bought paintings by both Jack and J.B. Yeats and by AE, he did not acquire a Hone. It was on his second visit to Ireland, in August 1903, that he bought his first works by Hone: two small pictures 'painted out in the open and not re-touched or enlarged' (Cat. nos. 1 & 2 below).[20] It is not possible to establish where Quinn acquired these. Reid[21] says that George Russell brought Quinn out to see Hone on this visit and that 'he bought a landscape'; but this is not the case. In a letter to Quinn dated 1 October 1908 Russell wrote, 'I only met Hone once' and the landscape which Quinn acquired on a visit to Hone was 'Bundoran Rocks' (Cat. no. 3 below) which he bought when J.B. Yeats brought him out to Hone in October 1904.[22] As his first letter to Hone on 21st December 1908 implies, this visit was probably the first occasion that the two met.

The correspondence between the two men - Hone and Quinn - is warm and affectionate.[23] Hone (1831 - 1917), who at the time was in his seventies, was a venerable and venerated figure in the Dublin art world as AE's letters make clear. Quinn, who at this stage was little more than a novice as far as art was concerned, was to become one of the greatest avant-garde art collectors of the 20th century. Quinn, who by American standards was never a wealthy collector, reveals in his letters the very qualities - persistence, tact, charm, and flattery - which made him such a successful patron. By these means, in his later dealings with such artistic giants as Braque and Picasso, Derain, Brancusi and Rouault, did he assemble his great collection.

Learning that it was Mrs. Hone who did not care for the painter's pictures to be sold, he established a rapport with her, enquiring after her peaches and garden, and sending her a Hokusai. (In her response Mrs. Hone demonstrated that she too was capable of great tact!). When Quinn feared that Hone might not allow him any more pictures, he flattered him with the promise of an exhibition or a critique in New York. As with most collectors, it was the chase rather than the catch which was most satisfying to Quinn. After a lengthy correspondence and endless tribulations, Russell secured a further three pictures for him and despatched them in March 1911. When two months had passed and he had received no acknowledgment, he wrote to Quinn on 6 May mildly expressing his hurt: 'Did the pictures arrive alright? Did you like them? I dare say you will tell me what you think when you have time.'

After his visit to Ireland in the autumn of 1904 when he visited Hone at St. Doulough's, the painter's home in Raheny near Dublin, Quinn did not return to Dublin for another five years. Then, in August 1909, he again visited St. Doulough's and bought six more pictures.[24] On this trip the Yeats sisters gave a party for Quinn to which the Hones as well as Jack Yeats, Sarah Purser, AE, and Sir Walter Armstrong (the Director of the National Gallery) were bidden.[25] With the purchase of three further pictures in 1911 - selected by Russell (Cat. nos. 15, 16, & 17 below) - Quinn's Hone collection of seventeen works was complete. In that same year, 1911 - the year of Roger Fry's 'Post Impressionist Exhibition' at London's Grafton Galleries (about which Quinn made diligent inquiries)[26] - he paid his first visit to Paris and thereafter his collecting moved into quite a different realm.

Quinn always valued his pictures by Hone. He included the three which he then owned among the seventy-eight works of Irish art which he lent to the Irish Industrial Exhibition at Madison Square Gardens in September 1905[27] and, much more significantly, he lent two - 'Hastings' and 'Lough Swilly' (Cat. nos. 5 & 9 below) - to the Armory show in 1913 where they hung among the greatest masterpieces of early 20th century art. On his death and by the terms of his will, his sister, Julia Anderson, was permitted to take any of his paintings by AE and Hone which she wanted: the remainder, like the rest of his great collection, were to be sold at public auction.

In the end Quinn had a total of seventeen paintings by Hone. All of these were exhibited in the Memorial Exhibition of Quinn's Collection held in New York in 1926 and thirteen of them were sold in the Quinn sale a year later.

Notes

1. James White, 'John Butler Yeats and the Irish Renaissance' (National Gallery of Ireland, Dublin, 1972).

2. The correspondence is among the extensive John Quinn Memorial Collection in the Rare Books and Manuscripts Division of New York Public Library (Astor, Lenox and Tilden Foundations). All letters which are here quoted are in this collection and are published by kind permission of New York Public Library.

3. For John Quinn see B.L. Reid, 'The Man from New York: John Quinn and his Friends' (New York 1968); for Quinn's collection see J. Zilczer, '"The Noble Buyer": John Quinn, Patron of the Avant-Garde' (Hirshhorn Museum, Washington, 1978).

4. Zilczer, op.cit., p. 9.

5. For J.B. Yeats and Quinn see Reid, op.cit., Zilczer, op.cit. and W.M. Murphy, 'Prodigal Father: the Life of John Butler Yeats (1839 - 1922)' (Ithaca and London, 1978).

6. In letters to Townsend Walshe dated 20 July 1909 and 22 July 1909.

7. Letter to Townsend Walshe dated 3 September 1909.

8. Ibid.

9. Zilczer, op.cit., p. 9.

10. 'International Exhibition of Modern Art, Association of American Painters and Sculptors, Inc.' held at the 69th Regiment Armory, New York, 17 February - 15 March 1913. See M. Brown, 'The Story of the Armory Show' (New York, 1963).

11. Reid, op.cit., p. 641.

12. 'Memorial Exhibition of Representative Works Selected from the John Quinn Collection', Art Center, New York, 7 - 30 January 1926.

13. 'Paintings and Sculptures. The Renowned Collection of Modern and Ultra-Modern art formed by John Quinn including many examples purchased by him directly from the Artists', American Art Association, Inc., New York, 9 - 12 February 1927.

14. 'Catalogue des Tableaux Modernes provenant de la collection John Quinn', Hotel Drouot, Paris, 28 October 1926.

15. For an up-to-date account of Hone see Julian Campbell, 'Nathaniel Hone the Younger, 1831-1917' (National Gallery of Ireland, 1991).

16. Reid, op.cit., p. 8 and Murphy, op.cit., p. 234.

17. Murphy, op.cit., p. 236.

18. In his first letter to Russell, dated 9 March 1903, Quinn wrote: 'I hope you have not forgotten John Quinn who spent some pleasant hours with you in September last'.

19. Russell's letters to Quinn and Quinn's to Russell are among the Quinn Memorial Archive.

20. See JQ to AE, 20 December 1908, below.

21. Reid, op.cit., p. 16.

22. See JQ to NH, 21 December 1908, below.

23. There are eleven letters from Quinn to Hone and nine from Hone to Quinn among the Quinn Collection. The letters, as published here, have been edited to abbreviate them for the purpose of publication but nothing of substance is omitted.

24. Hone's receipt for these, dated 17 August 1909, is among the Quinn correspondance.

25. Murphy, op.cit., p. 348, quoting a letter from Ruth Pollexfen to J.B. Yeats dated 28 September 1909.

26. Zilczer, op.cit., p. 21.

27. Reid, op.cit., p. 39.

The Correspondence

16 September 1904 John Quinn (JQ) to George Russell (AE)

My trip to Ireland this Autumn is off. I am of course bitterly disappointed ... I wanted to bring back ... a couple of pictures that I partly engaged of Mr. Hone. When I was there last summer he had three or four not finished and I asked him to send me two of them when they were finished but he said to wait until next summer when I came over and then he would have them finished; so I hoped to be able to select two this summer.

10 September 1908 JQ to AE

I am sorry for many reasons I couldn't get abroad this summer ... I want to get at least three more of Mr. Hone's portraits (sic). Do you ever see him? What do you think of selecting two or three of his landscapes for me? Would you care to do it? I think I would care to rely upon your judgement rather than upon that of any man I know in Ireland. I know that you are a great admirer of his work ...

1 October 1908 AE to JQ

I will gladly do what you want with Mr. Hone, if you will write to him, but I was speaking to Lane, of our Municipal Gallery, and he told me it is very difficult for anybody now to get pictures out of him, that his fame has been steadily growing, Lane having boomed him over in London and exhibited a number of his pictures, so that the dealers are crowding about him, and he has refused on several occasions to part with pictures at all, though he has a large number in his possession. He is a wealthy man and he likes his own pictures and likes keeping them, but I hope that if you write to him he will be induced to part with them to you. I have a most tremendous admiration and believe that there is not a living landscape artist of greater power than Hone at his best, and Lane tells me that the English art critics have come to the same conclusion. Personally I like the earlier pictures with their classic beauty of design, better than the later and more elemental visions, but all are good.

... I only met Hone once, but he knows all about me, and many of my friends are friends of his ...

20 December 1908 JQ to AE

I am much obliged for your offer about Hone ... I wanted to ... get three or four more of his paintings. I have one called, I think, 'Bendoran Rocks' (sic) for which I paid him £30, which was the price at that time that he stated he asked for his pictures of that size. Then I have two smaller ones, painted out in the open and not re-touched or enlarged, about 16 inches long and 12 inches wide. I paid him £10 for each one of these.

21 December 1908 JQ to Nathaniel Hone (NH)

I daresay you have forgotten John Quinn, of New York, who with Mr. John B. Yeats called to see you now four years ago and bought one of your pictures - Bundoran Rocks. The year before I had bought two small ones, just as you had painted them in the open from nature. When I was last in Ireland I told you I expected to 'return next year' and that I hoped then to bring back with me two or

John Butler Yeats
(1839-1922)
A.E. George W. Russell (1903)
(1867-1935)
NGI. Cat. No. 871

three more of your pictures, the same size as the one I bought. But four years have passed, I regret to say, and I have not been able to get over yet. I had all my plans made to go abroad this summer but business and politics combined kept me here in New York all summer.

One of the chief objects I had in mind in going abroad this summer was to call upon you and to endeavour to persuade you to part with three or four more of your pictures. The three of yours I now have, especially the large one, have been greatly admired by several artist friends of mine who have seen them. In despair at not being able to get abroad, I have written to my friend George W. Russell, whose work as an artist you doubtless know and some forty or fifty of whose pictures I have, and have asked him if he, as a favor to me, would not call upon you and, if you are still willing, as you were four years ago, to sell me three or four of your paintings, to select them for me. I know you like to keep your pictures to yourself, but if you knew the pleasure your pictures have given my friends and myself, I am sure you would consent to part with three or four. The price you used to ask was £30 but if the price has gone up to 40 or 50 pounds I will gladly pay that. I have sent to Mr. Russell a rough little pencil sketch of the large one I have, to give him an idea of its subject matter. Mr. Russell is familiar with the business of packing and forwarding and consular-invoice and so on and you would, therefore, have no trouble with that part of the business.

I do sincerely hope you will consent to part with three or four of your pictures.

John Butler Yeats
(1839-1922)
**Lily (Susan) Yeats
(1901)**
(1866-1949)
NGI. Cat. No. 1180

Some day I will have a Hone and Russell exhibit of pictures and I will never part with your pictures while I live.

... Mr. John B Yeats has been here in New York for now nearly a year. He likes America and seems to be having a pleasant, if not very profitable visit. He is robust and in good health. In a public lecture here last winter he paid a glowing tribute to your work.

10 January 1909 AE to JQ

I saw (Hone) yesterday and spent two hours going carefully over the pictures for sale. There was a very large number of half finished pictures which I do not suppose now will ever be finished for Hone is an old man like I say and his best days are over. I would have liked to get some of the early Hones but people have gleaned the studio before me and Hugh Lane has been out there many times and there is little good which escapes his eye.

... First of all I selected a beauty of rocks in sea, 'Kilkee' he calls it. This was the best in his room and I call it a real good Hone. Its price was £30. There was a second painting of rocks at Kilkee, rather smaller, which I thought finely composed, its price was £15. Then I selected a painting of 'Etretat', an earlier picture, better finished than anything he has done for years. It is a relic of his French period, cliffs with sun on them and fisherpeople below the cliffs, finely composed and very effective. The price of this was £30. There was also one of his land pictures, very desolate and Honeish of Donegal cliffs with waves breaking in the distance, the price of which was £30 and a beautiful little sketch of Dublin Bay which was a study for one of his largest and best pictures hanging in the Municipal Gallery here. The price of this is £10. Hone has put all of these on one side ...

If you wish to drop out any of these, I think it would be best to drop the Donegal Cliffs which is fine but you could have other cliff paintings in much the same mood. Nearly all his paintings for years are cliffs and seas breaking on them and it is difficult to get a change of subject as his triumphs are in this line and I never cared for his other pictures as much. There was a rather fine picture of Hastings which might be substituted for the Donegal picture. It is not so impressive but it is better painted ...

11 January 1909 JQ to AE

I was delighted to receive a letter from Mr. Hone a few days ago in which he said that he hadn't at all forgotten me, that he remembered my flying visit, and that: 'When George Russell comes down I daresay he will find some things suitable ... I should like to send you the best that I have. I am at present preparing pictures for our Dublin exhibition', etc. So I think that part of your work is done, namely, his consenting to part with four or five of his pictures and you will also see that he very generously says that he would like to send me 'the best he has' ...

Miss Lily Yeats wrote to her father the other day, and among other things told of a visit to their new place of Mrs. Hone who said that she remembered me with pleasure because I didn't 'try to buy the pictures off the walls'. I believe it is Mrs. Hone who hates to sell the pictures ...

27 April 1909 AE to JQ

... I would like to have taken one or two pictures off his walls, but I was warned by several people that the Hones did not like visitors trying to buy what is practically the furniture of the house, so I took the best of the pictures he had by him, and indeed I don't think I could have done much better even if I could have picked the pictures off the walls, with one exception of a gigantic landscape which would probably be much too large for you. I hope you will be pleased with them. I know I almost regretted having them sent out of Ireland I am so much in love with Hone's work, it is so large and elemental. I think he has painted his best pictures now, and the pictures of the last year or so have a looseness of handling which comes, I think, from failing vigour. He is a very old man. He painted with Corot and the Barbazon (sic) people in his youth, and exists here like some far wandered survivor of that school, and to my mind is equal to any of them.

The things of Hone's which I like best of any are small studies in a classical manner which were painted about 30 years ago. I have seen half a dozen of them here and there and they enchant me, but he has none of those by him.

13 May 1909 NH to JQ

I hope the pictures will please you when they reach you ... Russell ... asked me if I approved of them being varnished. I think that if pictures are covered by glass and well secured from dust by papers pasted at back that varnish does not improve them, if they are not under glass it is best to varnish them as they can be washed without injury, but varnish does not improve pictures.

31 May 1909 JQ to NH

... I note what you say about not varnishing. I think you are right about landscapes. All my pictures are under glass. But not all are covered on the back. I will take your hint and attend to that.

I am greatly your debtor for consenting to part with these pictures of yours ... You know I have one fairly large one and two small ones now; so these five will make eight of yours I have in all.

I hope to get abroad in July of this year ... I shall take great pleasure in calling on you and Mrs. Hone. I remember the peaches she grew in her garden. I drive out, as I did before; for the pleasure of the ride and to see if the country has changed any.

If ... I say it a little fearfully ... if I can tempt you to part with two more large ones when I am there, I am going to do so. So please, if any persons turn up to buy between now and about July 10th, please consider two large ones as spoken for.

30 June 1909 NH to JQ

I hope the pictures arrived all right and that they please you. If you come to Ireland and can come out here please write me a line before as I might be out driving. If you would write saying by what train you could go to Raheny station I could send for you, as there are plenty of horses here and send you back by any train that suits you.

8 July JQ to NH

... The paintings by you were finally delivered to me a week ago Saturday ... They are lovely, all of them. I like best the scene on the coast of Normandy and the Scene on the Coast of Hastings. The third of the three large pictures, that of the brown rocks and sea if quite similar to the one large picture which I bought from you when I was last in Ireland; but it is a beautiful picture and I am glad to have it.

... I expect to ... reach Ireland about the end of the first week in August. I will send you a note as soon as I reach Dublin, telling you what day and hour I expect to come out to see you.

I want, if I can, to induce you to part with two more of your large paintings.

I saw Mr. J.B. Yeats this morning. He seem to be still enjoying himself here very much. I suggested that he return on the steamer with me; but he thought he would like to stay on here to see what his chances would be for a little longer. He ought to have been a great general, instead of an artist. He never would have known what the thought of surrender was.

17 December 1909 JQ to Mrs Hone

I am sending for you and Mr. Hone, as a Christmas rememberance and a slight appreciation of my gratitude to me for parting with his pictures to me, a Japanese painting by the celebrated Japanese painter Hokusai. I bought it at the sale of the original art objects formerly belonging to John LaFarge. Mr. LaFarge is one of our best painters and workers in stained glass, and statuary and sculpture. He is an expert on oriental art ... The kakemono which I send you represents Brigands in the Mountains, enjoying a fire built on a cliff, on a cold winter day. It is painted on silk .. It is signed "Hokusai". I trust that you and Mr. Hone will like it. It is one of the best of those that I bought. Everybody admires Mr. Hone's pictures. I am having some magnificent frames made for them.

When I was in Dublin I got an extra copy of the catalogue of the Modern Gallery of Art. I sent it to Mr. James Huneker, the art critic of "The Sun". He wrote a short notice on it in which he referred to Mr. Hone's works as those "of a great and not well enough known landscapist" ... When I get all of Mr. Hone's pictures framed I am going to have Mr. Huneker write a special article on it. He has agreed to do it ...

Mr. Yeats is still here. He lectured the other evening at the studio of Robert Henri, one of our best painters. His lecture was a good success. I believe he made some $70 out of it. That would be about 14 pounds.

5 January 1910 Mrs Hone to JQ

I have been longer answering your kind letter and of acknowledging the arrival of the Japanese picture than I wished but so many people come and so many things have to be done at Christmas and New Year, I was very busy. I thank you very much for 'the Brigands in the mountains warming themselves', it is most curious and clever, and takes a while to understand, we have hung it on a carved screen we brought some years ago from Cairo and there is a Japanese flower pot on a brass table beside it, I think it looks quite at home! Mr. Hone is up painting now, but he will write just a note in this for you. He kept his word about the pictures for me. We have another Lough Swilly, hanging upstairs again; I am glad now you got these. As your art critic says his pictures are not well enough known. We are very well thank you and the weather is lovely like spring today. I hope you are not troubling yourself working at everything too hard! We are glad to hear of Mr. Yeats and that he is doing well. Will you kindly remember me to him when you see him. I thank you for saying you will send a copy of the paper with special article about your pictures, we shall be glad to get it. I am your sincerely,

Magdalen Hone

P.S. I am sending you yesterday's Irish Times. Read Mr. Tim Healy's speech at Dundalk about Mr. Redmond.

P.S. Mr. Hone sends you his very kind regards, he thinks the picture very interesting, he is off out now to see trees being planted. M.H.

5 July 1910 JQ to NH

Mr. James Huneker, a very accomplished man and one of our best critics, came to my apartment a week ago Saturday ... In Sunday's Sun there appeared a notice by him, a little bit flattering, I think, to my collection of pictures, because to a casual reader it would seem that I had more pictures than I really have. Mr. Huneker liked your things very much. What he especially liked about them was 'the absence of any trace of effort or exertion.' He didn't say this in his criticism and I am sorry he didn't; but he kept coming back and looking at them and admiring their fine colours and their breadth and depth and their ease of mastery.

John Butler Yeats
(1839-1922)
John Quinn (1912)
*(1870-1924)
Hirshhorn Museum and
Sculpture Garden,
Smithsonian Institution,
Washington D.C.
Museum Purchase 1976*

I am sending you three copies of this paper, as Mrs. Hone might care to have a copy and to send a couple of copies to friends.

15 July 1910 NH to JQ

Many thanks for the Sun paper which you have kindly sent me. Mr. Huneker has been very indulgent in his appreciation of my work. Of course my wife is delighted with him. We are both very glad that you are coming to Ireland and hope that you will stay a few days with us. In the country about here there are some things to see which would interest you so when you come you must not run away in a few hours as you usually do. I am glad to hear that Yeats is flourishing. I hope he is painting portraits which he can do very well though he too often tires his sitters being over conscientious about his work and dissatisfied with what is quite satisfactory. Though it is a good thing in painting to be never satisfied with your work the sitters should be considered.

23 July 1910 JQ to NH

... Indeed, Huneker was not indulgent in his appreciation; in fact, the whole article should have been about you in my view it could not be overdone. I am very glad that Mrs. Hone liked it.

Undated (Spring or later, 1910) AE to JQ

Old Hone had some fine pictures in this year's Academy in Dublin. He is a wonder. I thought the year before that he was failing but there were three splendid landscapes as good as anything he ever did almost. I wish we had young people to follow him. I don't see anybody. We have processions of poets but very few artists in Ireland. Orpen, Shannon and Kelly live out of the country and only Orpen is Irish by birth I think.

1 August 1910 JQ to AE

I am exceedingly glad to hear what you say about Mr. Hone's work this year. Mrs. Hone wrote me that he had painted a new picture of Lough Swilly, and that she was delighted with it and that she was glad I had the one I got last summer. I think I told you that I sent her a kakemono by Hokusai from the John LaFarge collection. I didn't want to send the work of an American artist, but I thought she would like this. She seemed pleased with it. I sent him a copy of the Huneker article, and I had a letter from him the other day about it. He said something with his accustomed modesty about the article being indulgent with his work, but added that: ' Mrs. Hone was delighted with it'; so that I am glad that I got Huneker to do it. As Charles Lamb said: 'A little taffy while one lives is much more satisfying than much epitaphy when one is dead!'

13 November 1910 JQ to NH

George Russell wrote me last Spring that he had seen some new pictures by you which he described as 'perfectly beautiful'. I meant to come over this summer, as I had written you. But two or three matters detained me here ...

... One of the things I wanted to come to Ireland for was to have the pleasure of seeing you and Mrs. Hone again, and if possible to induce you to part with two more of your pictures to me. Now that I am unable to come myself, I still am anxious to have the pictures if you are willing to part with them. I am writing to George Russell to write to you or to come out and see you and to pick out the two pictures, either two of the new ones that he referred to or any two that you care to part with ...

... Mr. Yeats is still here and is flourishing ... He is writing articles for Harper's Weekly and doing them very well. Every time he comes into my place he wanders around looking at your pictures and they please him more than anything I have.

I hope that this will find you and Mrs. Hone very well. I am so sorry that I could not have had another walk in her beautiful gardens.

24 November 1910 NH to JQ

... I have not seen George Russell lately. I believe he is very busy and I seldom go to Dublin. When he comes out here I will show him what I have. I have been painting lately the Co. Clare coast. Perhaps you might like this wild nature, it has never been well painted and is not commonplace. My wife asks to be remembered. Your Japanese work which you sent her is much admired.

24 December 1910 AE to JQ

I went out to Hone and rummaged over his pictures. I selected two for you but one of them provisionally only. He has six new pictures all of which promise well but are only in a half finished state now. One of them which I liked very much I asked for an option for on your behalf. I will see it at beginning of February again and by that time it will be finished with other pictures for Hibernian Academy exhibition and I will definitely make up your mind for you by proxy. You cannot get any of these new pictures until March when the Academy show is over. He wants these to be exhibited there. The other picture is an old one which hung in his hall which I thought better than the new ones. But if the new ones turn out finer I have no doubt he will let me take one of them instead for you. There is one very fine new picture but it has the same place, same rocks as one you have so I did not worry over it. If the new one turns out as well as I think it will, you will have a fine picture of boats on a tumbling sea. The price of each picture is £30. He is an astonishing man with power in his trembling old fingers yet and vision in his soul ...

... Old Hone is a splendid old fellow nearly eighty now and he carries on farming as a side vent to too much activity in his nervous system. He is very wealthy and I sometimes think he could have been a bigger artist if he had not so much money. But no, I think he is the biggest landscape painter living as it is it may be all right.

6 February 1911 JQ to AE

... In regard to the Hones, please use your own judgement. You know in a general way what I have ... The larger the pictures the better. He is a big man and I should be glad to have three pictures instead of the two ... above all I should be glad to have another large picture of the Loch Swilly size, if he will part with it ... The only precaution I have to suggest is not to get another one of the Bundoran Rocks, the brown rocks jutting out unto the sea, with the sea-weed gatherers, the donkey cart and the man and woman in brown, because I have two large ones and one small one of it ...

7 February 1911 JQ to NH

George Russell wrote me that he had been out to see you. I have written to him to please select three or four more of your pictures, if you cared to part with them. He said you had some fine new ones (not yet quite finished) ... it would be quite agreeable to me to wait till after the close of the Academy Exhibition ... I should very much like ... to have another large picture the size of the Lough Swilly - one to hang beside or opposite it. Mr. Yeats admires it immensely and is never tired of praising it. He goes up to it every time he comes to my place ...

I am sorry I could not get abroad this last summer. I should have liked to go out to your place two or three times and eat some of Mrs. Hone's peaches and go through her wonderful flower gardens.

16 February 1911 NH to JQ

... George Russell has been out here and I am sending to Egan's next Monday 3 pictures for you, two of them were selected by Russell and the 3rd coast of Clare was intended for the Academy Exhibition but owing to a mistake about a frame I have not sent it, so I send it to you thinking it would please you. I have not at present any picture of the size of Lough Swilly ...

16 February 1911 AE to JQ

You rather terrified me by what you said about Hone's rocks. The 'Cliffs of Kilkee', which is one of the pictures I selected for you, is not like the subject he has treated so often of a rock on the foreground and a big wave coming over it. Now that he is getting old he has a tendency to repeat forms of composition. I do not mind that very much myself because I think every artist of any individuality does the same thing. Corot painted misty trees all his life, and Rossetti one face. Whistler used a couple of tones, and, as far as I am concerned, Hone might go on painting his rock and his great wave for the remainder of his life and would not bore me.

... He has no picture so large as the one you got when you were there last. He was just beginning a sea picture which promises to be good when I was out there a few days ago, but as he says himself, he cannot paint for more than a couple of hours now, and there is a little looseness about the touch though there is, I think, a great surety still in the mind and one cannot be certain what the artistic value of the picture will be now until we see it completed. He is a great old man anyhow.

24 February 1911 AE to JQ

Just after I got your letter I got a note from Hone saying he had heard from you and was sending a third picture with the two I had selected. Remembering what you said about the rocks and seaweed gatherers, I borrowed a friend's motor and went out next morning and found the picture was one of the kind you wanted no more of. It was good of its kind but I selected a picture of a ferry boat going across a channel which I think is a very fine and austere composition unlike anything you have. I would have selected it at first but I believe he must have had it in some other room because I did not see it when I called on Hone before. It is good.

... I enclose Hone's note of the pictures (3 at £30) which I suppose you want.

5 March 1911 JQ to AE

Two years ago when I took the big Hone, 'Lough Swilly', with me to London and had it re-packed there by Dicksee & Co., they put a lot of heavy drawings in the big case on top of the large canvas, without any protection between, and the result was that 'Loch Swilly' was badly marked and creased by the smaller, heavier things, and I had to send it to an expert to have it re-lined and have the creases taken out ...

... I thoroughly agree with you about Mr. Hone. He is 'a great old man'. If you think that of the pictures which he sent to the Hibernian Academy (apart from the three which he sent to me) that there are one or two more that I ought to have, if he will part with them, I shall be glad to have them. However, they can be attended to later on. I mean especially if he has any large one, the size of 'Loch Swilly' ...

... The only thing that reconciles me at all to having bothered you about Mr. Hone is that he is a lovable, great old man, and I think he likes you very much, from the way he writes about you to me, and I know if I were you I should want to see the old man as much and as often as I could. It is too bad that someone doesn't get him to talk about his early reminiscences of the painters - Corot, Diaz, Millet and others, - and get him to tell something of his earlier experiences and something of his views on art, and publish it in an article or a book about him. He is a great enough painter to have a book done on him. Why don't you try to do it - get him to give you his reminiscences of his early days, who he studied with, his views on painting, and so forth? A good book could be done in this way, and you could write the criticisms. The illustrations could be taken care of well, and you could put enough personal reminiscences into it to make it very interesting. I mean just that. I should be very glad to guarantee something for the publication of it, if the publisher wanted a guarantee. Why don't you think it over, and if it appeals to you sound the old man on the subject?

20 March 1911 AE to JQ

I think Old Hone conceives his pictures as well as ever and has the same sentiment but his handling is a little fatigued and is not so direct as it was when he was younger. He has six pictures in the Hibernian Academy this year but I like yours better than any of them except one which was his favourite waves on rocks and you have enough of this kind already.

18 March 1911 NH to JQ

... I sent some pictures to the Hibernian Academy, most of them have found purchasers. We look forward to seeing you in summer.

2 June 1911 JQ to NH

I received yours of March 18th. I also received the three pictures ... I am delighted with them! The large marine picture which you call 'Coming Home' I think I like the best of the three. Others prefer the 'Rocks of Kilkee', still others 'The Ferryboat'. I have had them all framed and they look very fine and striking.

12 June 1911 NH to JQ

I am glad you and your friends are pleased with the pictures ...

..My wife asks to be remembered. We hope you will come here in August and stay a few days if you can, there are some curious antiquities about here which I would like to show you.

Catalogue of Paintings by Hone in the John Quinn Collection

(The date given below is an amalgam of information derived from the correspondence, Hone's receipts, and the catalogues of the Memorial Exhibition and the Quinn Sale. The Quinn Hones were sold at the New York auction in February 1927 and the descriptions quoted below are from the sale catalogue. In 1909, $70 was the equivalent of about £14 - see Quinn's letter to Mrs. Hone of 17 December 1909.)

1. *Sands at Malahide*
    12 x 18 ins.
    Signed, lower right, N. Hone R.H.A.
    Purchased, 1903. (£10)
    Lot 66, Quinn sale, ($140)

'Prospect of blue sea with small sailing craft, under a deep blue sky. In the foreground a stretch of rose-tinted sands'.

2. *Sheep Grazing, Malahide*
    13 x 18 ins.
    Signed, lower left, N.H.
    Purchased, 1903. (£10)
    Lot 203, Quinn sale, ($65)

'Impressionistic view of richly wooded and fragrant landscape, under a sombre ivory sky suffused with misty light casting shades of violet. In the foreground sheep are browsing'.

3. *Bundoran Rocks*
    24 x 40 ins.
    Signed, lower right, N.H.
    Purchased, October 1904. (£10)
    Lot 109, Quinn sale, ($120)

'Atmospheric rendering of rugged rocks, with deep prospect of greenish-blue sea, under a lavender sky. At the right are faintly discernable figures and a gray mule; in the foreground brown-tipped gulls.'

4. *Chalk Cliff, Etretat, Normandy*
    24.5 x 40 ins.
    Signed, lower right, N.H.
    Purchased, January 1909. (£30)
    Lot 97 in Quinn sale, ($120)

'Painted more than twenty years ago' according to Hone's receipt, dated 18 April 1909.

'Centring the composition a huge cliff with a flying buttress jutting into the sea, in the foreground animated fisherfolk and three fishing smacks, and to the right a vista of deep blue sea with a reflection of a sinking sun. Charming work possessing a rare quality of unity and atmosphere'.

Nathaniel Hone the Younger
(1831-1917)
Hastings
The Metropolitan Museum of Art, New York

5. *Hastings, Sussex where William the Conqueror landed with his Army*
   27.5 x 42 ins.
   Signed, lower right, N.H.
   Purchased, January 1909 (£30)
   Lot 350, Quinn sale, ($100)

Exhibited, 1913, 'The Armory Show, New York, Cat. no. 586 where said to date from 1890.

'Painted more than twenty years ago' according to Hone's receipt, dated 18 April 1909.

'In the middle distance the cliff shadowing the small village, and the strand fringing the bay dotted with fisherfolk drawing in their nets, while to the right is a vista of the open sea; under an angry gray sky with hanging clouds'.

6. *Coast at Bundoran*
   24 x 40 ins.
   Signed, lower right, N.H.
   Purchased, January 1909 (£30)
   Lot 239, Quinn sale, ($100)

'Rugged coastline, with figures loading a cart to which is harnessed an old gray horse. In the middle distance the white-crested waves are seen breaking over the rocks, and various gulls with brown-tipped wings, and beyond a view of blue-grey sea, under an ivory-blue sky tinged with violet tones'.

7. *Coast at Kilkee*
   18.5 x 28.5 ins.
   Signed, lower right, N.H.
   Purchased, January 1909 (£15)
   Lot 329, Quinn sale, ($120)

150

'Subduedly-lit view of jagged coastline, with grayish-green water and the white-crested curl of an incoming breaker. Two figures are faintly discernible at the edge of the rock, under a sky heavily laden with nimbus clouds of cumuluous form; in the foreground graceful gulls'.

8. *Dublin Bay*
   12 x 18 ins.
   Purchased, January 1909 (£10)

Said in the letter from AE to JQ dated 10 January 1909 to be a study for a picture in the Dublin Municipal Gallery.

9. *Lough Swilly*
   55 x 35 ins.
   Purchased, August 1909 (£50)

Exhibited, 1913, 'The Armory Show', New York, Cat. no. 585 where said to date from 1895.

10. *Glenmalure*
    24 x 40 ins.
    Purchased, August 1909 (£30)
    Lot 240, Quinn sale ($100)

'Misty view of mountainous country, under a romantic sky, flecked with cirrus clouds. In the middle distance, rising pasture lands of russet-brown tones, and cattle with their shepherd cloaked by a beam of sunlight. At the left behind a stone wall, a donkey peering into space'.

11. *Shore at Malahide*
    26 x 40 ins.
    Purchased, August 1909 (£30)
    Lot 488, Quinn sale, ($210)

'In the foreground an inlet of placid water reflecting the tones of a deep cloudy blue sky, and the crescent of a rainbow. By the bank is a fishing smack. Charming rendering of reflected lights'.

12. *Strayed Cattle*
    28 x 36 ins.
    Signed, lower right, N.H.
    Purchased, August 1909 (£30)
    Lot 498, Quinn sale, ($120)

'Impressionistic view of richly-wooded country enveloped in autumn foliage. In the foreground two massive elms, and grazing and resting cattle, flecked by innumerable lights and shades; at the upper left, a vista of deep blue sky'.

13. *Shore Malahide*
    26 x 37 ins.
    Purchased, August 1909 (£30)

14. *Road near Marlotte, France*
    21 x 25 ins.
    Purchased, August 1909 (£25)

'The picture was painted thirty years ago' according to Hone's receipt, dated 17 August 1909.

Nathaniel Hone the Younger
(1831-1917)
Shore Malahide, Co. Dublin
The Metropolitan Museum of Art, New York

    15. *Coming Home*
          26 x 38.5 ins.
          Signed, lower left, N.H.
          Purchased, January 1911 (£30)
          Lot 243, Quinn sale, ($60)

Said in a letter from AE to JQ dated 24 December 1910 to be an 'Old picture which hung in hall' at St. Doulough's.

'A vast expanse of blue-green sea with three sailing craft steering for home under a limitless stormy sky. In the foreground graceful gulls are skimming the water'.

    16. *The Ferryboat*
          24 x 40 ins.
          Signed, lower left, N.H.
          Purchased, January 1911 (£30)
          Lot 351, Quinn sale ($100)

'The foreground is occupied by the rich green waterway, with the ferryboat carrying various white-capped figures, steering for the far shore, upon which other figures are seen, shadowed by the richly-wooded banks. Gulls are gliding and cresting the water; under an ivory-blue sky'.

Nathaniel Hone the Younger
(1831-1917)
The Ferryboat
The Metropolitan Museum of Art, New York

17. *Rocks at Kilkee*
    24 x 40.5 ins. (Said in Memorial Exh. Cat. to be 33 x 40)
    Purchased, January 1911 (£30)
    Lot 492, Quinn sale, ($95)

'Misty view of an azure sea under an ivory-blue sky; to the right massive cliffs casting deep shadows. Around are numerous graceful gulls. Though few colors are used in the composition, the artist has divided them into an infinity of tints, obtaining an amazing effect of depth and recession'.

Jack Butler Yeats
(1871-1957)
**The Liffey Swim
(1923)**
NGI. Cat. No. 941

THE NATIONAL GALLERY OF IRELAND'S COLLECTION OF PAINTINGS BY JACK B. YEATS.

'SEEMINGLY HAPHAZARD ... A PICTORIAL ACCIDENT OF THE HAPPIEST KIND'

Hilary Pyle

The quotation in the title for this article is taken from a review of Jack B. Yeats's new work in 1927 written by Thomas Bodkin[1], who was shortly to become Director of the National Gallery of Ireland; and it seems to sum up the way in which the National Gallery has gradually acquired its collection of the artist's work, a total of 43 paintings and drawings.

The first pictures by Jack B. Yeats to come into the Gallery's permanent holding were *The Liffey Swim* and *A Morning in a City*, gifts of the Haverty Trust in 1931 and 1941 respectively. Bodkin in fact was one of the trustees of the Haverty Bequest when *The Liffey Swim* was purchased from Yeats's studio, in December 1930. Thomas Haverty, who died in 1916 at the age of 92, had left instructions in his will that a Trust be created to encourage Irish art and particularly painting. The Trustees - the President of the Royal Hibernian Academy, the Director of the National Gallery of Ireland, and the Lord Mayor of Dublin were to purchase works by painters of Irish birth who lived in Ireland, with a preference for Historical or Fancy Subjects and ignoring landscape, 'except perhaps an occasional landscape of a very high order.'[2] Works purchased by the Trust would be lent to public galleries, and every five years allocated permanently to some Irish institution.

Thomas Bodkin was one of the first trustees, acting with Dermod O'Brien and John J. Reynolds, the Curator of the Municipal Gallery, who filled the third position on the Trust until the office of Lord Mayor was actively revived. Bodkin was a friend as well as an enthusiastic critic of Yeats, and Yeats was an obvious artist to buy, though he did not exactly fulfil the terms of the Haverty will. He was living in Ireland, in Dublin at the time; but he had not been born there. He had been born in 1871 in London of Irish parents, and so was not technically 'of Irish birth'. He did not paint 'historical superior art' in the sense that his earlier compatriot, James Barry, and, no doubt, Thomas Haverty, born in 1824, would have understood it.[3]

Fortunately the Trust did not quibble, Yeats was obviously the outstanding modern Irish painter. From the start AE (George Russell), who had a good eye as a critic, had called him 'a millionaire of fancy',[4] comparing him with Millet. He had been likened to Goya when he exhibited with the *Salon des Independents* in Paris.[5] Yet if he seemed obvious to the Haverty Trust, how did he fit in with the National Gallery's objective of (in the words of Hugh Lane) 'buying pictures of deceased painters of established merit'?[6] The Gallery's acquisition of works by living Irish artists had been limited to accepting donations of some portraits by Doyle, Purser,

Lavery, and O'Conor, and an exceptional landscape by Hone given by the artist in 1907.

Bodkin and his colleagues, however, were determined to put a painting by Yeats in the National Gallery. For the Dublin Municipal Gallery they would have selected one of Yeats's more recent paintings, one of the pictorial accidents, executed in the 'rapid, seemingly haphazard brushwork', whose originality Bodkin admired. But they chose *The Liffey Swim*, a work painted at the peak of Yeats's more conventional period in the early twenties, when the changeover into a thoroughly modern style was only vaguely apparent, and they offered it to the National Gallery under certain conditions in February 1931 when the offer was accepted. The painting, completed in 1923, had been awarded a silver medal in the Paris *Olympic Exposition* the following year, and had been received well at the Royal Hibernian Academy and at subsequent showings in London and Liverpool. Yeats regarded it as a major work and priced it accordingly. The Haverty Trustees, rather than waiting five years to allocate it, presented it immediately to the Gallery, and it was later loaned - because of its modernity - to the Dublin Municipal Gallery of Modern Art.[7]

While *The Liffey Swim* probably falls into the category of a landscape or cityscape, it is without doubt a landscape 'of very high order': and though it is not a history painting in the original meaning of the term, it might be regarded as a history painting in the twentieth century sense, when the effects of post-impressionism had made particular incidents of a moment redolent of some indefinable eternity. There is a spontaneity about the picture, which has always made it popular with viewers. A crowd is gathered on Bachelor's Walk in Dublin to see the annual swimming competition. People push for a view from the tops of passing trams, or crane over the parapet of O'Connell Bridge seen in mid-distance and over the near wall of the Walk. The strong diagonal lines of the compositional structure, echoed by the broad flowing lines of the paint, lend a freedom to a sympathetic interpretation of an ephemeral event.

Such an event was of significance in a Dublin, which was in the first years of independence at the time of the painting, finding its identity as the capital of a free nation, with a regard for its cultural pastimes as well as for its political dimension. Yeats's inclusion of himself, picked out in a brown hat among the near crowd, with a lady who is probably his wife, puts the picture in the tradition of landscapes two or three centuries before, where, to pinpoint the scene in history, the artist placed himself at his easel in the foreground.

In *A Morning in a City*, the city of Dublin, not long after dawn, has the same feeling of history. It is a casual moment in the early morning, a moment that could be savoured every day of a lifetime, yet a moment that, in the artist's interpretation in the wake of Manet, becomes an eternal moment through the figure of the artist which lingers on the eye. He wanders through the centre of the painting, unhurried like the early busy ghosts who move with determination towards some objective. The light from the broken sky begins to reveal more solid forms in the carmine shade thrown by the Georgian buildings. Exhibited first in 1937 at the Royal Hibernian Academy, the picture was bought from the artist by the Haverty Trust - whose National Gallery representative was now the new director Dr. George Furlong - the following February. On this occasion they observed the intentions of the will, and the painting was not presented to the National Gallery for another three years.

Apart from two works by Keating and MacGonigal donated twenty years later, these are the only pictures presented to the National Gallery by the Haverty Trust. Yeats's genius, and his importance as a national artist, were next recognised, during the following decade, by the committee which organised the first major retrospective of his work. The exhibition may have been precipitated by the joint exhibition with Sir William Nicholson at the National Gallery in London in 1942, organised by Sir Kenneth Clark in connection with a Sickert exhibition as a triangular showing of the anti-academic elements in British art of the twentieth century. Clark knew Yeats had nothing in common with Nicholson except 'youth and ...independence', as he wrote in the catalogue. Even in their black and white illustrations, which were the only works shown side by side, Nicholson's blacks were masses while Yeats's blacks were lines. Yet the fact that Yeats - who despite his deeply felt nationalism was used to exhibiting under the British as well as the Irish umbrella - was given such an honour was a reminder of his international standing.

Clark contrasted Yeats's symbolism and lawless colour with the cool realism and urbanity of Nicholson (which Yeats had admired in his earlier days),[8] selecting 34 of Yeats's paintings of the 1920s and 1930s. The National Loan Exhibition, mounted at the National College of Art in Dublin in June and July 1945, set about representing Yeats comprehensively, and showed 179 works, most of them oil paintings, with some important watercolours.

With the remains of the proceeds from the exhibition, the committee chose a new painting from Jack Yeats's studio for presentation to the National Gallery of Ireland in 1946. Like the two Haverty Trust canvases, it was eminently suitable for the national collection. *Men of Destiny* in composition ressembles *Two Travellers* of 1942, which was exhibited in London in the winter of 1946, and bought by the Tate Gallery. The latter in its picaresque nuance of two men on life's journey is universal in its application while undoubtedly Irish in origin. But *Men of Destiny* has an extraordinary seriousness, and prophetic intensity. It is a simple painting of some fishermen, walking up the point after securing their hooker. They walk relaxedly, with their hands in their pockets, yet their faces and bodies are aflame with more than the glow of the setting sun: they walk with intent, reminiscent of the men W.B.Yeats met

> *'at close of day*
> *Coming with vivid faces*
> *From counter or desk among grey*
> *Eighteenth-century houses.'*

Jack Yeats knew the ancient name for Ireland was Inis Fáil, 'Island of Destiny': and there is a local poetry in the painting. But he was painting as a world war was coming to an end, and in this work projected a meaning far wider than the shores of Ireland alone. 'Men of Destiny', he is saying, are the men of vision for all mankind.

Not content with this donation, Father Senan, OFM.Cap., the Chairman of the National Loan Exhibition, with 'a group of private citizens', presented a further work by Yeats to the National Gallery in 1947. Father Senan, who wrote the foreword or *reamhscéal* to the catalogue in Irish, felt it fitting that Yeats should be thanked in Irish, *'toisc go bhfuil nár measc fear gur féidir leis stair ár dtire a's tréithe ár náisiúin do thabhairt go huasal a's go solusmhar'* ('because there is a man in our midst who can represent our country's history and our nation's customs

Jack Butler Yeats
(1871-1957)
**Men of Destiny
(1946)**
NGI. Cat. No. 1134

with nobility and light.') The picture he chose conjures up what is a common enough scene in Yeats, a fair day, with the jostling crowd of farmers, tinkers and townspeople. But *Above the Fair*, raised high on an enormous grey, is a gold-haired child, as prophetic for the future of man as are the *Men of Destiny*. Both paintings were chosen to be shown in a posthumous Yeats exhibition, at the Venice Biennale in 1962, when - apart from Louis le Brocquy who was chosen in 1956 - it was thought that there was no one sufficiently modern to represent Ireland.

During the 1950s, the National Gallery collection of Jack Yeats's more than trebled, due to donations and bequests which included other living Irish artists, some superb paintings by Leech and Swanzy, as well as the Keating and a MacGonigal presented by the Haverty Trust. Evie Hone, the painter and stained glass artist, now owned *The Small Weir, Coole*, dating from Yeats's visit to Coole Park in 1923, and lent by Mrs. Josephine MacNeill to the National Loan Exhibition. A small vibrant panel, one can understand how it appealed to Hone, with her broad treatment of glass, and her appreciation of strong translucent tones. The study of cows grazing beside the weir on Lady Gregory's estate in County Galway has the character of a sketch made *en plein air*. The black rocks wear ruffs of foam, as the high water all but submerges them.

The painting came into the gallery with the rest of the Evie Hone Bequest in 1955. Two years later, the year that Yeats died, Mr. and Mrs. Raymond French donated *The Power Station*, a less romantic painting than *The Small Weir*, of 1930, depicting the Pigeon House Power Station on the South Wall of Dublin port. This small atmospheric picture, with the shapes of the Dublin hills sweeping behind the stiff vertical chimney with its flag of smoke, was one of the last of the realistic views of Dublin which Yeats perfected during the 1920s. Three more of these

Jack Butler Yeats
(1871-1957)
**Many Ferries
(1948)**
NGI. Cat. No. 1550

views were added to the Gallery collection through the Richard Irvine Best Bequest in 1959, *Draughts* (1922), which is a study of sailors relaxing at the Grand Canal Dock, *In the Tram* (1923), a Lucan scene, and *Islandbridge Regatta* (1925), a view of spectators and competitors not unlike *The Liffey Swim*, though more transcendental in mood. The final work by Yeats from the Best Bequest dates from the visit to Coole in 1923, when he painted a subject he had often described in watercolour in his early days, a West of Ireland regatta. Within a small panel measuring 23 x 36 cms., Yeats managed to convey the sense of infinite space, of the sky surrounding the depth of open blue water with small boats gathered on it, near grass and gorsey shore and the hump of mountain, the whole scene lighted by a cloudy sun.

Two other paintings, of Yeats's late period, came into the Gallery through the Friends of the National Collections of Ireland. The Friends of the National Collections, founded in 1924 for the purpose of seeing that a permanent modern gallery be provided to house the Lane pictures in Ireland,[9] also undertook the task of obtaining works of art and objects of historic value for the public collections of Ireland. *The Cavalier's Farewell to his Steed* (1949) owned by Mrs. Dorothea Case, and *Many Ferries* (1948), by Mrs. Julia Egan, were bequeathed through the Friends in 1958 and 1960.

Both are romantic paintings and they refer to memories of the artist's youth, recast so as to acquire a new meaning. For *The Cavalier's Farewell* the artist takes the title of a poem he learned like all his generation, *The Arab's Farewell to his Steed* by Caroline Norton, a poem of deep emotion about the relationship between a man and his horse. Not only does he alter the title, but he seemingly treats the subject frivolously, representing the 'cavalier' as a small boy, translated into a hero by means of his fancy dress and his imagination, flourishing his hat in farewell to his 'steed' - a piebald on a merry-go-round. Using the humorous fun and the fantasy colour of the fairground, Yeats manages to convey an emotion and elation that parallels the deeper sentiment of the poem, and he captures the innocence and high idealism of childish imaginings as no other Irish artist has ever done.

Many Ferries recalls the journey he had made with John Millington Synge around the 'congested districts' of Connemara and Mayo forty years before in 1905. It is an amazing painting of green/blue sunlit memory, an image painted on the mind. There was no incident or story, only a character, the ferryman of Dinish Island near Gorumna, off the coast of Connemara, who caught the imagination of Synge as well as of Yeats. The man rowed them from Furnace to Dinish, talking all the time about his years in America earning his living as an interpreter for the Irish emigrants. 'Afterwards he took us up to the highest point of the island', wrote Synge, 'and showed us a fine view of the whole group (of islands) and of the Atlantic beyond them, with a few fishing-boats in the distance, and many large boats nearer the rocks rowing heavily with loads of weed'.[10]

Mrs Julia Egan bequeathed a second painting through the Friends, a picture which has turned out to be the most popular in all the Yeats collection, and has been reproduced on cards and posters since Yeats's copyright ban on reproduction came to an end. *Before the Start* is a canvas of Yeats's first oil period, when he created strong evocative images of aspects of life in the West of Ireland, a theme that preoccupied him for about twenty years. Three jockeys are silhouetted against the sky, beside the flag which marks the starting point of the race. Yeats no doubt owed much in his horse racing paintings to Degas: but while there are stylistic similarities in the early watercolours, he quickly developed a strong personal manner, which matured in its own idiosyncratic way, nourished by what he saw, but always independent of any formal group. *Before the Start* has a certain archaism in the way narrative plays a part - perhaps this is one reason for its popularity. But it arises from a belief in the narrative of life, and grows out of actual observation, rather than being a literary intervention from some secondary source.

Thomas MacGreevy was Director during the 1950s, and was no doubt partially responsible for these donations and bequests of that period. His literary and artistic affiliations led him to promote Irish art more than any director since Henry Doyle in the 1880s. About 1958, he purchased a bundle of cartoon designs by Jack Yeats for the sodality banners at Loughrea Cathedral, which were embroidered at Dun Emer in 1903.[11] Miss Hyland who owned them had been assistant to Lily Yeats, who supervised the embroidery. Dr. MacGreevy distributed the cartoons where he saw fit, giving the *St. Asicus*, for example, to Sligo Museum, since Asicus is the patron saint of the Diocese of Elphin. To the National Gallery he donated two of the linen transfer designs, that for the *St. Asicus*, and *St. Colmcille*. Since they have been cleaned and restored, they provide an interesting insight into practical aspects of the Arts and Crafts movement in Ireland at the beginning of the century.[12]

The Last Dawn But One (1948), a picture of a circus striking camp, purchased by the National Gallery in 1969, came from MacGreevy's personal collection: but, before he retired, he bought an important early oil for the Gallery from Dr. Eileen MacCarvill. *The Double Jockey Act*, painted in 1916, is the only other circus painting by Yeats in the National Gallery. For an artist whose interpretation of the circus as a metaphor for life parallels that of Rouault, and some of whose greatest and most poignant works picture circus scenes and characters,[13] this is an unfortunate gap. *The Double Jockey Act*, first exhibited at the Royal Hibernian Academy in 1917, is especially interesting because of its stylistic anticipation of the expressionism of ten years later. The paint is used thickly, with broad lively brushwork, still within figurative bounds, but exaggerating representational elements so as to foster the high pitched emotion. The emotion of tenuous triumph and soaring elation is created by the pair of jockeys balancing perilously on the rump of the galloping piebald, silhouetted against the darkness of the tent top and lit by invisible flares; and this emotion is sustained by the counterpoint of the clown who gallops alongside, enjoying a parallel triumph, enlarged because of its addition of comedy and pathos.

Dr. MacGreevy could buy Yeats for the Gallery because after 1957 Yeats was a 'deceased painter of established merit'. But the only sign of an attempt at a policy for acquiring Yeats in a serious way appeared with James White, who became Director in 1964. Immediately he set about buying works by Yeats, *About to Write a Letter*, purchased from the estate of Richard MacGonigal a month after his appointment, *The Lying-in-State of O'Donovan Rossa* and *Grief* in 1965, a group of important watercolours - the first examples of this vital aspect of Yeats's work to enter the Gallery - in 1967, and *The Last Dawn but One* in 1969.

With hindsight, it can be readily seen that, in the euphoric atmosphere of the 1960s, when the Shaw Bequest was at last giving the Gallery some purchasing power, and the completion of the new extension was drawing in the public as never before, it was the time to buy Yeats's works which were accessible and comparatively modest in price. Leo Smith, of the Dawson Gallery, was the first art dealer in Ireland to recognise Yeats's importance. Victor Waddington, Yeats's main agent after Sir Kenneth Clark's exhibition, moved to London after Yeats's death, where he organised regular exhibitions of his work: and he presented the National Gallery with a key work in Yeats's development - a full length pencil *Self-Portrait* (c. 1920) - in 1961, showing his interest in the collection. With his brother, who had a gallery in Montreal, and Leo Smith in Dublin working in conjunction with him as well, he promoted and commanded the Yeats market. When works like *The Breaker Out* (1925), *The Bus by the River* (1927). *The Clown among the People* (1932), *The Face in Shadow* (1946), and many more now in private collections, were available, it now seems a pity that the National Gallery did not acquire them. Yeats's stature as a European master of the first half of the twentieth century, despite Kenneth Clark's tentative attempts, had not then been fully estimated.[14]

But it is important to emphasise that during Dr. White's directorship, more than half the present collection of Yeatses came into the Gallery. Like Thomas MacGreevy, James White was an enthusiast for Yeats's work and a personal friend of the artist. He was responsible for encouraging donations, which included a unique design for theatre, the Mountain Backcloth intended for W. B. Yeats's play, *The King's Threshold*, in 1913, presented by Victor Waddington in 1968: and, looked at as a group, his purchases of watercolours, drawings and designs, are satisfying. *The Lying-in-State of O'Donovan Rossa*, the Cork patriot who was exiled in America, and whose remains were brought back to Dublin in 1915, depicted an event of enormous political significance at the time. Yeats joined the crowd who paid homage at the bier in the City Hall, and with the assistance of his own notes

Jack Butler Yeats
(1871-1957)
**About to Write a Letter
(1935)**
NGI. Cat. No. 1766

from memory, and a newspaper photograph, he made the drawing. This was purchased from Leo Smith for the Gallery in 1965, in time for the 50th anniversary of the Rising. With the *Self Portrait* referred to above it is one of Yeats's most important pencil drawings.

1966 and 1967 expanded this area of small works considerably due to the William Cadbury Bequest and a far-seeing watercolour purchase from Victor Waddington. The three watercolour paintings, *On the Broads* of Norfolk in England, of 1899, show Yeats's watercolour technique at its finest, when he manipulated fluid pigment on its own in perfect accord with his subject. No titles or theme were necessary. Three different aspects of yachting are imaged in a vivid and immediate manner. Yeats never exhibited them, unlike the three other paintings of this 1967 purchase, which are excellent examples of Yeats's middle and late period watercolours. *The Man from Aranmore* (1905) was a result of Yeats's now historical journey around the Irish speaking districts of Connemara with J. M. Synge in June 1905. It is a typical character study in his *Pictures of Life in the West of Ireland* series, influenced somewhat by his collusion with Synge, who in words had been doing what Yeats was doing in pencil and paint, and whose book, *The Aran Islands*, Yeats illustrated the following year.

Lough Gill, County Sligo is a strong and atmospheric watercolour landscape, painted in 1906, the year when Yeats was beginning to work seriously in oil. The watercolour is the size he maintained throughout his life when painting the majority of his oil landscapes without figures; the style and handling of paint are similar to his first oil landscapes. *The Circus Chariot* (1910) shows Yeats working in watercolour when oil was now his preference. From the translucence of the early period, and the tonal staining and strong imagery of the middle style, he has moved to a more solid form of watercolour expression, interested in stylisation of form and light, as he was in his oils.

Jack Butler Yeats
(1871-1957)
Grief (1951)
NGI. Cat. No. 1769

Counter-balancing the watercolours, the drawings for illustration provided by the William A. Cadbury Bequest of 1966, fill out another area of Yeats's activity. *The County of Mayo* (1903), is a fine example of Yeats's pen and ink illustration for his own inspired publication, *A Broadsheet*, issued by Elkin Mathews from 1902-3. *A Broadsheet* was followed by *A Broadside* (1908-15), published by Yeats's sister Lolly from Dun Emer and the Cuala Press: and *A Wake House* and *The Pilot* are drawings for this. The Bequest included an illustration for Synge's *Aran Islands* as well as three drawings for Yeats's own book of drawings of 1912, *Life in the West of Ireland*, to which a fourth, *The Poteen Makers*, was added in 1979 from the Seamus Kelly Bequest. The Cadbury Bequest included what is perhaps the best of the oil illustrations to *Irishmen All*, by George Birmingham, *The Priest* (1913).

Dinner Hour at the Docks (1928), donated by Mrs. R. M. Smyllie in memory of her husband in 1966, and *Flower Girl, Dublin* (1926), presented by International Business Machines, New York in 1969, swelled the number of oil paintings, adding to Yeats's survey of contemporary Dublin and Dublin life. But the most important acquisitions of the 1960s were both purchases, *About to Write a Letter* (1935), from the McGonigal collection, and *Grief* (1951), bought from Victor Waddington in 1965.

About to Write a Letter is a major middle period oil in which Yeats combines fantasy and reality in a rich visual metaphor, which borders on melodrama, but has an actuality that is human and moving. *Grief* is charged with a less personalised emotion. It ranks with Picasso and Dali in the revulsion for war it permeates through the simple image of an Irish village - something Yeats had painted numerous times over his long life - now under military attack. The grief of the stricken family group in the foreground must reach out to all who see it.

1971 was the centenary of Jack B. Yeats's birth, celebrated by an exhibition at the National Gallery. Not quite as large as the National Loan Exhibition in 1945, it

Jack Butler Yeats
(1871-1957)
In Memory of Boucicault and Bianconi (1937)
NGI. Cat. No. 4206

was perhaps more representative, showing some of the early black-and-white drawings as well as more than fifty paintings executed after 1945, nearly all of them major works. Perhaps in commemoration of the centenary, Mrs. Mabel Waddington presented *No Flowers*, a tender meditative work of 1945 shown in the exhibition, to the Gallery.

Two fine oil paintings were added to the collection in the late 1970s, *In Memory of Boucicault and Bianconi* (1937), an inimitable memory fantasy, presented by John Huston in 1977, and *For the Road* (1951) given by Mr. and Mrs. F. L. Vickerman in 1978. The latter, a fresh and emotional horse painting, like *Grief* helped to make up for the complete absence of works from the 1950s, when Yeats was revered internationally.

The final Yeats acquisition in the National Gallery of Ireland, came during the directorship of Homan Potterton[15] - the wonderfully lyrical canvas of 1949, *The Singing Horseman*, bequeathed by Máire MacNeill Sweeney, in memory of John L. Sweeney. In an astoundingly free image, a *tour de force* drawing in oil of a mounted horseman in a fertile landscape, it fashions a view of life that is at once visionary and philosophical. The man's head and hands are lit with gold. The horse is gold, set amid an ecstasy of colour, its eye opaque with insight.

Nothing by Yeats has been bought by the Gallery during the last twenty years: and indeed, with such limited resources, and the inflated prices that the recent highlighting of Irish artists has precipitated, it seems unlikely that the Gallery's collection can be enlarged and improved other than by welcome but chance donations and bequests.

The pictures of the National Gallery of Ireland's Yeats collection each have an individual significance, which has made them popular both in Yeats exhibitions, and in group exhibitions of Irish art. Some have travelled to exhibitions as far apart as Los Angeles, Helsinki, Venice and Bonn. With new attitudes to conservation, it is unlikely that they will be seen abroad in the future except on very rare occasions. Happily, however, in 1990, the oil paintings were brought together for the first time in what can be called a 'Yeats Room' in the refurbished Irish rooms of the Gallery's Milltown Wing. This 'seemingly haphazard' collection of works by Ireland's unsurpassed twentieth century genius can now be appreciated fully by visitors to the Gallery.

Notes

1. *Studio* 93 (1927 May) pp. 362-4.

2. Papers of the Haverty Trust in the RHA Archive, published by kind permission of the President of the Royal Hibernian Academy, Mr. Thomas Ryan.

3. *Lectures on Painting by the Royal Academicians, Barry, Opie and Fuseli*, ed. R. N. Wornum (1848) p. 88.

4. *Freeman's Journal* (1901 October 23) p. 5.

5. H. Pyle, *Jack B. Yeats*: a biography (1970, revised edition 1989) p. 165.

6. *National Gallery of Ireland: Illustrated Summary Catalogue of Paintings*, with an introduction by Homan Potterton (1981) p. xxviii.

7. Information about accessions from the Board minutes, by kind permission of the Board of Governors and Guardians of the National Gallery of Ireland. See also James White, *The National Gallery of Ireland* (1968) pp.36-7. The painting is listed in the *Municipal Art Gallery, Dublin: Illustrated Catalogue* (1958) no. 36, p. 291. *A Morning in a City* was also loaned to the Dublin Municipal Gallery, when it was acquired in February 1944; and *Men of Destiny*, donated by the Committee of the National Loan Exhibition in July 1946, was offered on loan to the Dublin Municipal Gallery 'during the life time of the artist'.

8. H. Pyle, op.cit., p. 164.

9. T. Bodkin, *Hugh Lane and his Pictures* (1956) pp. 62-8.

10. J. M. Synge, *Collected Works* II (1966) p. 306.

11. *Irish Arts Review*, Vol. I no. 4 (Winter 1984) pp. 24-8 (ill.), 'The Dun Emer Guild', by P. Larmour; H. Pyle, *Jack B. Yeats in the National Gallery of Ireland* (1986) pp. 10-13.

12. See *Irish Women Artists from the 18th century to the present day* (National Gallery of Ireland catalogue, 1986) pp. 22-7 (ill.), 'Women and the Arts and Crafts Revival in Ireland c. 1886-1930' by N. Gordon Bowe.

13. *The Circus Dwarf* (1912), *The Haute Ecole Act* (1925), *The Clown among the People* (1930), *The Clown of Ocean* (1945), *The Great Tent has Collapsed* (1947) etc., all in private collections. *The Singing Clown* (1928) is in Sligo Museum and Art Gallery.

14. The attempt by the National Gallery to concentrate on the exhibition of old masters, by sharing a system of loan/exchange with the Dublin Municipal Gallery of Modern Art, may be an explanation: though this could not have been the case after 1971, when Yeats technically became an old master.

15. Although Homan Potterton, who was Director 1980-1988, bought no works by Yeats, he commissioned the descriptive catalogue of the collection, illustrated in colour, Hilary Pyle, *Jack B. Yeats in the National Gallery of Ireland* (1986).

Jean-Jacques Bachelier
(1724-1806)
The Death of Milo of Croton (1761)
NGI. Cat. No. 167

THE FALL AND RISE OF JACQUES-LOUIS DAVID IN DUBLIN

Robert Rosenblum

By a series of happy and unexpected coincidences, James White's professional biography, the rapid growth of scholarly knowledge concerning Jacques-Louis David, and my own adventures in art history all converged in one place, the National Gallery of Ireland.

The first part of the story has to do with cleaning of the Augean stables of David misattributions; the second, with the search for lost treasures by the master himself. Part One was prompted by my very first visit, in 1958, to Dublin, where, after setting my bags down in a hotel, I rushed to the National Gallery and was immediately stopped in my tracks by a huge painting that bore, so I read, a nameplate identifying it as a work by David totally unfamiliar to me. The subject, nevertheless, was a familiar one in French art, especially sculpture; the horrendous death of the Greek athlete, Milo of Crotona, who, his hand trapped in a tree trunk, fell prey to wild animals. But as a passionate enthusiast for David, and as a zealous young scholar of his work who had never before come upon a reference to such a painting, I could only be dumbfounded. The picture, to be sure, was unforgettable in its heroic rhetoric of physical anguish inspired by the Laocoön, and clearly had something to do with the mixture of modern passion and antique marble that helped to define David; but in every other way, it eluded the master's grasp. Awkward foreshortenings, fussy landscape detail, all too prominent wolves, and a total absence of edifying moral purpose made the attribution move from implausible to impossible. Yet the sheer size and authoritative presence of the Dublin painting kept nagging at me for an explanation. Who could have painted it and when? Its dimensions and ambitious look certainly suggested a painting that might have appeared at one of the biennial Salons of 18th-century Paris. A hunt was irresistible.

One day, several years later, the needle in the haystack appeared. Lo and behold, not only was there a painting of this very subject shown at the Salon of 1761 by a painter, Jean-Jacques Bachelier, who specialized in animals but wanted to elevate his stature to a "peintre d'histoire" by essaying a classical subject; but even better, the dimensions in the Salon *livret* corresponded to the Dublin painting. And better still, the virtuoso 18th-century French draughtsman, Gabriel de Saint-Aubin, had troubled to make a swift drawing after the painting in the margin of his own copy of the little catalogue. My detective work turned out to be one of those rare open-and-shut cases in which conflicts of interest or connoisseurship could not muddy the issue.

In 1965, one year after James White assumed the directorship, my publication of what seemed to me a tidy and definitive piece of scholarship appeared in a series of essays honoring my own professor at New York University, Walter Friedlaender.[1] How the new director of the National Gallery of Ireland felt about this demotion is not for me to say; but looked at positively, it could be considered that what would have been at best a minor painting by a major master, David, had been transformed into a major painting by a minor master, Bachelier. Nevertheless, this not only left the National Gallery without a David; but it also meant that at the time, the 1960s, no other public collection in Ireland or, in fact, the United Kingdom could claim to have a painting by the master. To see one, either the Channel or the Atlantic Ocean had to be crossed.

Such deflations of the Davidian corpus were typical of the scholarly purges that began most sensationally in 1951, when Charles Sterling unsettled unquestioned assumptions by disattributing a favourite painting by David at the Metropolitan Museum of Art, a portrait of Mlle. Charlotte du Val d'Ognes, which he hoped to demonstrate was, in fact, not by the master but by one of his many women students, Constance Charpentier.[2] Although in fact, this new attribution was to be seriously questioned (I, for one, never found it convincing), it set off a domino series of enquiries about David attributions that proved especially fruitful in the 1960s, when one museum after another, whether in Dublin, New York, or the French provinces, had to relinquish the happy fiction of a "David" to the sober scholarly fact of a lesser attribution to artists whose names were often barely known. I myself, after turning the Dublin "David" into a Bachelier, went on, in 1968, to resolve an equally vexing David problem at the Museum in Valence, where a painting no less fascinating than the Dublin *Milo* - an illustration to Dante's grisly tale of Count Ugolino in the Tower of Starvation, presumably signed and dated by David in Rome in 1786 - turned out to be something quite different, a painting from the Salon of 1800 by Fortuné Dufau;[3] and with similar goals of purification in mind, many other scholars succeeded, especially in the domain of portraiture, in unseating David's authority by turning up far lesser-known masters as the authors of paintings long treasured as being by the hand of the master. The Frick Collection in New York, for example, turned out, in 1962, to have a beautiful portrait of the Italian musician Antonio Bruni painted not by David, as the label had always claimed, but rather by one of his women students, Mme. Césarine Davin-Mirvault, who showed the painting at the Salon of 1804.[4]

For most museums, the clear light of scholarly truth meant that their pantheon of great artists was reduced by one major master; and so it was in 1965 at the National Gallery of Ireland, a year after James White took the reins. But the story does not come to an end here with a whimper, but concludes with a bang. Some

Jacques Louis David
(1748-1825)
**The Funeral of
Patroclus (1779)**
NGI. Cat. No. 4060

seven years later, in 1972, the lure of the hunt beckoned again. The prominent London art historian and dealer, Andrew Ciechaonwiecki, asked me whether, as a scholar of late 18th-century French painting, I would be good enough to have a look with him at what seemed to be an important, but unattributed painting in a venerable and aristocratic collection in Naples. We flew down to Rome together, and then drove on to Naples to visit this mysterious canvas in a grand and ill-lit palazzo; and there, on June 11, 1972, I had one of the great Eureka experiences of my professional life. Any knowledgeable student of David's work knew that for his first Paris Salon, that of 1781, he exhibited an ambitious Homeric painting, the *Funeral of Patroclus*; but that this work had soon disappeared from sight. But if there was no print after it, there were, at least, several related drawings to help us imagine what the lost work might have looked like. Could it possibly be that this large, grimy canvas, with its odd oblong format, had somehow ended up on the walls of a large *salone* in Naples? In fact, the connection with the drawings I remembered seemed as certain as the connection I had made between the Dublin *Milo* and the drawing of it by Gabriel de St. Aubin. After a few dazzling and unbalancing moments, I told Andrew that, hard as it was to believe, this murky painting simply had to be the lost David. Andrew bought it and had it cleaned, and thrilling to say, an inscription, *J. L. David f. Roma 1779*, appeared in the lower lefthand corner. The attribution case was decisively closed with the happiest of verdicts.

Happier still was the fact that the *Funeral of Patroclus* filled a major gap in our understanding of David's evolution; for it was the only ambitious painting on a classical theme that he executed during the five years, 1775 to 1780, that he spent in Rome as a student at the French Academy. Buoyed by this discovery, I rapidly published in 1973 a full account of the documentary evidence surrounding the lost painting as well as an effort to explain the pivotal, Janus-like role the canvas played in the drama of David's successful attempts to purge himself of his Rococo past and to espouse a new vision of antique tragedy and epic grandeur that would continue to fire his genius both before and after the Revolution.[5] But so swift was the pace of David's resurrection of the classical world that he quickly felt embarrassed by his *Funeral of Patroclus*, which seemed retrograde by comparison with the newer masterpieces - *Belisarius, Count Potocki, St. Roch* - that he also showed at his Paris Salon debut in 1781. Legend has it that he even used the painting as a luncheon table before selling it off to a Montpellier collector in 1782.

Jacques Louis David
(1748-1825)
**The Funeral of
Patroclus (1779)
(Detail)**
NGI. Cat. No. 4060

Posterity has not agreed with the master, and when the canvas was offered on the art market in London in 1972, it was obvious that a major David had unexpectedly reappeared. It was clear, too, that the work could fill an enormous gap in any museum collection, not only because of the name of the artist but because this particular painting encapsulated the thrilling story of French art a decade before the outbreak of the Revolution, perfectly poised, as it was, between a fluttering Rococo past and an austere, classicizing future. Astutely, James White seized the chance to acquire immediately this mirror of individual genius and communal history for the National Gallery of Ireland, which was soon able to share the painting with the world in 1974-75, at the exhibition *De David à Delacroix; La peinture française de 1774 à 1830.*[6] As for me, David, and Dublin, the tale had the best of endings. The false David I had taken away from the collection in 1965 was replaced, in 1973, by the real thing.

Notes

1. "On a Painting of Milo of Crotona," in *Essays in Honor of Walter Friedlaender* (edited by Marsyas, Institute of Fine Arts, New York University), Locust Valley, New York, 1965, pp. 147 - 51.

2. Charles Sterling, "A Fine David Reattributed," *Bulletin of the Metropolitan Museum of Art*, IX, January 1951, pp. 121-32.

3. "Who painted David's 'Ugolino'?" *The Burlington Magazine*, CX, November 1968, pp. 621-26.

4. Georges Wildenstein, "Un Tableau attribué à David et rendu à Mme. Davin-Mirvault: 'Le Portrait du Violiniste Bruni' (Frick Collection)," *Gazette des Beaux-Arts*, LIX, February 1962, pp. 93-7.

5. "David's 'Funeral of Patroclus' ", *The Burlington Magazine*, CXV, September 1973, pp. 567-76.

6. Paris, Grand Palais, No. 27. The painting then travelled with the exhibition to the Detroit Institute of Arts and the Metropolitan Museum of Art. It was sent off again in 1989 to the great bicentenary exhibition, *Jacques-Louis David, 1748-1825*, Paris, Musée du Louvre, no. 31.

Claude Lorrain
(1600-82)
Hagar and the Angel
(1656)
Private Collection, on loan to the National Gallery of Ireland

THE IRISH CLAUDES

Alistair Rowan

In the modern age it is perhaps not very often that lines or a line of poetry invade our consciousness as we look at a work of art. The Victorians were much given to this kind of cultural correlation, printing a few verses or a rhyming couplet beneath an oleographic plate to promote some literary association which today may seem obscure or else perhaps over contrived. We do not do this much nowadays and yet I invariably find that before the two landscapes by Claude Lorrain now in the National Gallery of Ireland, *Hagar and the Angel* and *Juno confiding Io to the care of Argus*, the solemn, measured opening of Gray's *Elegy written in a country churchyard* comes always to my mind. The tug of the poetic language is insistent:

> 'The curfew tolls the knell of parting day,
> The lowing herd winds slowly o're the lea,
> The ploughman homeward plods his weary way,
> And leaves the world to darkness and to me.'

Gray establishes in his opening lines an immediate image - vivid and timeless - of the unchanging pastoral landscape of eighteenth-century Europe. It is a poetic response to Nature, as poignant in its precise observation as in the resigned meditation on the condition of the rural poor which the evening countryside evokes. Gray is an eminently pictorial poet and it is perhaps for this reason that his words seem to marry spontaneously with the artistic visions of Claude Lorrain, perhaps the most supremely poetic painter ever to touch landscape.

Claude's pictures are not of real places. He does not set up his canvas in the countryside and give us a view of the Tiber near Rome, where he lived, nor of the Alban hills. His aim is to create a landscape of the imagination, not a particular view which his contemporaries might recognise, but a timeless ideal world in which what we accept as true is not the topographical detail but the very essence of the painter's vision. The places shown in the two Irish Claudes are not real in themselves but the elements out of which they are composed, the animals, plants shrubs and trees - and the light and atmosphere - are absolutely real and completely convincing. This is a world which we can all know and experience. Claude is one of the very greatest artists and these two paintings, though not physically large, will amply repay the visitor who pauses to give them the attention they deserve.[1]

Claude Lorrain
(1600-82)
Juno Confiding Io to the Care of Argus (1660)
NGI. Cat. No. 763

Like many northern artists Claude travelled to Italy in early adolescence and after a period of experimentation, with different masters and different types of painting, fixed on landscape as his chosen means of expression. In fact he became a specialist. Though in his earlier work he was often content to paint pastoral scenes of no particular subject or intention, perhaps some peasants relaxing in the countryside or the Holy family resting during the journey to Egypt, as his art matured, the subject came to have much more significance for the artist. The two paintings in the National Gallery are good examples of this trend. Both are mature works and each is painted to illustrate a precise subject: an angel appearing to Hagar in the wilderness, which Claude painted in 1656, and Juno leaving a white heifer in the care of the herdsman Argus, painted four years later in 1660.[2] Claude was 56 and 60 years old when he created these ideal landscapes. They are works which distil a lifetime's experience of the real countryside and it is perhaps this very understanding of nature which gives them their special appeal.

Claude, as an artist, was totally absorbed in the natural world. His interest in painting did not express itself in extravagant Baroque images of people or in grandiose architectural views but in the meticulous and loving record of plants and trees, of inanimate nature and the effects of light and shade. Joachim von Sandrart, the German painter and writer who mixed for some years with the community of foreign artists in Rome, gives a lively account of visits with Claude, Pieter van Laer and Nicolas Poussin to a farm which Poussin rented north of the city beyond the Ponte Molle. These meetings could on occasion be boisterous yet the impression which is given of Claude is of a shy, retiring man, an introverted personality sitting quiet in the company of others, and someone who needed time to be alone. Such a person draws energy and inspiration from moments of isolation and it was no doubt this aspect of his personality that led Claude regularly to withdraw into the countryside and there to study and record with graphic precision the infinite variety of nature. Claude's drawings in the open air, in pencil, pen, body colour, ink and sepia wash provided the raw material from which his landscapes were created.[3] Thus the elements with which we are presented are of observed reality, of light obscured by dense foliage or filtered through the lighter fronds of sapling trees, as in the clump that rises behind Juno, Io and Argus, a subtle and carefully observed juxta-position of effects which is typical of Claude. Both paintings also reflect the almost botanical fascination exhibited by the artist in describing plant forms. The foreground of each is filled, in a way which Claude had learnt from the example of Adam Elsheimer, with detailed and quite charming studies of a variety of plants commonly found in wasteland or undergrowth: there are briars with serrated pinnate leaves in both pictures, bright spots of a plant like colt's foot in the painting of Hagar and plantains and a large mullein in the first year of its growth in the foreground of the Io picture.

Both pictures are enlivened by quite beautiful studies of animals; not painted simply for the sake of painting an animal or for demonstrating a particular skill as a Dutch artist might do, but absorbed sympathetically into the landscape as elements of it. Claude's animals often appear only in part: the little flock of goats behind Io, or the head and high backs of the cattle that have gone foraging in the ditch behind Argus. This is the painting of an artist who understands and has noticed the habits of cattle: we are surprised by the hint of their presence as can happen in real life when an unseen herd suddenly reveals itself over the lea of a hill. It is common enough for cattle to seek moist damp places in the summer and Claude places Io's companions in exactly the right sort of place within his picture. It is a group of deer, delicate fragile creatures who gently crop the grass, that point up the naturalness of the scene in the painting of Hagar's story. Once again three are shown as no more than the upper half of an animal, peeping up above the rise of a bank, but Claude knows how deer behave at evening time and has shown them with up-turned ears, continually flicking and on the move to prevent flies from settling.

All these minutely observed studies of trees, plants and animals are combined into a single image and given pictorial coherence by Claude's greatest single quality, his manipulation of light. Claude's paintings breathe a real atmosphere, and once again, the accuracy of the effect is achieved by detailed studies that lead the artist to the perfection of a particular skill. Claude's skies shimmer, changing from a brilliant pale colour of great luminosity at the level of the horizon - coral pink in the painting of Hagar and pale cream in the Io story - to a rich deep blue at the top of the canvas. Unlike Poussin, and most other seventeenth-century painters who treated landscape, the gradations of colour are not juxtaposed in bold contrasts but merge imperceptibly one with another in a technique that is quite special to Claude. Let the eye jump from the horizon to the top of either picture and the change in tone and density will be most clearly appreciated but the gradations of tone are so subtle and so carefully worked that they can hardly be detected at any spot on the canvas. What Claude does is to scumble one colour over another so that a thick layer of paint is laid upon the under surface and

Claude Lorrain
(1600-82)
Juno Confiding Io to the Care of Argus
(1660)(Detail)
NGI. Cat. No. 763

dabbled over it; immediately above this dabbled surface another shade or tone is introduced and gradually the gradation of tone and colour is built up. It is an immensely complex process and one which, apart from close inspection, can not be detected when the eye is at the proper distance to read the painting as a whole. It is this technique which gives the special luminosity to Claude's skies.

In one area alone the artist is sometimes deficient: the drawing of human figures. The little group of Juno, Io and Argus has a certain static grace and it certainly gains from its position directly in front of a group of protective trees - for Claude, like Domenichino, always sets his figures in a conscious way within a composition - but Hagar and the angel leave rather more to be desired. There is something a little awkward in the view we are given of the angel's wings, which do not 'grow' convincingly out of its body and Hagar herself seems inordinately tall. She is kneeling on the ground yet already betrays the elongated form, which became a mannerism of Claude's late work, as if an extra length of perhaps as much as a foot had been let into the trunk of the body. Indeed if we imagine Hagar standing up, her height will be extraordinary. It has sometimes been suggested that the elongation of Claude's figures reflects his dependence on the engraved work of a fellow Lorrainer, Jacques Callot, but where Callot absorbs the fashion within his work as a whole, in Claude it can seem odd. The figures are nonetheless essential to the story of both pictures and that story is usually the starting point for the image the painter creates.

The biblical tale of Hagar attracted Claude on more than one occasion for it provided a theme of exactly the right type to appeal to seventeenth-century

Claude Lorrain
(1600-82)
Hagar and the Angel (1656)(Detail)
Private Collection, on loan to the National Gallery of Ireland

sensibility, a touching tale of a hardship and injustice borne by an innocent young woman. We first encounter Hagar, in *Genesis* chapter 16, when as an Egyptian slave girl and maid to Abraham's wife Sarah she is given to Abraham as a concubine and conceives a child by him. Sarah, who was at that time childless, became jealous. She fancied that Hagar would soon despise her mistress and treated her so badly that the girl ran away soon after she had become pregnant. Travelling through the wilderness on the way to Shur, Hagar was found by an angel who told her she should return to Abraham's household, submit to Sarah's harshness and that she would bear a child Ishmael whose descendants would be countless. Hagar returned but the rivalry between Sarah and her maid erupted again after Sarah herself had given birth to a son, Isaac. Sarah caught Ishmael teasing the baby and now insisted that the boy and his mother should be banished. Thus Abraham was obliged to send Hagar once more into the wilderness where, after the food and water which she had brought were finished, she was forced to abandon her son under a bush as she could not bear to watch him dying of thirst. Once more an angel came to the rescue of the distraught mother and child pointing out a well which saved both their lives. Ishmael settled in Paran and became famous as an archer.

Claude illustrated the story of Hagar five times. At first he was attracted to the earlier part of the tale when the angel appears to Hagar in the wilderness on her own; he made two versions of this subject in 1646 and 1654 before designing the Dublin picture which also illustrates this part of the story. Later, in 1668, he produced the most closely inter-related pair of paintings of his entire career to

Claude Lorrain
(1600-82)
Landscape with Abraham Expelling Hagar and Ishmael (1668)
Trustees of the British Museum

illustrate Abraham banishing Hagar - watched by a vindictive Sarah from a parapet above - and, the subsequent part of the story, when the Angel appears to Hagar and Ishmael in the wilderness. The second Dublin picture of Juno, Io and Argus is another illustration of a touching story and here once again Claude is elaborating on a theme whose subject had already attracted his attention in 1644 and 1646. The Dublin picture is Claude's last version of this subject and it is in fact the first of a pair of paintings which tell the story of Io as a whole.

While the history of Hagar has a happy ending the episode of Jupiter's love for Io, told in the bitter-sweet poetry of the first book of Ovid's *Metamorphoses*, is full of sadness. Io was a water nymph, the daughter of the River God Inachus. She was loved by Jupiter who cast a dark cloud around her to trap her and then, appearing out of the mist, seduced her. Juno, who was well used to her husband's infidelities, noticed the extraordinary cloud on a bright clear day and, suspecting that she was being duped, 'came gliding down from the top of heaven' to see what was going on. Jupiter who sensed his wife's arrival had just time to turn Io into a white heifer though according to Ovid 'even in this form she was still beautiful'. When the god gave no satisfactory answer as to whose herd the lovely creature came from, Juno's suspicions were confirmed. Quite out-manouvering her husband and to thwart any further affairs she boldly asked for Io as a gift. Not to surrender the heifer would have uncovered what had actually happened so Io, now transformed, was given by a reluctant Jupiter to Juno who confined her for safe keeping to the herdsman Argus, a man whose 'head was set about with a hundred eyes, which took their rest in sleep, two at a time in turn'. Poor Io! 'When she strove to stretch out suppliant arms to Argus she had no arms to

Claude Lorrain
(1600-82)
Landscape with Mercury and Argus (1660)
Trustees of the British Museum

stretch, and when she attempted to voice her complaints, she only mooed'. For a while it seemed that Juno had triumphed but Jupiter was so irritated by his wife's success that he ordered Mercury to find Argus, and kill him. Disguising himself as a goatherd, Mercury first caught Argus's attention by his skillful playing of pan pipes, lulled him to sleep until all his eyes were closed and then cut off his head. Juno was furious: in revenge she created a stinging fly to plague Io and chase her round the world, while in pity she gathered Argus's hundred eyes and set them in her peacock's tail.

It is the second part of the Io story which is more commonly shown in art, with Argus, 'perched apart on a high top, keeping watch on every side'. Claude's two first versions are of this subject and the pendant - or pair - of the Dublin picture shows Argus and Io with Mercury and a herd of goats which the murderous god had collected to provide himself with a credible disguise. The scene shown in the Dublin painting, *Juno confiding Io to the care of Argus*, is unique.

Claude's determination to specialise in landscape proved highly successful. By the time he was in his middle thirties he was already a celebrated painter to such an extent that other artists began to replicate his style and even to paint fake Claudes. The artist's response to this situation - to make a drawn record of each of his paintings before it left the studio - brought into being one of the most unusual documents in the entire history of art, the *Liber Veritatis*, now in the British Museum, which contains a collection of 195 drawings by Claude and records all his finished work from about 1635 until the time of his death in 1682.[4]

The designs in the *Liber Veritatis* make up a unique category in the history of drawing for they are neither sketches, individual studies, nor designs produced in

Claude Lorrain
(1600-82)
Landscape with Juno Confiding Io to the Care of Argus (1660)
Trustees of the British Museum

the evolution of a composition, which is the usual status of most drawings, nor are they copies by other artists *after* Claude. They are original copies by the artist himself and copies in which he is clearly prepared to adjust the proportions of a composition to make it accord better with the pre-determined shape of the pages of the book in which he set out to record the appearance of his paintings. This is of course an artistic activity innately extending the drawing beyond the bounds of mere record so that the relative scale of the figure groups is increased and proportions are altered. There can never be any doubt as to the identity of the picture recorded by Claude for that was his essential purpose in creating the volume, yet equally the artist's freedom in design is left unimpaired. The *Liber Veritatis* drawings of the two paintings of the Io story demonstrate the use of the book clearly. They allow us to see the composition of the pendant picture of Mercury, Argus and Io (this painting is now in a private collection in South Africa) and here the temple on the left and the figure group are both drawn larger than in the finished picture. In the case of *Juno confiding Io to the care of Argus* the painting and the drawing are remarkably similar yet even here a careful comparison will establish differences: the town in the middle distance is proportionally larger in the drawing while the group of trees behind Juno and Argus is slightly altered in the silhouette and the handling of their trunks is different. Claude even adds three birds in the drawing wheeling in the sky above the town though no trace of them can be found in the actual painting. Nonetheless a comparison of the goats and cattle in the two versions, the drawing and the painting, will prove the remarkable care taken by Claude to include every relevant detail in his drawing even to the tiny figures on the bridge and the man in a boat rowing on the river.

Claude Lorrain *(1600-82)* **Landscape with Hagar and the Angel (1656)** *Trustees of the British Museum*

The drawing for the painting of Hagar and the Angel provides a contrast. This is one of the most altered of all Claude's *Liber Veritatis* drawings. The canvas of the painting is of a tall format, almost square but a little taller than it is wide, while in the drawing taken from the picture Claude has expanded the composition laterally to fill an oblong space: the proportion of foliage in the tree tops and sky is about the same in both images but the shape is radically different and though the figures are identifiably similar the animal details in the background are quite sketchy in the drawing. In passing we may note the distinctly different 'feel' that the oblong drawing conveys beside the more intimate structure of the taller painting.

The Irish Claudes complement each other in a number of ways. In the first place they illustrate the two main sources for subject matter which the artist used throughout his life: the bible and classical poetry. They are painted on a different scale. Though it is the more intimate subject, the scene showing Hagar is considerably larger: it is painted on a coarser canvas with a diagonal weave and it has to be viewed from a little further away than the Io picture which is meticulous, jewel-like in its finish and infinitely delicate. One surface glows like enamel while the other seems almost flat and is more thinly and more freely painted. The two pictures also differ in mood for the angel appearing to Hagar is optimistic and makes use of a warm palette while Juno, Io and Argus inhabit a landscape which is full of foreboding and is described, in consequence, in cooler, even chill, colours.

In this contrast we can appreciate the extent to which the artist relied on the subject matter for his artistic inspiration for there can be no doubt that the variety of moods in his mature work comes as a direct consequence of the stories which he illustrates. Each landscape is devised to support, if in a subliminal way, the poetic message of the text. In the case of Hagar we are shown an evening scene. A convention of Baroque art, possibly originating in the theatre, suggested that a scene in which light comes from the left-hand side was set in the morning while a light from the right meant that it was evening. Thus in Claude's last versions of the Hagar story in 1668, Abraham sends Hagar and her son out into an eerie early-morning landscape, with a low sun throwing long shadows from left to right while the pair are saved by the angel at evening time. In the Irish picture a warm evening light is flooding the scene, catching the tops of the brushwood that grows around the base of the larger trees, casting the long reassuring shadows that mark the end of a fine day, and fringing Hagar's head with light as, crossing her hands in greeting, she turns to face the angel. The stillness, the peaceful scene of distant mountains and the sea, and the peach and coral glow of the sky all convince us that Divine assistance is at hand.

In the case of Juno, Argus and Io, the intervention of the gods is anything but benign. The tale offers a criticism of the havoc which can be caused by unbridled self-will. Io and Argus are its innocent victims and so, in the opening stage of the story, Claude shows us a landscape of surpassing beauty, yet one which is tinged with impending sadness. It is morning. A cool light illuminates the group of figures, Juno commanding with up-raised arm, Io meek with a beautiful big eye, and Argus kneeling, frightened or astonished, by the demands of Jupiter's queen. The long shadows that are cast here carry no reassurance; no warm light tinges the tops of the bushes or brightens the plant forms in the foreground while a chill wind tosses the tops of the trees and twists the stems of the willow branches immediately behind Juno and Io. On the bridge behind, and on the roadway that leads to the town, tiny figures stroll by- some no more than dots of creamy pink paint to suggest the head and shoulders of a figure passing behind a bank that obscures our view of the road. In populating a landscape, Claude was an absolute master. In his many sea-port scenes tiny figures peer down from parapets upon the quays and boats below and, in the case of this particular picture, the little distant figures certainly add poignancy to the scene. They are there to underscore the continuity of ordinary life, a continuity which, at times of personal sadness or tragedy, can seem to be almost an affront. While mischievous gods send Io and Argus on a relentless course to destruction, the life of an unheeding ordinary world continues in the background.

A number of Claude's drawings, in the *Liber Veritatis* and elsewhere, provide precise page references to contemporary editions of the texts which he chose to illustrate. There can be no doubt therefore that his created ideal landscapes were intended to be an expression, through natural forms, of the ideals and emotions suggested by the stories themselves. In Claude's art we encounter a painter who regarded his subject not simply as an excuse to paint a conventionalised view but as the starting point for the creation of an ideal landscape that would be both true and sympathetic to its poetic source. The Irish Claudes amply support this view and it is no doubt for this reason that they can still stir poetic memories in the mind. If the scene with Juno, Io and Argus evokes 'the breezy call of incense-breathing morn' with swallows 'twittering from the straw built shed', Hagar takes us at once to that magic time at the very end of a day when light in long striations falls across the fields and tiny boats lie motionless upon a distant sea:

'Now fades the glimmering landscape on the sight,
And all the air a solemn stillness holds,
Save where the beetle wheels his droning flight,
And drowsy tinklings lull the distant folds'.

Notes

1. The primary source of reference on the paintings of Claude is the Critical Catalogue by Marcel Röthlisberger, *Claude Lorrain, The Paintings*, New Haven, 1961, 2 vols. (revised and up-dated 1979).

2. The landscape with *Hagar and the Angel* is the property of The Lady Dunsany and is on loan to the National Gallery of Ireland. *Juno confiding Io to the care of Argus* was bequeathed to the National Gallery of Ireland in 1918 by Sir Hugh Lane (Cat. No. 763).

3. The major work on Claude's drawings is Marcel Röthlisberger, *Claude Lorrain, The Drawings*, University of California, Los Angeles, 1968, 2 vols.

4. A complete facsimile edition of the *Liber Veritatis*, with an Introduction and catalogue by Michael Kitson (including five extra drawings added after Claude's death) was published by British Museum Publications Ltd., London, in 1978.

Attributed to Edgar Degas
(1834-1917)
**Portrait of
George Moore**
*(1852-1933)
Ashmolean Museum,
Oxford*

GEORGE MOORE AND DEGAS

Denys Sutton

After his father died, George Moore's mother asked him whether he wanted to go to Oxford or Cambridge University, but he made the correct decision by opting to cross over to Paris so as to study painting. Thus the young man accompanied by his valet William Moloney set off for the French capital in 1873, thereby embarking on aesthetic and other adventures that coloured his life and provided him with a stock of memories and ideas that remained with him for ever.

One of Moore's talents was a gift for evoking the spirit of the place, as he does in his memorable description of his arrival in Paris. 'We all know', are his words in his admirably entitled book *Confessions of a Young Man* (1888), 'the great grey and melancholy Gare du Nord at half-past six in the morning; and the miserable carriages, and the tall, haggard city. Pale, sloppy, yellow houses; an oppressive absence of colour; a peculiar bleakness in the streets.' This vivid picture, not unlike a canvas by Raffaëlli, helps to explain Moore's sympathy for art, and eventually for that of the avant-garde.

In this early autobiography, Moore describes his first steps as an art student and his visit to the painter Alexandre Cabanel who told him that he did not accept private pupils and advised him to attend the Ecole des Beaux-Arts. It says much for the agreeable atmosphere of those days that Moore took a cab to the British Embassy, where the Ambassador, Lord Lyons, 'an elegant old gentleman', received him and arranged for the requisite documents to be sent to the Ministry of Fine Arts. However, the Ecole des Beaux-Arts did not please Moore and eventually he ended up at Julian's famous school in the Passages des Panoramas, where the students included no fewer than eight or nine English girls.

Romance was in Moore's blood. He was apt to embroider the truth so that it is by no means easy to establish the facts concerning his life in Paris, where, except for an occasional absence, he remained until about 1880, and it is even not clear where he resided at specific periods. He muddled the details about his relations with various artists, as Douglas Cooper pointed out in *Horizon* (1945), but he certainly visited the third Impressionist exhibition of 1877 where, among other works, mentioned in the *Confessions*, he saw Monet's *Dindons* (Musée d'Orsay, Paris), although at that stage he and his friends did not appreciate these masters. 'Then', he wrote, 'we stood and screamed at Monet, the most exquisite painter of blond light'.

Moore kept up his lessons for a year or so, but then, to quote him, 'I laid down my charcoal and said "I will never draw again". That vow I have kept.' His days in Paris were happy, above all, he discovered modern French literature, Baudelaire and through Gautier, he came to love Balzac, 'the great moral influence of my life.'

He also enjoyed cafés, meeting the poet Villiers de l'Isle Adam at Le Rat Mort and becoming an habituée of the Nouvelle Athènes in the Place Pigalle and in a delicious passage he evokes the smells and sounds of café life. His meeting with Villiers de l'Isle Adam was fortunate for through him, he was introduced to Mallarmé. He wrote about him in the *Butterfy* (Summer 1909) and the French poet appears in Moore's novel *Seymour and Some Women* (1917).

Exactly when Moore came across such stars as Manet and Degas is difficult to determine, if his claim is exact that he first met Manet when this artist was installed in his studio in the rue d'Amsterdam then this must have been after 1878, when he moved there. It is sometimes claimed that Moore first encountered J.E. Blanche, that pillar of the Entente Cordiale, in Manet's studio, but Blanche denied this, suggesting that they may have met one another at the painter Henri Gervex, with Henner and Ary Redon, or even at Dieudonne's hotel in Ryder Street, London.[1]

Manet appealed enormously to Moore who wrote about him in an appreciative manner, his hero even made three portraits of him, one of which depicts him seated in the Nouvelle Athènes (The Metropolitan Museum of Art, New York). Yet Moore never devoted a full-length essay to Manet and his art.

Of all the French avant-garde, Degas stimulated Moore to his most sustained effort as an art critic, possibly because the painter is an enigmatic personality. The date of the first encounter between Degas and Moore is uncertain: an entry in the artist's *Notebook No. 27*, which specifically states on page 28 that Moore was staying or intended to stay at the Hôtel Victoria, suggests that he was correct in saying that their meeting occurred in 1876. In *Avowals* (1919) Moore claims that he came across Manet for the first time at the Nouvelle Athènes when in the throes of correcting proofs. These were presumably of his book of poems, *Flowers of Passion* published in 1878; his earliest recorded appearance in a periodical came in 1880. According to Moore, Degas was in the café on the same occasion, but, as no mention is made of Manet introducing the two men, it could well be that they already knew one another and thus that a date for their meeting prior to 1878 is right. Moore is alleged to have lived in the rue de la Tour des Dames, but Jean C. Noel in his extensive volume on Moore (1966) can unearth no evidence that, in fact, he resided in this street. However, if he did live there he would have been a neighbour of Degas, the Halévys, Fromentin and Madame Howland.

Moore got to know Degas relatively well, visiting his studio, eating with him and seeing him at the Nouvelle Athènes. He related in *Hail and Farewell* (1911) that he introduced his rather astonishing friend, Lewis Weldon Hawkins, a minor academic painter, to Degas who was much tickled by his conversation, telling the master that Jules Lefebvre 'sums up all the qualities an artist should possess'. Degas burst into laughter and when they left he whispered into Moore's ear: *'Votre ami est très fort. Il m'a fait monter l'échelle comme personne'*. And on coming across Moore some days later in the Rue Pigalle Degas asked after Hawkins.

Moore and Degas visited the Exposition Universelle together in May 1889[2] and according to Moore, the painter enjoyed the French translation of *Confessions of a Young Man* so much that he was invited to join him for breakfast.[3] Degas's own comments on Moore are few, but according to Sickert, he found him 'very intelligent.[4] Daniel Halévy reported the master as recalling that they talked a great deal at the Nouvelle Athènes. However, when in the summer of 1890 he lunched with Ludovic Halévy and Degas,[5] Daniel Halévy noted[6] 'Good old Moore becomes silent the instant Degas appears and watches him with the eyes of a child' Unfortunately the slight pencil drawing of Moore in the Ashmolean Museum, Oxford is no longer accepted as by the artist, but it does provide a portrait of him during his Paris period.

At the start, Moore did not appreciate Degas's work, and after his earliest visit to the artist and looking at his portraits, at his marvellous ballet-girls, and the washerwomen, 'he understood (his own words); nothing of what I saw.'[7] His blindness to Degas alarmed him, as he told Manet, who only 'murmured under his breath that it was very odd, since there were astonishing things in Degas'.

He soon learnt to appreciate Degas and on 3 February 1886 he wrote to his mother that while spending a pleasant fortnight in Paris, he persuaded Edward Martyn to buy two pictures.[8] It is generally, and probably correctly, assumed that these were Degas's *Deux Danseuses dans la Loge* and *Les Deux Arlequins*, both of which were bequeathed by Martyn to the National Gallery of Ireland. Weight is given to this contention by the fact that (as Joseph Hone first observed in his life of Moore (1936)), John Norton, a character in Moore' novel *A Mere Accident* (1887) is based on Martyn who is described as possessing pictures by 'the four great painters, Manet, Degas, Monet and Renoir.' Martyn, a distant relation of Moore, owned two pictures by Corot and Monet and did much on behalf of the Irish Revival. Champion of the reform of sacred music in Ireland, he financed the Palestrina choir, and wrote about this composer in *The Speaker* at the early date of 1895. He was a passionate Wagnerian, a taste that emerges from Moore's acccount of him in *Hail and Farewell*, when they were at Bayreuth together.

In the same year (1886) an article on the last Impressionist exhibition appeared in the *Bat* (25 May 1886), a small magazine of the type described by Moore in his novel *Mike Fletcher (1889)*. Although the piece is unsigned[9] the content suggests Moore's hand as was first proposed by Edwin Gilcher in his excellent Bibliography of the writer (1970). 'The four studies from the Nude', to quote Degas, 'are at once a terror and a delight to behold'. 'His account of these pastels betrays his sympathy for the poor and downtrodden which is one of the most attractive aspects of his early fiction and reflects the influence of Zola; thus he writes 'The short, coarse, thick thighs of the poor working woman, deformed by the toil of modern days, has never been seen on canvas before; she is passing her chemise over her lumpy shoulders. A little to the right of her we have a woman sponging herself in a ten-and-six-penny tin bath, but the chef d'oeuvre is the short legged lump of human flesh who, her back turned to us, grips her flanks with both hands. The effect is prodigious. Degas has done what Baudelaire did - he has invented a frisson nouveau. Terrible, too terrible, is the eloquence of these figures. Cynicism was one of the great means of eloquence of the middle ages, and from Degas' pencil flows the pessimism of the early saint, and the scepticism of these modern days.'

The first of these nudes described by Moore is probably *The Woman washing herself* (The National Gallery of Art, Washington D.C.), and the second is *Femme à son Lever: La Boulangère* c. 1866 (The Henry and Rose Pearlman Foundation, on loan to the Princeton University Art Museum).

Edgar Degas
(1834-1917)
Two Ballet Dancers in the Dressing Room (c. 1880)
NGI. Cat. No. 2740

The attribution of this article to Moore, therefore, seems justified on several counts: its style possesses verve, though lively writing was then the order of the day; moreover, the laudatory reference to Seurat's *'Un Dimanche à la Grand-Jatte* (Art Institute, Chicago) is echoed in a rather lower key in an essay on 'Monet, Pissarro, Sisley and the Decadence' published in *The Speaker* in 1892 and reprinted in *Modern Painting* (1893).

Moore's view of Degas's nudes - powerful works indeed - are more or less identical with those expressed in *Confessions of a Young Man* in which he emphasised that the artist's genius lay in infusing 'new life into the worn out theme of the naked woman'. Many years later in *Ave*, the first volume of his autobiography *Hail and Farewell* (1911), Moore added a piquant detail about the woman who posed for *La Boulangère*. He did so when referring to a woman in Dürer's *Fortune*, which he had seen in Germany, observing that 'Degas more than once drew a creature as short legged and as bulky, and the model he chose was the wife of a butcher in the Rue de la Rochefoucauld.'

Moore's account of the circumstances of this woman appearing at the artist's studio (as he recounted to Martyn in the book) is almost worthy of Feydeau. 'The poor creature arrived in all her finery, the clothes which she wore when she went to Mass on Sunday, and her amazement and her disappointment are easily imagined when Degas told her he wanted her to pose for him naked. She was accompanied by her husband, and knowing her to be not exactly a Venus de Milo, he tried to dissuade Degas, and Edward who has had little experience of life, expressed surprise that a husband should not guard his wife's honour more vigilantly; but he laughed when I told him that Degas had assured the butcher that the erotic sentiment was not strong in him, and he liked my description of the poor, deformed creature standing in front of a tin bath, gripping her flanks with both hands - his bias towards ecclesiasticism enables him to sympathise with the Middle Ages, and its inherent tendency to regard women as inferior, and to keep them out of sight.' His words echo those of the article in *Bat*.

Moore's experience of the Parisian world was reflected in several of his early novels, and Ronald Pickvance[10] has drawn attention to the echoes of French avant-garde art discernable in *A Modern Lover* (1883), *A Mere Accident* (1887) and *Mike Fletcher* (1889). The third book mentions 'a picture of ballet-girls bought in France', which is possibly a reference to the painting acquired by Martyn in Paris. The hero of the book declares that 'I know of no more degrading spectacle than that of a woman washing herself over a basin. Degas painted it once. I'd give anything to have that picture'. According to Ronald Pickvance, this work may be identifiable with the rather minor *La Toilette* (Lemoisne 767), which was in the Alexander Reid sale of 10 June, 1898. (Lot 56).

As is only to be expected an observer of the human scene such as Moore needed only a few deft sketches to bring Degas to life. In the *Confessions of a Young Man* he describes sitting next to him in the Nouvelle Athènes, writing that he was a 'round shouldered man in a suit of pepper and salt. There is', he went on, 'nothing very trenchantly French about him either, except the large neck tie, his eyes are small and his words are sharp, ironical, cynical.'

His main opportunity to discuss Degas came with his excellent piece in the *Magazine of Art* in 1890, which he rightly considered to be his best article on art which is illustrated with the *Répétition d'un ballet sur la Scene*, of 1874 (The Metropolitan Museum of Art, New York), then belonging to Walter Sickert, the *Ballet from 'Robert le Diable'*, owned by Constantine Ionides, (now in the Victoria and Albert Museum), and a group of mounted jockeys.

This essay is one of the most lively contemporary accounts of the master, who was then forty-six, with its references to 'the vast canvases of his youth' piled up 'in formidable barricades.' Moore noted the 'great wheels belonging to lithographic presses', and 'much decaying sculpture', including dancing girls 'modelled in red wax': these were 'strange dolls - dolls if you will, but dolls modelled by a man of genius.'

With a light touch Moore evokes the pleasant breakfast they enjoyed in the artist's apartment in the Rue Pigalle 'overlooking a courtyard full of flowering chestnut trees'. It was characteristic of Degas that he should have told Moore of his delight in a recent acquisition - a red chalk drawing of a hand by Ingres. His words were: 'That's my idea of genius, a man who finds a hand so lovely, so wonderful, so difficult to render, that he will shut himself up all his life, content to do nothing else but indicate finger-nails.'

Moore was quick to report the artist's usually trenchant and individual remarks: thus Degas maintained that literature has only done harm to art: 'You puff out the artist with vanity, you inculcate the taste for notoriety, and that is all: you do not advance public taste by one jot ...' Then he added: 'You do not even help us to sell our pictures.'

Degas recounted to Moore his happy memories of Manet and his displeasure of 'la vie de parade, so persistently sought by Mr. Whistler.' He said of this artist

Edgar Degas
(1834-1917)
La Boulangère (Etude de Nu, Femme à son Lever)
The Henry and Rose Pearlman Foundation, Inc., on Loan to the Art Museum, Princeton University

when he was having many photographs taken: 'You cannot talk to him; he throws his cloak around him - and goes off to the photographer.' He quotes, too, one of Degas's pointed works to a young man 'hungering for drawing room success' *'Jeune M ... dans mon temps on n'arrivait pas, dites?'*

One of Moore's most intriguing recollections is Degas's remarks to a landscape painter, whom he met at the Cirque Fernando: *'A vous il faut la vie naturelle, à moi la vie factice'*. Degas reminded Moore that his art was 'the result of reflection and study of the great masters; of inspiration, spontaneity, temperament - temperament is the word - I know nothing.'

The belief that Moore had no eye for art is strongly contradicted by his observations about Degas's works in this article; he appreciated the visual qualities of the race course scene, as when he noted that 'A race-horse walks a white post which cuts his head in twain'. This may well be a reference to *Jockeys before the Race* c. 1878-79, (Barber Institute, Birmingham).

Moore's judgement is displayed in his comments on Degas's artistic treatment of the ballet-girl. 'Artists', he said, 'will understand the almost superhuman genius it requires to take subject-matter that has never received artistic treatment before, and bring it at once within the sacred pale. Baudelaire was the only poet who ever did this; Degas is the only painter.' He was especially taken by *Dancers practising at the Bar*, c. 1876-77 (The Metropolitan Museum of Art, New York), noting that 'The arrangement of the picture is most unacademical, the figures are half-way up the canvas, and the great space of bare floor is balanced by the watering pot.'

Edgar Degas
(1834-1917)
The Rehearsal of the Ballet on the Stage (1874)
The Metropolitan Museum of Art, Gift of Horace Havemeyer, 1929. The H.Q. Havemeyer Collection

This exquisite picture was shown in the 1877 Impressionist exhibition which Moore visited, but as it is hard to believe that he remembered it some thirteen years later, he presumably saw it either in the artist's studio, or in the collection of Henri Rouart, to whom it was given by the artist.

He praised the picture of washerwomen, but considered that perhaps Degas's 'most astonishing revolution of all was the introduction of the shop window into art', referring to 'a large plate-glass window, full of bonnets', with 'a girl leaning forward to gather one.' His description of this picture led Moore to reflect on the years of 'servility and obeisance to customers' it expressed.[11] Although rather far fetched Moore's interpretation is a reminder that he was the author of that heart-rending naturalistic novel of a servant girl *Esther Waters* (1894). However, following on the point already made in his earlier writings, Moore affirmed that 'the most astonishing of all Degas's innovations are his studies of the nude.' He quoted Degas's famous saying *"La bête humaine qui s'occupe d'elle même: une chatte qui se lèche"*. 'Yes, it is the portrayal of the animal life of the human being, the animal conscious of nothing but itself.' Another citation from the artist apropos of a woman washing her feet led to the famous words: 'It is as if you looked through a key-hole', which has given rise to much unfortunate speculation on Degas as a 'voyeur'.

In the version of this essay published in *Impressions and Opinions* (1891), Moore added three long paragraphs concerning the pictures that especially appealed to him, among them *Leçon de Danse*, then in the possession of his friend Blanche and now in the Burrell Collection, Glasgow. He detected in this a 'certain analogy' with Watteau, 'the grace and lightness and air of fete remind us of

Watteau, the exquisite care displayed in the execution reminds us of the Dutchmen'. For Moore, Degas's portrait of the artist's father and Lorenzo Pagans (Museum of Fine Arts, Boston) recalls Holbein, and he much admired the portrait of Manet: 'Those who knew Manet well cannot look without pain upon this picture; it is something more than a likeness, it is as you saw the man's ghost.' The portrait of Mlle. Malot brought to mind 'certain Spanish painters'. (Degas painted from portraits of this dancer, Lemoisne 419-22). He perceptively noted that in Degas's studies of the nude there is a frankness which seems borrowed from the early Italians' and fully grasped the way in which Degas's art was 'based upon a profound knowledge of the great masters.'

Unfortunately this admirable assessment of Degas got him into trouble as the painter was furious about the allusion to his having assisted his brother over financial matters. Degas complained to Blanche about Moore's indiscretion in mentioning his private life. 'I am sorry that Degas is cross', Moore wrote to his friend,[12] who had furnished him with information, 'It is really too stupid of him. He will have to get over it but I will take your advice and refrain from sending him the article.' But the painter had seen it; Moore was dropped.

Despite his *contretemps*, Moore continued to support Degas, even claiming in a piece on 'Art Patrons' (*The Speaker*, 27 June, 1891) that he had advised collectors to buy his works, another article in this paper (5 December, 1891) provides a valuable account of *Répétition d'un Ballet sur la Scène* (The Metropolitan Museum of Art, New York). Moore correctly believed it to be originally a drawing done for the *Illustrated London News*; 'but the *News* could not make use of the drawing on account of the rectory circulation.' Degas, he continued, on receiving it back, 'began painting upon it in oil, very thinly - so thinly that the original drawing is still visible through the paint'.

That Degas's subject matter greatly appealed to Moore was shown by his comment on *At the Milliners*, 1882, (The Metropolitan Museum of Art, New York), when it was shown at Mr. Collie's rooms in Bond Street in 1892 (*The Speaker* 2 January, 1892) which enabled him to castigate the 'middle class woman'. Needless to say, there is no precise evidence concerning the woman's background', she could come from the upper reaches of society!

His novelist's love of commenting on what he took to be the theme of a picture rather led him astray when the famous *Au Café* (Musée d'Orsay, Paris) was lent by Arthur Kay to the Grafton Gallery in 1893. In his articles in *The Speaker* (25 February, 1893),[13] while realising that the man was his old friend Marcel Desboutin, Moore failed to grasp that the woman was the actress Ellen Andrée. Letting his imagination get the better of him, Moore declares that she was at 'the Elysée Montmartre until two in the morning, then she went to the *ratmort* and had a *soupe aux choux*; she lives in the Rue Fontaine, or perhaps the Rue Breda; she did not get up till half past eleven; then she tied a few soiled petticoats round her, slipped on that peignoir, thrust her feet into those loose morning shoes, and came down to the café to have an absinthe before breakfast. Heavens "what a slut". A life of idleness and low vice is upon her face; we read there her whole life. The tale is not a pleasant one, but it is a lesson.' The picture and the article caused a considerable stir and provoked a lengthy correspondence in the periodical press. Moore realising that he had gone much too far and was wrong in his interpretation made a handsome apology in three articles (*The Speaker* 25 March, and 8 April,

Edgar Degas
(1834-1917)
Au Café (1876)
Musée d'Orsay, Paris

1893), with the title 'The New Criticism' that reveal his skill and elegance as a formalist critic.

Another opportunity to render tribute to Degas came when in 1905 Hugh Lane arranged an exhibition in aid of the Gallery of Modern Art in Dublin; this was comprised of the Staats Forbes collection, strong in Corot and the Barbizon masters, a group of Impressionists from Durand-Ruel and paintings given by artists for the establishment of a Gallery should it come into being.

Moore was then living in Dublin at No. 4 Upper Ely Place, and already had shown an interest in Irish art, writing a preface for the catalogue of an exhibition of Nathaniel Hone's landscape painting held at No. 6 St Stephen's Green. Lane hoped that Moore would devote an article to the Gallery exhibition, but he declined to do so, although he agreed to deliver a lecture.

He had to face an audience which included several of the leading members of the Celtic Renaissance, among them W.B. Yeats, just back from New York and clad in a fur coat. The elder Yeats had painted Moore's portrait that year and said that his mind was the most stimulating he had ever come across and considered him to be a born fighter.

As was only to be expected, Moore's lecture was vivid and full of fascinating titbits of information.[14] Manet received the most attention, Degas was accorded less praise than in the 1890s, but Moore provided his audience with a selection of the master's witticisms and used passages that had appeared in his writings, such as the account of the painter at the Nouvelle Athènes.

Moore compared Degas with Leonardo da Vinci, both he claimed, being intellectual artists, and he found that this was true of the *Mona Lisa* and *Leçon de Danse*; 'they were painted with the brains rather than with the temperaments; and what is any intellect compared to a gift like Manet's?' 'He maintained that 'The intellectual pleasure that we receive from a mind so curiously critical, inquisitive and mordant as Degas's withers, but the joy we get from the gift of painting like Manet's is a joy that lasts for ever.' He found, too, that there were far too many 'quips'; in Degas's art: 'I include in my list of quips a great number of ballet girls and race horses.' Moore's comparison to *Mona Lisa* and *Leçon de Danse* was also made in *Memoirs of my Dead Life* (1900). After Degas's death in 1917 Moore republished his *Magazine of Art* article on the master in *The Burlington Magazine* (1918) with a short preface which adds a few significant details to his relationship with the artist. He recounts that at the end Degas 'under the power of remembrance' sent him word that 'he would be glad to see me when I came to Paris again. But it is difficult to renew a friendship that was as close as ours after several years; I did not feel that it could be renewed, and never saw Degas again'.

After Moore had given Paul Lafond of the Bibliothèque Nationale, who published a two volume book on Degas (1918-19), a copy of *Impressions and Opinions* (with his article on Degas), the latter wrote to him that 'Degas lives alone and almost blind, seeing nobody, without any kind of occupation.' Moore's sympathy for humanity is not in doubt, and he related how he 'fell to thinking of the old man of genius hearing of his pictures selling for thousands and unable to see them, sitting thinking, weary of his life.' Always keen on a good story, Moore went on to recount that Robert de Montesquiou (his name is not in fact supplied) succeeded in getting to see Degas. ' "Why Monsieur Degas," he asked, "do you remain always at Montmartre: why not let me take you to the Faubourg St Germain". The answer he got was: "Monsieur le comte de.... leave me upon my dunghill." '

These were by no means Moore's final words about Degas. In 1931 Daniel Halévy presented him with a copy of Degas's letters edited by Marcel Guèrin, for which he had written a preface. Moore, ever punctilious replied in English (18 August, 1931), praising Degas the correspondent because he painted his own portrait in his letters. 'The daily life of the man is related as Dürer might have related his', are his words, and he claimed that all his life Degas who admired the Middle Ages tried to 'equal Dürer and he was unable to do so. Nobody can ever equal Dürer'.

In a second long letter (1 September, 1931), Moore said that nobody but Jean Jacques Rousseau 'could have given a portrait of such intensity, and he was the least self conscious writer I ever remember'. In a revealing passage, Moore also declared that these letters reveal the real Degas: 'For a reason unknown to himself, Degas - never did a more sensitive human nature breathe beneath our skies - took devilish pains to persuade the world that he was an old bear incapable of finding a friendly word for anyone. The exact opposite is the truth.' Moore believed that nobody could ever write Degas's life. 'These letters' he maintains, 'are his autobiography; even if they do not give everything, and a first class writer, Balzac for example, could write some pages about a man who cannot resist the temptation of adorning himself out of coquetterie, with the mask of an old bear. What an innocent perversity'.[15]

During his time Moore saw a considerable number of works by Degas; his close friend Sir William Eden, to whom he dedicated *Modern Painting*, owned three of Degas's pictures one of which was that refined masterpiece *Washerwoman*, called by the baronet my own 'immaculate Degas.' Moore himself owned a pastel (unidentified) by Degas which hung on the staircase in his house, 121 Ebury Street, London.[16] He also gave Arthur Symons two lithographs by Degas as a wedding present in 1901.[17]

One of Moore's lesser known publications is his introduction to an anthology of what he terms 'pure poetry' (1924), and it is in keeping with this interest, that he was able to appreciate both the realism (such as it is) of Degas's works as well as their more abstract qualities. The sharp observer of human foibles who prided himself on his awareness of Balzac and Zola was also the imaginative Celtic dreamer, and it was not the least of his achievements that, despite reservations, he grasped much about the art and personality of a major artist of his period.

Notes

1. *Mes Modèles*, 1928, p. 209.

2. *The Hawk*, 24 December, 1889.

3. *The Burlington Magazine*, xxxii, 1918, p. 22.

4. 'Degas', *The Burlington Magazine*, xxxi, 1917, pp. 183-92.

5. *My Friend Degas*. Translated and edited by Mina Curtiss, 1966, p. 41.

6. Op.cit., p. 36.

7. It was first published by R. Pickvance, 'A New Discovered Drawing by Degas of George Moore', *The Burlington Magazine*, CV, 1963, p. 271-80.

8. Joseph Hone, *The Life of George Moore*, 1936, p. 123.

9. The text is reprinted in *Impressionists in England. The Critical Reception*, edited by Kate Flint, 1984, pp. 68-71. See also Kate Gruetzner 'Degas and George Moore. Some observations about the Last Impressionist Exhibition' in Degas, ed. R. Kendall, 1985. pp. 32-39.

10. *The Burlington Magazine*, CV, 1963 pp. 276-80.

11. *Apollo*, (111. 1976 p. 170.) quoted by Denys Sutton, 'The Vase and the Wash-Tub.'

12. The original article and the three subsequent pieces in *The Speaker* are reprinted by Flint op. cit. For an account of the controversy see R. Pickvance, 'L'Absinthe', *Apollo*, LXXVI, 1963, pp 395-98.

13. The lecture was published as *Remininiscenes of the Impressionists*, 1906, as a Tower Press Booklet, 38 Cornmarket, Dublin. For a convenient reprint of the text see *Hail and Farewell*, 1911, edited by Richard Cave, 1976, pp. 647-63.

14. These letters, originally written in French, were published in the twelfth edition of Daniel Halévy's, *Pays Parisien*, 1931, in the 1945 edition of *Lettres de Degas*, ed. Marcel Guerin and in the English translation, *Degas Letters*, 1947, where presumably they were rendered into English from the French text.

15. See J. Hone *op. cit.*, p. 298.

16. Kate Gruetzner, op. cit., suggests that the picture is identifiable with *The Hatshop Window* (Lemoisne 683) which means that Moore would have to have seen it in the studio. It is not particularly large, measuring 65 x 50cm.

17. See Denys Sutton, *'Degas et L'Angleterre'. Degas Inédit*, 1989, p. 288. note 7.

Jonathan Fisher
(fl. 1763-1809)
**A View of the Lower
Lake, Killarney**
NGI. Cat. No. 1797

ACQUIRING IRISH PAINTINGS
1964-1980

Michael Wynne

During the period 1964 to 1980, the years of James White's Directorship, he deliberately set himself the task of strengthening the Irish School of Painting in the National Gallery of Ireland. In addition to purchases, some really fine gifts and bequests arrived and a receptive climate was created to encourage such generosity.

From 1964 to 1980, works by many hitherto unrepresented Irish artists entered the collection. Looking, firstly, at eighteenth century artists, in 1965 neither Richard nor Robert Carver were represented in the Gallery. In 1973 a large Robert Carver, was bought from Leger of London for £4,500. In 1966 a superb small Jonathan Fisher of *The Lower Lake, Killarney,* a painting engraved in aquatint, was purchased from Anthony Thompson of Belfast, for £100. A second unquestionable Fisher, depicting *The Eagle's Nest, Killarney* a slightly tired canvas by an artist who painted thinly, to judge by his best known works, was acquired from the same Belfast dealer in 1967 for £350.

Views of Dublin are always popular, even to those who can not claim to be Dubliners. A view of Dublin Bay from the boat house of the University of Dublin, at Ringsend, by the scarcely known Thomas Snagg, was bought from James Gorry of Dublin in 1970 for £50. The modest price reflects the irretrievably lost paint areas, but the picture adds much to the knowledge of the social scene of Dublin in the eighteenth century. Six years later a magnificent pair of large panoramic views of Dublin by William Ashford, first President of the Royal Hibernian Academy, were purchased through Spink's of London from a member of the Camden family for £12,000. One was an extensive view of Dublin from Clontarf, while its pair showed Dublin from the village of Chapelizod, just west of the city, nestling under the Phoenix Park. An ancestor of the vendor had been Lord Lieutenant of Ireland in the last decade of the eighteenth century, and thus there is every likelihood that the paintings were ordered by that Lord Camden, as a worthy memento of his Dublin assignment. Unfortunately, prior to being offered to the Gallery, the paintings had been subjected to the then current London art trade lining technique which could be coded "roll of linoleum". Nonetheless, there was more than enough remaining to make such panoramas of the capital city an imperative buy. In passing, one may observe that many Irish landscape painters's techniques in the eighteenth century were relatively thin, and sometimes included glazes, which means that restorers must approach them with great care until they

Nathaniel Hone the Elder
(1718-84)
The Conjuror (1775)
NGI. Cat. No. 1790

have built up experience of their styles; Fisher, Roberts and early Ashfords fall into this category.

A superb view of the inner section of the great harbour of Cork, with the city itself on the horizon, painted in a large work by Nathaniel Grogan, was purchased from Oscar and Peter Johnson of London in 1973, at a cost of £9,800. Five years later a similarly large Grogan of a harbour scene was purchased from Richard Green of London, for £15,000. To this day the precise location of the view is debated, the original designation of Kinsale being rejected. Since Grogan was a Cork man, and painted in the environs, the harbour is undoubtedly related to the area. The answer may well lie in artistic licence or creativity. While the view leads one here or there in the many notable harbours of the Cork area, the finished canvas may well be *A Harbour View* taking elements from local land and seascape. A picture of this scale was certainly not begun and finished out of doors in one place. Indeed, in the earlier acquisition, Grogan's houses and follies on the right hand side of the painting do not conform precisely to the well-documented area of the inner portion of Cork harbour. In both paintings, the figures are extremely well drawn to populate the views. Before the acquisition of these two works there was no painting by Grogan in the Gallery, a serious omission for an artist of his calibre.

In 1972, the acquisition of *An ideal landscape* by Thomas Roberts, for £8,000, from Leonard Koetser of London, greatly reinforced the modest holding of works by this talented landscape painter who died of consumption at the age of thirty in

1778. While Roberts had no first hand knowledge of Italian landscape, which is at the base of his composition, Solomon Delane spent several years in Italy. The landscape by Delane purchased from The Cynthia O'Connor Gallery of Dublin in 1977, for £3,500, must surely depict a particular scene, as yet unidentified, particularly as it is relatively small. Again, this was the first picture by the artist to enter the National Gallery. Thomas Robinson was a Yorkshire man who came to Ireland and made his career here. His portrait of the horse "Paddy Whack" may be considered with landscapes, because of the delightful setting of horse and groom. This painting was acquired at Adam's of Dublin in 1979, for £2,210.

A number of eighteenth century subject paintings were also acquired, of which the most significant must surely be *The Conjuror* by Nathaniel Hone the Elder, purchased in 1966 from Colnaghi of London for £2,500. The story of this satire on Reynold's compositional methods is well known, and the picture was studied and displayed with great skill at the major Reynolds exhibition at the Royal Academy, London. Even before this special "exhibition within an exhibition" by John Newman, this painting was frequently loaned to exhibitions of British Art of the second half of the eighteenth century. Another interesting, but tiny panel painting, a James Barry copy of a classical painting by Poussin, executed in Rome, was purchased from the Albany Gallery of London in 1969, for £375. In 1972 a slightly salacious painting *Sylvia, a courtesan* by Matthew William Peters was acquired from Leger of London, for £1,800. Yet again, this was the first painting of Peters, who was extremely proud of his Irish parentage, to enter the Gallery. In 1975, three lunettes by Jacob Ennis, after designs of Pietro da Cortona, which had graced a house in Rutland (now Parnell) Square, were bought from George Laffan of Dublin, for £1,600; sadly their condition leaves much to be desired, and the fourth lunette, in better condition, escaped. Again this was a first representation in the national collections.

The Gallery's collection of eighteenth century portraits was similarly reinforced. A Charles Exshaw portrait of an unidentified man was bought from Hibernian Antiques of Dublin in 1972, for £300, while a portrait of Sir William Robinson, Bt., by Matthew William Peters was acquired from Mr F Vickerman of Dublin, for £1,500. The latter portrait was engraved in the eighteenth century.

A portrait of Jane Seymour Conway, in the reclining pose traditionally described as *melancholia*, a good work by Charles Jervas, was purchased from Charles Rothenburg of London in 1974, for £2,000. In 1975, at a Christie's auction, a full length portrait of Eaton Stannard by James Latham cost £670. As the price might suggest this was not an exhilarating image, but its art historical importance lay in the fact that it was engraved. It may seem strange to a younger generation that even in 1975 many scholars of British and Irish painting were gaily attributing to Hogarth genuine works from the brush of James Latham. The articles by Andrew O'Connor, developed more recently by Anne Crookshank, have clarified this potential minefield.

When Malahide Castle was being sold up by the Trustees of the late Lord Talbot de Malahide, the opportunity was taken to acquire prior to auction a large number of portraits by Irish artists, and others of interesting Irish sitters, painted by foreign artists. Malahide Castle was noted for its strength in this area. Paintings by Garrett Morphey, Gaspar Smitz, and James Latham greatly enhanced the national patrimony. Many of them were loaned to the Castle when Dublin Tourism

William Davis
(1812-73)
A View of the Rye Water Near Leixlip
NGI. Cat. No. 4129

undertook to open the Castle to the public, after it was purchased together with its demesne by Dublin County Council. For divers historical reasons Malahide Castle became the home of portraits of families other than Talbot, mainly through marriage. Thus one finds O'Reillys, Wogans, O'Neills, and Segraves. The thirty-seven portraits cost the nation £7,000. This represented a much higher figure because the proceeds were exempt from tax; nonetheless, it must be acknowledged that the Trustees erred on the generous side. This is an excellent example of the manner in which meaningful collaboration between private individuals, or their representatives, and public institutions can have felicitous results. Today Malahide Castle and park is a wonderful amenity for Dublin, and especially for the ever-expanding towns of Malahide and Swords. Would that some similar arrangement could have been elaborated when Carton was sold; what a wonderful role it could have played about fifteen miles to the west of the city, serving also the townships of Lucan, Leixlip and Maynooth.

Nineteenth century Irish painting requires further study and much has yet to be discovered, but, in the years from 1964 to 1980, many additions of value were acquired by the National Gallery of Ireland. The first work by Limerick born Jeremiah Hodges Mulcahy to enter the collection was an attractive view of Curragh Chase, home of the de Vere family, purchased from Anthony Thompson of Belfast in 1966, for £275; later, in 1973, this was joined by a view in the forest of the same County Limerick estate, acquired from Hibernian Antiques of Dublin, for £736. The man on horseback is variously described as a poacher or game-keeper; there is a slight difference! Another first entry was William McEvoy's *View of Dublin Bay* bought from Dublin dealer, George Laffan in 1968, for £140.

A superb opportunity to reinforce the collection of works by James Arthur O'Connor came when, in 1970, the distinguished London theatrical personality, Courtney Kenny, offered four paintings by private treaty for £1,800. They depicted

Ballinrobe House, home of Mr Kenny's ancestors, two views in the park of the same house, and a view of Lough Mask. These early works of the artist filled a lacuna in the Gallery's holding, and may be compared to larger series commissioned for Westport House and Portumna Castle.

Another first was *Tête du Chien, Monaco* by Richard Whately West, unsung in his homeland, but with an entire gallery devoted to his work at Alassio on the Ligurian coast. This large canvas of a view in Monaco was bought in 1975 from Hibernian Antiques of Dublin, for £660. Yet another first was *Rye Water, near Leixlip* by William Davis, a wonderfully fresh and painterly depiction of a scene in County Kildare. It was purchased from the Cynthia O'Connor Gallery of Dublin in 1975, for £1,750. Davis is highly regarded in Liverpool where he settled, but the works on view there are a form of Victorian banality that is utterly unrelated to the undated view in County Kildare. At a Mealy's auction in Dublin, again in 1975, the range of Gallery pictures by the Mulvany family was increased with the purchase of a *Mountain rivulet*, a signed work of Thomas J Mulvany, which cost £287.50.

The nineteenth century was par excellence a century of social comment by painters as well as writers. In 1971 an Irish vendor, who wished to remain anonymous, sold to the Gallery *Death of the Queen*, a large canvas by Thomas Moynan, a view at College Green, Dublin, showing a news sheet announcing the demise of Queen Victoria. The cost was £100. In 1975 a charming picture *Children dancing at a crossroads* by Trevor Thomas Fowler was purchased from Dublin dealer, Wolfe Cherrick, for £900. Unusually cheerful, its attraction is derived in no small measure from the light colours used. One year later, a rare work by Robert Fox, *Head of an oriental*, was acquired from the Cynthia O'Connor Gallery, for £770.

For a nation so addicted to the Turf, Ireland produced very few painters of horses, racing or hunting. A competently executed portrait of "The Fairy Queen" by George Nairn was bought from Robin McConkey of Dublin, for £3,000 in 1977. Thomas Robinson, to whom reference was made earlier, was a naturalised Irishman.

Straddling the nineteenth and twentieth centuries was Roderic O'Conor from County Roscommon. At an early stage he abandoned his legal studies and devoted himself to painting. He went to France and remained there for the rest of his long life, dying in 1940 at the age of eighty. During James White's directorship, the Gallery's holding of O'Conor was greatly strengthened. In 1973 *Landscape with rocks*, a genuine Fauve picture with vibrant colours, was purchased from Seán O'Criadáin of Dublin, for £2,700. This was an appropriate development of the collection following *La ferme de Lezaven*, acquired by Thomas MacGreevy in 1961. In between, in 1966, came the purchase of *A quiet read*, a gentle painting using a subdued Fauve palette. This work cost £1,000, and was bought from a private collector through a firm of solicitors. Another interesting addition to the holding of O'Conor's work was *A reclining nude*, bought from Roland, Browne and Delbanco of London, in 1971, for £2,000. This is a painting directly inspired by Velázquez's famous Rokeby Venus in the National Gallery, London.

From the Crane Kalman Gallery of London came *La jeune bretonne*, a typical study of a young Breton lady in traditional costume. This was bought for £2,100,

Roderic O'Conor
(1860-1940)
A Reclining Nude Before a Mirror (1909)
NGI. Cat. No. 4038

in 1975. The last O'Conor to enter the collection was one of the few very early works to survive, *Between the cliffs, Aberystwyth*, a painting which shows the artist straining to break away from the style of, say, Nathaniel Hone the Younger. The vendor was Peter Lamb of Dublin and the price £1,500.

Two other artists from a similar period are Walter Osborne and William Leech. The former, who died young in 1903, was represented further by one delightfully moody view of the Four Courts, purchased from Anthony Thompson of Belfast in 1969, for £350. A lovely portrait of the young John William Scharff was presented by Miss M Hutton in 1970, while *A landscape with cattle*, a typical work of 1892, was presented by Mrs T Moorehead in 1978.

A reasonable holding of the work of William Leech was reinforced by the acquisition of a self-portrait and a portrait of the artist's wife, known as *Au cinquième*, both from the Dawson Gallery, Dublin. A landscape in Quimperlé, known as *The goose girl*, purchased in 1970 from the Gorry Gallery, for £500, has proved to be one of the Gallery's most popular pictures, to judge from the sales of reproductions of it.

Sir William Orpen is well represented in the Gallery, but the opportunity to buy *The Holy Well* from the Agnew Somerville Gallery of Dublin in 1971, for £1,500, was seized upon very wisely. This large canvas depicted Ireland's Celtic heritage with a sardonic eye, in an extremely accomplished way, using a type of tempera technique which included ground down marble.

Two important decorative schemes were saved. The room in the house on Merrion Square which contained wallpaper totally painted by George Russell (AE) was in dire need of treatment. The Irish Agricultural Organisation Society Ltd

William Leech
(1881-1968)
A Self-Portrait (1966)
NGI. Cat. No. 1914

(successors to the co-operative movement founded by Horace Plunkett), presented the wallpaper to the Gallery in 1974. Firstly, the paper had to be removed from the walls, and then a delicate task of conservation ensued, conducted by a small team under the direction of Maighread McParland. The wallpaper is full of symbolist, mystical and spiritualist figures.

The second decorative scheme was from St Mary's Church, Haddington Road, Dublin, where the authorities had thrown out the decoration of two side chapels. They happened to be the work of Harry Clarke, who had painted in a tempera technique, on linen, some beautifully drawn angels, treated in light colours with a most delicate brush. They were rescued and carefully treated in the Gallery's Department of Conservation. The man who reported the "find" on the rubbish heap was given a modest reward.

The Gallery's small holding of the work of Paul Henry was reinforced in 1968 by the acquisition of two works from Mrs Kathleen Henry, a relative of the artist by marriage, for the sum of £500 (for both). *Launching the currach* must be one the painter's finest figurative paintings. One really does get the feeling that the men are straining to get the craft into the sea. *Potato diggers*, the second picture, was also a most welcome addition to the collections. In 1974 the holding was well filled by the generous bequest of Mrs Mabel Henry, the artist's widow by his second marriage.

To represent a very conscious phase in Irish painting, three abstract pictures by Mainie Jellett were bought in 1968 from the Dawson Gallery, for £288.15.0.

William Orpen
(1878-1931)
The Well of the Saints
or **The Holy Well**
(1916)
NGI. Cat. No. 4030

Subsequently, in 1979, the Gallery received under the terms of the will of Miss R S R Kirkpatrick, of Dublin, six outstanding similar Jelletts. Studying under Albert Gleizes in Paris for a short period in nine successive years, both Mainie Jellett and Evie Hone produced high quality paintings in the fully evolved Cubist tradition. To this day there is no example of Evie Hone's work in this mode; but there were some really fine pictures and abstract works in glass in the great Memorial exhibition, held in Dublin and London in the year following her death. Indeed, there are some younger critics who maintain that Evie Hone did not fully understand the idiom. Perhaps the best answer to this is the fact that on more than one occasion, Mr Leo Smith, proprietor of the Dawson Gallery, had trouble in attributing unsigned examples to either Mainie Jellett or Evie Hone. Having made up his mind he would point out his reasons for his decisions. A man with a most sensitive eye, he was agent for both artists, and after their death always tried to have some of their work in stock.

In the period under review the Gallery acquired some notable additions to the national portrait gallery. It is sufficient to cite a few instances of this ongoing process. In 1975 Mr Ciarán MacGonigal presented a most sensitive study of the head of General Richard Mulcahy, by Patrick Tuohy. In 1972 a self-portrait by Gerard Dillon was purchased from members of his family, for £300. A small head of the poet Seamus Heaney by Edward McGuire was bought from the Dawson Gallery in 1974, for £485. In 1977 the Gallery was presented with a fine portrait of the distinguished writer Seán O'Faoláin, also by Edward McGuire, funded by a committee organised by Seán Mulcahy and Father Cyril Barrett, SJ.

Paul Henry
(1876-1958)
Launching the Currach (1910/11)
NGI. Cat. No. 1869

The artist who was to become the most individualistic, and the most unclassifiable Irish painter in the first half of the twentieth century, Jack B Yeats, was already substantially represented in the national collections. But during James White's years at the Gallery, this artist of world stature had his holding greatly reinforced, through a mixture of purchase and public generosity. In 1965 *Grief* was purchased for £6,300. This was a late work of 1951. In 1969 the multinational firm IBM presented the Gallery with a delightful canvas called *The flower girl*, from the artist's middle period. Alas, this example did not lead to gifts from other major corporations, and in a later chapter, it was IBM who sponsored the very successful exhibition 'The Irish Impressionists', and, in 1991, the exhibition of works by Nathaniel Hone the Younger.

What greater honour to the artist and the donor could one imagine than John Huston's gift in 1977 of *In memory of Boucicault and Bianconi*. This painting is totally redolent of the Irish spirit and its characters. *For the road* depicts a very fine horse; it was presented in 1978 by two lovers of the Turf, Mr and Mrs Frank Vickerman, of Dublin. The acquisition of these works, and others by Yeats, enabled the Gallery, in 1990, to dedicate an entire room to the artist, showing some early paintings right through to his late work.

From the above review, it is abundantly clear that during his directorship, James White was very active indeed in pursuing a great enrichment of the Gallery's Irish School, adding major works, but not neglecting the archival aspect of a National Gallery in obtaining minor works which will not be shown regularly, but which are absolutely necessary in building up the history of Irish art. What has been described is far from a complete catalogue of acquisitions, and undoubtedly some readers will miss mention of some of their favourite works. But it is ample evidence to show that we are very fortunate that James White paid such attention to the acquisition of Irish paintings.

Notes on the Contributors

Bruce Arnold is a journalist, author, critic and art historian whose publications include *A Concise History of Irish Art* (1969) and *Orpen: Mirror to an Age* (1981).

Dr. Nicola Gordon Bowe lectures at the National College of Art and Design, Dublin. She has published widely on early twentieth century arts and crafts and is author of, among other publications, *The Life and Work of Harry Clarke* (1989).

Dr. Marion Burleigh-Motley is Head of the Office of Academic Programmes at the Metropolitan Museum of Art, New York, and is an expert on modern art, especially that of the Soviet Union.

Dr. Julian Campbell lectures at the Crawford School of Art, Cork, and has published a number of scholarly catalogues of successful exhibitions including *The Irish Impressionists* (1984), *Mary Swanzy* (1986), *Frank O'Meara* (1989) and *Nathaniel Hone the Younger* (1991).

Ciarán Carty is Arts Editor of *The Sunday Tribune* and author of *Robert Ballagh* (1986).

Anne Crookshank former professor of the History of Art, Trinity College, Dublin, has written extensively on Irish painting since 1600, and has been active in the promotion of exhibitions of contemporary art.

Paul Durcan one of Ireland's premier poets, is the author of numerous volumes of poems including *The Selected Paul Durcan* (1982), *Daddy, Daddy* (1990, Whitbread Prize for Poetry), and *Crazy About Women* (1991).

Brian Fallon is Chief Critic (Literature and Art) of *The Irish Times* and author of a number of publications including the monograph *Tony O'Malley* (1984).

Tony Gray has enjoyed a distinguished career as a journalist, critic and author. His latest book is *Mr. Smyllie, Sir* (1991).

Dr. Seamus Heaney is an internationally acclaimed poet, essayist and lecturer whose most recent volume of poems is titled *Seeing Things* (1991).

Dr. Eileen Kane lectures in the History of Art Department at University College, Dublin, and her specialist interests include the art of the Middle Ages.

Raymond Keaveney Director of the National Gallery of Ireland, has a particular interest in drawings and his publications include *Master European Drawings from the National Gallery of Ireland* (1983) and *Views of Rome from the Thomas Ashby Collection in the Vatican Library* (1988).

Dr. Brian P. Kennedy Assistant Director of the National Gallery of Ireland is the author of *Alfred Chester Beatty and Ireland 1950-1968: A Study in Cultural Politics* (1988), *Dreams and Responsibilities: The State and the Arts in Independent Ireland* (1990) and *Jack Butler Yeats* (1991).

Benedict Kiely is one of Ireland's best-known journalists and broadcasters and is a celebrated author of novels, short stories and works of non-fiction.

Louis le Brocquy is an internationally respected artist whose work is to be found in many celebrated public and private collections. He has been the subject of a monograph by Dorothy Walker in 1981 and of a number of retrospective exhibitions including a major show in Dublin organised by the Arts Councils of Ireland in 1987.

John Montague is a leading Irish poet whose publications include: *Poisoned Lands and Other Poems* (1961), *Tides* (1970), *The Rough Field* (1972), *A Slow Dance* (1975), *Selected Poems* (1982), *The Dead Kingdom* (1984) and *Mount Eagle* (1988).

Homan Potterton was Director of the National Gallery of Ireland from 1980 to 1988 and has published extensively including *Irish Church Monuments 1570-1880* (1975), *The National Gallery, London* (1977), *Canaletto* (1978) and *Dutch Seventeenth and Eighteenth Century Paintings in the National Gallery of Ireland* (1986).

Dr. Hilary Pyle is the foremost expert on the work of Jack Butler Yeats; among her many publications are *Jack B. Yeats* (1970), *Jack B. Yeats in the National Gallery of Ireland* (1986), and *Images in Yeats* (1990).

Robert Rosenblum Professor of Fine Art at New York University, is an internationally renowned scholar whose publications include *Ingres* (1967), *Modern Painting and the Northern Romantic Tradition* (1975) and *Art of the Nineteenth Century* (with H.W. Janson, 1984).

Dr. Alistair Rowan was Professor of the History of Art at University College, Dublin, from 1977 to 1990 and is now Principal of Edinburgh College of Art. He is a leading expert on the architecture of Robert Adam about whose work he lectured as Slade Professor of Fine Art at the University of Oxford, 1988-89.

Denys Sutton (1917-1991) was Editor of *Apollo* from 1962 to 1987, the author of numerous publications, an organiser of exhibitions, a noted art authority and an enthusiastic admirer of the National Gallery of Ireland.

Dr. Michael Wynne Keeper, National Gallery of Ireland, is an expert on Irish art, especially stained glass, and his books include *Irish Stained Glass* (1963, with James White), *Fifty Irish Painters* (1983), and *Later Italian Paintings in the National Gallery of Ireland* (1986).

Index

Illustrations are in italic; **extended references are in bold.**

Abbey Theatre ix, xiv, 21, 25, 133
Académie Royale 97
d'Acigné, Pierre 91
Adler, Jankel 72
Aiken, Chetwood 40
Albers, Josef 27
Allen, William 61
Andrea del Sarto 59, 62
Andrée, Ellen 192
Andrews, Provost 61
Annesley, Mabel 4
Anouilh, Jean 70
Ardizzone, Edward 9
Armstrong, Sir Walter 15, 136
Ashford, William xiv, xvi, 197, 198
Auden, W.H. 54
Ayrton, Michael 26
Bachelier, Jean Jacques; *The Death of Milo of Croton 166*, 167, 168
Bacon, Francis 32, 75
Baldwin, Provost Richard *61*
Ball, Maude 8
Balthus 48, 71
Balzac, Honoré de 186, 195
Barlach, Ernst 71
Barre, Bertrand de la 93
Barry, James 25, 155, 199
Baselitz, Georg 53
Bassano, Jacopo 23
Bassano, Leandro 60
Baudelaire, Charles 186, 187, 190
Beale, Robert 57
Beatty, Sir Alfred Chester 25, *106*, **107-19**
Bedford, Duke of 60
Behan, John 50, 51
Beit, Sir Alfred xi, xv, 24, 26
Bell, Graham and Vanessa 9
Belloc, Hilaire 121
Bellow, Saul 55
Beresford, Archbishop Lord John 62
Berkeley, Bishop George 61
Bernard, Émile 37
Bindon, Francis 63, 65; *Provost Richard Baldwin 61*

Birmingham, George 163
Blanche, Jacques Émile 186, 191, 192
Blythe, Ernest 70
Bodkin, Thomas xi, 16,17, 22, 26, 29n, 155, 156
Bonnard, Pierre 10,19, 21, 23
Borée, Philipot 92
Bores, Francisco 23
Botterell, May 37, 45n
Boudin, Eugène 29n
Bourke, Brian xv
Brancusi, Constantin 136
Braque, Georges 10, 11, 71, 79, 136
Burke, Edmund 62
Burrell, Sir William 111, 118n, 191
Butts, John 59
Cabanel, Alexandre 185
Callot, Jacques 176
Campbell, George xv, 51, 70, 71, 72
Campbell, J.J. 126
Carbery, Ethna 124
Carpione, Giulio 59
Carracci, Ludovico 59
Carver, Robert xiv, 197
Catterson Smith the Elder, Stephen 61, 62
Cézanne, Paul 18, 110, 135
Chagall, Marc 19
Challoner, Luke 57
Chambers, Sir William 17
Chapman, James 59, 61, 62
Charpentier, Constance 168
Chesterton, G.K. 124
Childers, Erskine 4, 24, 25
Chillida, Eduardo 54
China 1732; *The Diamond Sutra (Jade Book) 112*
Chinnery, George 25
Chirico, Giorgio de 10, 19
Cigoli, Ludovico xvi
Clare, Lord 61
Clark, Sir Kenneth 21, 26, 157, 161
Clarke, Austin 69
Clarke, Harry 203
Clarke, Margaret 4, 12
Claudel, Paul 70

209

Claude Lorrain **172-183**; *Hagar and the Angel* **172-183**, *172, 177*; *Juno Confiding Io to the Care of Argus (oil)* **173-183**, *174, 176,* (drawing) *180*; *Landscape with Abraham Expelling Hagar and Ishmael 178*; *Landscape with Mercury and Argus 179*
Cocteau, Jean 70
Coffey, Florence ix
Cogniat, Raymond 78
Coldstream, William 9
Collins, Michael 127, 129
Collins, Patrick 70, 72
Cologne Art Fair 73
Colum, Padraic 123
Comerford, John 16, 18
Connolly, Cyril 71
Connor, Jerome 23
Conor, William 8
Contemporary Irish Art Society 26, 27
Contemporary Picture Galleries ix, x, 9
Cooke, Barrie 54
Corot, Jean-Baptiste Camille 29n, 141, 147, 187, 193
Cosgrave, William Thomas 17
Costakis, George Marian 33
Courbet, Gustave xvi
Courtauld, Samuel 17
Courthion, Pierre 78
Coyne, Fr. Edward xi
Craig, Michael 28
Cranfield, John Smith 60
Cranfield, Richard 59, 61, 63
Crowley, Nicholas 21
Cullen, Cepta x, 3
Curran, Con 4, 21, 22, 24
Cusack, Cyril 70
Cusack, Ralph 7
Dagnan-Bouveret, Pascal; *Breton Women at a Pardon* 38, *39*
Dali, Salvador 163
Dargan, William 15
Daubigny, Charles 23
Daumier, Honoré 29n

David, Gerard; *Le Jugement de Cambyses* 130,131
David, Jacques Louis, **167-171**; *The Funeral of Patroclus* xiv, xvi, *169, 170*
Davin-Mirvault, Césarine 168
Davis, William; A *View of the Rye Water near Leixlip 200*, 201
Degas, Edgar 18, 29n, 110, 160, **184-195**; *Au Café* 192,*193*; *La Boulangère (Étude de Nu, Femme à son Lever)* 187, 188, *190*; *Portrait of George Moore 184*; *The Rehearsal of the Ballet on the Stage* 189, *191*, 192; *Two Ballet Dancers in the Dressing Room* 187, *188*
Delane, Solomon 199
Derain, André 10, 12, 19, 135, 136
Desmarais, François **97-105**
De Valera, Éamon 7, 17, 18, 107, 126
Diaz de la Peña, Virgilio Narcisse 147
Dibbetts, Jan 48
Dietz, Ferdinand xvi
Dillon, Gerard 70, 204
Dombet, Guillaume 93
Domenichino 62, 176
Doyle, Henry 155, 160
Du Berry, Frank xiii
Dubuffet, Jean 50, 71
Dufau, Fortuné 168
Dufy, Raoul 10, 19, 71
Dunsany, The Lady 26, 183n
Dunoyer de Segonzac, André 22, 23
Duquesnoy, François xvi
Dürer, Albrecht 188, 194
Duveen, Lord 17, 118n
Edwards, Hilton 70
Egan, Daniel 63, 146
Eliot, T.S. 4
Elizabeth I, Queen 59, 60, 61, 62
Elsheimer, Adam 175
Ennis, Jacob 199
Epstein, Jacob 25
Eumorfopoulos, George 113
Exshaw, Charles 199
Fallon, Gabriel 124

Farrell, Michael 53
Fergusson, R.C. x
Fernández, Juan xvi
Feydeau, Georges 188
Figgis, R.R. ('Bobs') 12, 22, 24
Fisher, Jonathan 198; *A View of the Lower Lake, Killarney 196*, 197
Foras Eireann x
Forbes, James Staats 193
Fowler, Trevor Thomas 201
Fox, Robert 201
Fragonard, Jean Honoré xiv, xvi
Francastel, Pierre 78
Frederick, Prince of Wales *63*, 64, 65n
French School xvi
Friends of Modern Dublin 28
Friends of the National Collections of Ireland **15-30**, 159
Frink, Elizabeth 27
Fromentin, Eugène 29n, 186
Frost, Terry 26
Fry, Roger 136
Furlong, George xi, 9, 19, 21
Gaiety Theatre ix, 3
Gainsborough, Thomas 60
Ganly, Brigid 24
Gauguin, Paul 18, 37, 39, 40, 135
Gautier, Théodore 186
George I, King 62
George II, King 63
George III, King 60
George IV, King 22
Gérard, Baron François xiv, xvi
Gertler, Mark 10
Gervex, Henri 186
Ghiberti, Lorenzo (Workshop) xvi
Giacometti, Alberti 71
Giotto 87
Giovannetti, Matteo 87
Giovanni di Paolo; *Crucifixion* xiv, xvi, *66*
Gleizes, Albert 10, 11, 12, 204
Glenavy, Lady 21

Gogarty, Oliver St. John 4, 16
Golub, Leon 55, 56
Gonzales, Eva xvi
Goulding, Sir Basil 24
Goya, Francisco de xiv, xvi, 155
Graham, Patrick 51
Granard, Earl of 16, 20
Grant, Duncan 9, 18
Grattan, Henry 61
Gray, Thomas 173
Greacen, Robert xi
Greenberg, Clement 53
Greene, Graham 50
Gregory, Lady Augusta 17, 134, 135, 158
Gris, Juan 10, 12
Grogan, Nathaniel xvi, 198
Guinness, May 12, 19, 21
Gulbenkian, Calouste 109, 118n
Guttuso, Renato 27
Gwynn, Denis 25
Hall, Kenneth 7
Hall, Patrick 52
Hamilton, Eva 20, 21
Hamilton, Hugh Douglas 25
Hamilton, Letitia 4
Hammer, Armand xiv
Hanlon, (Father) Jack ix, 3, 4, 7, 71
Harrison, Sarah Cecilia; *Sir Hugh Lane 14,* 16, 29n
Hatch, J.D. xiv
Haughey, Charles 27
Haverty (Thomas) Trust 18, 19, 155, 156, 157, 158, 165n
Hawkins, Louis Weldon 186
Healy, Tim 143
Hearst, Randolph 109
Hendricks, David 27, 54
Henner, Jean Jacques 186
Henri, Robert 143
Henry, Françoise 21, 24
Henry, Paul ix, 8, 72; *Launching the Currach* 203, *205*
Heron, Patrick 79

Hewitt, John xi, 122
Hickey, Thomas *An Indian Girl 25*
Higgins, Frederick Robert x, 3
Hill, Derek 25
Hill, Nathaniel 39
Hilton, Roger 26
Hitchins, Ivon 27
Hoffmann, Hans 52
Hogarth, William 199
Hokusai 136, 142, 143, 145
Holbein the Younger, Hans 192
Holloway, Joseph 7
Home, Robert 61
Hone, Evie ix, x, 4, 12, 21, 23, 25, 27, 70, 71, 127, 158, 204
Hone the Elder, Nathaniel 21; *The Conjuror,* xiv, xvi, *198,* 199
Hone the Younger, Nathaniel **133-153**, *134,* 193, 202, 205; *The Ferryboat 153; Hastings 150; Shore Malahide, Co. Dublin 152*
Hopper, Edward 48
Hoppner, John 61
Houghton, John 65
Howald, Ferdinand xiv
Hudson, Thomas; *Frederick, Prince of Wales 63,* 64
Huebler, Douglas 48
Huneker, James 143, 144
Hunt, John 25
Hussey, Philip xvi
Hyde, Douglas 3, 133, 134, 135
Image, Selwyn 18
Independent Artists 73
India 1855; *Maharao Ram Singh of Kotah on a White Charger Attacking a Water Buffalo 114*
Ionides, Constantine 189
Iran 17th century; *Binding of Persian Manuscript 109*
Irish Exhibition of Living Art x, 22, 24, 70
Irish Museums Trust 28
Irvin, Albert 27, 54
Jaquerio, Giacomo 94n
Jellett, Mainie ix, x, **2-13**, 21, 22, 70, 71,127, 203, 204; *Achill Horses* 5, *6;* A *Composition 11; Decoration 2; The Virgin of Éire 10*

Jervas, Charles 199
John, Augustus 4, 25, 135
John, Gwen 135
Johnston, Nevill 70
Jordan, Eithne 54
Judd, Donald 52
Keating, Seán 4, 9, 25, 72, 75, 124, 157, 158
Kelleher, D.L. 124
Kelly, Elsworth 54, 55
Kelly, Gerald Festus 145
Kelly, Oisín 51, 70, 71, 72
Kernoff, Harry 9
Killanin, Lord 25
King, Archbishop William 61
King, Richard 126
King-Harman, Anne 26
Kingston, Richard 32
Kirkeby, Per 53
Kirkwood, Harriet 4
Klee, Paul xvii
Kooning, Willem de 55
van Laer, Pieter 174
La Farge, John 142, 145
Lagrenée l'aîné, Louis Jean François 97
Lamb, Charles 4,145
Lane, Sir Hugh xi, xvn, 14, 15, 16, 17, 26, 27, 29n, 62, 64, 138, 155, 193
Lastman, Pieter 59, 64
Latham, James 199
La Tour, Etienne de xvi
Lavery, Sir John 156
Lawless, Matthew James; *The Sick Call 82,* 83
Leask, Ada 21, 23
le Brocquy, Louis xii, xv, 22, 70, 158
Le Clerc, Pierre Thomas; *Illustrations for Desmarais' poem Jérémie* **97-105**, *99, 101, 102, 103*
Leech, William John **36-45**, 158, 202; *A Convent Garden, Brittany* **36-45**, *36; Portrait of a Girl 43; A Self-Portrait 203; The Sunshade 42,* 43
Lefebvre, Jules 186
Léger, Fernand 52
Lemass, Seán 117

Leonardo da Vinci 194
Leslie, Sir John 16, 20, 21
Lewis, Wyndham 4
Lhote, André 32
Lifar, Serge 79
Little, Ernest x
Little, Patrick J. 24
Loftus, Chancellor Adam 57
Longford, Jack 8, 9
Longford, Lord 26
Lüpertz, Markus 53
Lurçat, Henri 19, 23
Lutyens, Sir Edwin 17
MacBride, Maude Gonne 124
McCormack, John 124
MacDonagh, Donagh 69
McEvoy, William 200
MacGonigal, Maurice 4, 9, 75, 157, 158
MacGreevy, Thomas xi, xii, xiii, 21, 24, 27, 75, 77, 79, 81, 124, 125, 126, 160, 161, 201
McGuinness, Norah 22, 24, 29n, 70, 71, 72
McGuire, Edward 4, 204; *James White 128*
McGuire, Senator Edward A. xii, 4, 9, 22, 79
McIlhenny, Henry 25
MacIlwaine, John Bedell Stanford 40
McKenna, Siobhán 70
MacLiammóir, Micheál 27, 70
Maclise, Daniel 25
MacManus, Seamus 124
MacNeice, Louis 9
Maconchy, Elizabeth x, 3
Madden, Samuel 59
Maguire, Brian 51
Mahaffy, Provost John Pentland 62
Mahon, Sir Denis 110
Malevich, Kazimir 34, 52
Mallarmé, Stéphane 186
Manessier, Alfred 71
Manet, Eugène 29n, 156, 186, 187, 194
Marcel, Gabriel 70
Maron, Anton 61
Marquet, Albert xvi, 10

Martin, Sir Alec 26
Martini, Simone 87, 88, 94n
Martyn, Edward 135, 187
Martyn, Ferenc 26
Mathews, Elkin 163
Matisse, Henri 12, 18, 21, 23, 52, 71, 135
Matta, Roberto 71
Maxwell, Constantia 21
Mayer, Lady Dorothy 26
Meninsky, Bernard 18
Merrill, Charles 27
Michelangelo 59
Middleton, Colin 53, 70, 71
Millet, Jean François 147, 155
Miro, Joan 52
Mola, Pier Francesco 59
Molyneux, William 61
Mondrian, Piet 52
Monet, Claude 29n, 41, 42, 185, 187, 189
Montherlant, Henri de 70
Moore, George 135, **184-195**, *184*
Moore, Henry 24, 71, 81
Morandi, Giorgio 71
Morgan, John Pierpont 110, 118n
Morisot, Berthe 21, 29n
Morphey, Garrett 199
Moynan, Richard Thomas 201
Moyne, Lord 26
Moynihan, Father Senan **120-127**, *120*, 157
Mulcahy, Jeremiah Hodges 200
Mulcahy, Michael 47, 49, 56
Mulvany, Thomas James 201
Murphy, Seamus x
Myers, Graham 60
Myles na Gopaleen (Brian O'Nolan) 69, 70
Nairn, George 201
Nairn, J.C. 62, 64
Nash, John 18
Nevinson, Christopher R.W. 10, 18
New Artists Group 50
Newman, Alec x
Newman, Barnett 48

Newman, Maureen x
Newton, Eric 21
Nicholson, Ben 71
Nicholson, Sir William 157
Nolan, Sydney 28
Norton, Caroline 159
Novoa, Leopoldo 27
Nyons, François de 90, 91
O'Brien, Dermod 9, 16, 20, 21, 22, 29n, 155
O'Casey, Seán 17, 70
O'Connor, James Arthur 21, 200, 201
O'Connor, Patrick xii
O'Conor, Roderic xvi, 37, 156; A *Reclining Nude Before a Mirror* xvi, 201, *202*
O'Curry, Peadar x
O Dálaigh, Cearbhall xvn, 25
O'Faoláin, Seán 69
O Faracháin, Roibeard 124
O'Higgins, Michael 124, 126
Oireachtas Art Exhibition 73
O'Kelly, Aloysius 38
O'Kelly, Seán T. 3, 79, 117
O'Mahony, Eoin (Pope) 125
O'Malley, Tony 70
O'Neill, Daniel 70, 72
Oppenheimer, Sir Ernest 113
O Rahille, Aodhaghan 123
O'Rourke, Horace 18
Orpen, Sir William xiv, 13, 18, 37, 49, 145; *The Well of the Saints, The Holy Well* 202, *204*
Osborne, Walter 26, 37, 40-41, 202; *Nathaniel Hone 134*
O'Sullivan, Seamus 7
O'Sullivan, Seán 122, 123, 124; *Father Senan Moynihan 120*
Ovid 178
Palma (Vecchio) 59
Panofsky, Erwin 34
Penni, Gianfrancesco 59
Perrins, Charles Dyson 113
Peters, Matthew William 199
Petit, Paul; *Frame 63*, 65

Petit, Roland 79
Picasso, Pablo 10, 11, 18, 21, 23, 50, 52, 53, 71, 136, 163
Pietro da Cortona 18, 199
Pilkington, Moira ('Deirdre McDonogh') 9
Piper, John 9
Place, Francis xvi
Pollock, Jackson 48, 52
Poussin, Nicolas 174, 175, 199
Power, Albert 18
Power, Arthur x, 127
Price, Archbishop Arthur *64,* 65
Provoost, Jan xvi
Purser, Sarah 12, 15, *16,* 17, 18, 19, 20, 21, 27, 29n, 136, 155
Puvis de Chavannes, Pierre 29n
Quinn, John **132-48**, *132, 144*
Quost, Ernest 16
Raffaëlli, Jean François 185
Rákóczi, Basil 7, 23
Rambert, Marie x
Ramsay, Allan 60
Ramsay, James 60
Read, Herbert 32, 78
Redmond, John Edward 143
Redon, Ary 186
Reid, Nano 4, 25, 70, 72
Reinhardt, Ad(olph) 53
Rembrandt 26
Reni, Guido 62
Renoir, Auguste xvi, 29n, 187
Reynolds, Sir Joshua xvi
Ribera (Lo Spagnoletto) 59
Ricci, Sebastiano 59, 62
Richards, Ceri 26
Richier, Ligier xvi
Rigby, Richard 60
Ringling, John 109
Roberts, Thomas xiv, 198, 199
Robinson, Dolly and Lennox 4
Robinson, Thomas 199, 201
Roslin, Alexander xvi

Rosse, Earl of 21
Rossetti, Dante Gabriel 147
Rothenstein, Sir John 22, 25
Rothschild, Lord 113
Rothko, Mark 53
Rouault, Georges 23, 49, 161; *Le Christ et le Soldat 20*, 21, 24, 136
Rousseau, Jean Jacques 194
Royal Hibernian Academy x, 4, 9, 37, 75, 144, 145, 146, 147, 148, 156
Roxburghe, John Duke of 113
Russell, George ('AE') 16, 19, 29n, 32, 127, 134, 135, 136, 137n, **138-148**, *139*, 202
Rynne, Stephen 7, 9, 127
Sacchi, Andrea 59
Saint-Aubin, Gabriel de 168, 169
St. Gaudens, Augustus 25
Salmon, Provost George 62
Salon, Paris 37
Sandrart, Joachim von 174
Sao Paolo Biennale 73
Sargent, John Singer; *Carnation, Lily, Lily, Rose 41*, 42
Saurine, Elizabeth 43, 45n
Schopenhauer 10
Scott, Patrick 73
Scott, William 26
Sears, David xi, 127
Seurat, Georges 135
Shannon, Charles Haslewood 145
Shaw, George Bernard *viii*, xiv, 16, 125
Shaw, Mrs G.B. (Charlotte Payne-Townsend) x, 16, 21
Sheehy, Edward 127
Shigemasa, Kitao; *Two Bullfinches on the Branch of a Cherry Tree 116*
Sickert, Walter 10, 157, 187, 189
Smith, Leo 161, 162, 204
Smitz, Gaspar 199
Smyllie, Robert Maire 69, 76, 125
Snagg, Thomas 197
Society of Dublin Painters ix, 3, 10

Sogliani, Giovanni xvi
Somerville, Edith 38
Souter, Camille 73
Lo Spagnoletto (Ribera) 59
Spencer, Stanley 19
Steer, Philip Wilson 10
Stella, Frank 48, 55
Strickland, Walter G. 16
Stuart, Gilbert 61
Sutton, Denys xvi
Swanzy, Mary 21, 158
Sweeney, James Johnson 32
Swift, Jonathan 61, 65
Synge, John Millington 70, 134, 160, 162, 163
Thaddeus, Henry Jones; *Market Day, Finistère 38*
Thompson, Henry Yates 111
Titian 59
Tonks, Henry 10, 19
Tracy, John and Edward 62
Troubetzkoy, Prince Paul; *George Bernard Shaw viii*
Tuohy, Patrick 204
An Túr Gloine 15
Turner de Lond, William 22
Ussher, Archbishop James 57, 60, 61, 62
Utrillo, Maurice 21, 23
Valencian School xvi
Valois, Ninette de x
Van Gogh, Vincent 18, 31, 41, 110, 135
Van Nost the Younger, John 25
Vasarely, Victor 71
Vasari, Giorgio 47, 48
Velázquez, Diego 201
Venturi, Lionello 32, 78
Vere White, Terence de 24, 30n
Veronese, Paolo 59
Victoria, Queen 201
Villabrille y Ron, Juan Alonso xvi
Vlaminck, Maurice 10, 12, 21
Vouet, Simon xvi
Vuillard, Edouard 23, 29n
Waddington, Victor ix, 22, 70, 72, 79, 127, 161, 162, 163, 168, 171

Walsh, Maurice 123
Warhol, Andy 55
Watteau, Jean Antoine 191, 192
West, Richard Whately 201
Westropp, Dudley 21
Whistler, James Abbott McNeill 147, 189
White, James **viii-xvi,** *viii,* 3, 13, 22, 24, 25, 26, 27, 28, 29n, 30n, **31-35,** 49, 56, 70, 73, **75-81,** *80,* 85, 117, 126, **127-129,** *128,* 133, 161, 167, 168, 201, 205
White, Thomas ix
Wilkinson, John and William 59
Wilson, Benjamin; *Archbishop Arthur Price 64*
Woodrow, Bill 27
Woods, Sir Robert 16
Wyeth, Andrew 48
Yarrow, Lady Eleanor 123
Yeats, Jack ix, xi, xiv, xv, 9, 20, 25, 26, 71, 75, 124, 125, 127, 134, 135, 136, **155-165,** 205; *About to Write a Letter* xvi, *162,* 163; *Grief* xvi, *163,* 164; *The Liffey Swim 154,* 155, 156, 159; *In Memory of Boucicault and Bianconi 164; Many Ferries 159,* 160; *Men of Destiny 157, 158*

Yeats, John Butler xiv, xv, 33, 133, 134, 135, 137n, 138, 140, 142, 143, 145, 146, 193; *Portrait of Sarah Purser 16; John Quinn 132, 144; AE, George W. Russell 139; Lily (Susan) Yeats 140*
Yeats, Lily (Susan) *140,* 141
Yeats, Lolly (Elizabeth Corbet) 163
Yeats, William Butler xiv, 17, 125, 135, 157, 161, 193
Yeats, Mrs W.B. (George Hyde-Lees) 16
Yoyusai; *Two Swallows Flying Past Willow Fronds (Inro) 108*
Yverni, Jacques **85-95;** *The Annunciation* xiv, xvi, *84, 86; Madonna and Saints Triptych 88-89,* 90
Zola, Émile 187, 195